MASTERS OF THE
ENGLISH REFORMATION

MASTERS OF THE
ENGLISH REFORMATION

by

Marcus L. Loane

HODDER AND STOUGHTON
LONDON   SYDNEY   AUCKLAND   TORONTO

British Library Cataloguing in Publication Data

Loane, Marcus L
   Masters of the English Reformation.
   1. Reformation – England – Biography
   I. Title
   274.2   BR378

   ISBN 0-340-33202-6

And they overcame by the blood of the Lamb,
and by the word of their testimony; and they
loved not their lives unto the death."

Rev. 12:11

To

The Venerable Archdeacon

RICHARD BRADLEY ROBINSON,

Friend, Host, and Guide,

with Gratitude and Affection

this book is

inscribed

" O the joy that the martyrs of Christ have felt in the midst of the scorching flames! Surely they had life and sense as we, and were flesh and blood as well as we; therefore it must needs be some excellent thing that must so rejoice their souls while their bodies were burning: when Bilney can burn his finger in the candle and Cranmer can burn off his unworthy right hand; when Bainham can call the Papists to see a miracle and tells them that he feels no more pain than in a bed of down and that the fire was to him as a bed of roses; when Ferrar can say, If I stir, believe not my doctrine: think then reader with thyself in thy meditations; surely it must be some wonderful foretasted glory that can do all this."

RICHARD BAXTER,
"The Saints Everlasting Rest",
Works, Vol. XXIII, p. 393.

INTRODUCTION

It was Martin Luther who declared that the doctrine of Justification by Faith Only is the article of a standing or falling church. The recovery of this doctrine was the key to the Reformation in Europe. It was the corollary of the translation of the Bible into the language of everyday life and its circulation in the homes and hands of ordinary people. These two momentous factors were to penetrate the Realm of England during the reign of Henry VIII and will for ever be associated in a special sense with the names of Thomas Bilney and William Tyndale. These two, and many others as well, were to die at the stake as a result of their unswerving loyalty to the doctrines of Grace as made known in the Word of God. Nor did they die in vain. The supreme authority of Holy Scripture in all matters of faith and conduct was written into the sixth of the Articles of Religion; and the doctrine of Justification by Faith Only was summed up in unforgettable language in the Eleventh Article. Those two "Articles of the Christian Faith" are the bedrock on which the history of the Church of England since the Reformation must stand or fall.

But the pivot of the Reformation in England during the reign of Edward VI was the doctrine of the Lord's Supper. Ridley's discovery of the work of Ratramnus led him to reject the doctrine of Transubstantiation and the Sacrifice of the Mass as totally foreign to the teaching of the New Testament. Ridley was able to convince Cranmer that Ratramnus was right; they came to believe that the bread and wine are "the pledges" of God's redeeming love and that the presence of the Lord Jesus is not to be found in an earthly altar, but in the hearts of those who feed on Him by faith with thanksgiving. Ridley was to expound this doctrine with clarity and dignity in his Treatise on the Lord's Supper, and Cranmer was to defend it with great learning in his controversy with Gardiner. This was the doctrine enshrined in the Source of the Holy Communion in the Book of Common Prayer in 1552.

When Queen Mary came to the throne, Ridley, Latimer and Cranmer were the outstanding Reformers who were thrown into prison. In all the debates which ensued, in their trial and condemnation for heresy, and in the sentence of death which consigned them to death by fire, the one basic issue was their doctrine of the Lord's Supper as opposed to the dogmas of the church with regard to Transubstantiation and the Mass. If the Church were right and they were wrong, they were not only condemned to a terrible form of death as heretics but were doomed to a lost eternity. Their real greatness was seen in the fact that they dared to stand by their convictions, formed as a result of intensive study of the Scriptures, and to die at the stake rather than yield to the pressures that were brought to bear on mind and feeling. And the candle they lit is one which by the grace of God will never go out.

What happened more than four hundred years ago is still vitally relevant. The integrity and authority of the Bible have been under constant assault from many quarters and it is no longer the one Book in the homes and hands of all. Many people today think that a good life, a good name, and a good reputation will somehow make them acceptable to God. And the reformed doctrine of the Lord's Supper has been obscured by an emphasis on the Real Presence which approximates more and more towards medieval teaching and practice. Let Bilney and Tyndale speak again; let Latimer and Ridley and Cranmer be heard afresh. They witnessed "a good confession" for their heavenly Master and sealed it with their lives. May this book renew the impact of their life and death on another generation "in the name of the Lord Jesus and by the Spirit of our God" [1 Cor. 6:11].

M. L. LOANE

MASTERS OF THE
ENGLISH REFORMATION

Masters of the English Reformation was first published in 1954, in preparation for the 400th anniversary of the martyrdoms of Latimer and Ridley in 1555 and of Cranmer in 1556. It tells the gripping story of the English Reformation from 1516 to 1556 through the eyes of five of its chief protagonists – Bilney the early martyr, Tyndale the Bible translator, Latimer the popular preacher, Ridley the theologian and Cranmer the statesman and liturgical scholar. I remember quite well the impact which this book made on me at the time. I felt thankful – even proud – to belong to a church whose formularies had been fashioned by such men, and I was challenged by their theological clarity, conviction and courage.

During the quarter-century (and more) which has elapsed since the book's original publication, the Anglican Communion has passed through a period of great change. The Book of Common Prayer (which, though dated 1662, is substantially Cranmer's second Prayer Book of 1552) remains an indispensable standard of Anglican doctrine. Yet it has been displaced in the common use of many churches by a variety of modern service books. While welcoming these books' contemporary language and feel, it is not inconsistent at the same time to deplore the growing ignorance of the theology of their ancestor, the Book of Common Prayer.

Change has come to Rome as well as Canterbury. The Second Vatican Council (1962-5) opened the windows of the Roman Catholic Church to the fresh air of ecumenical encounter. Only three months after its conclusion Archbishop Michael Ramsey visited Pope Paul VI in Rome, and their Common Declaration led in due time to the setting up of the first Anglican-Roman Catholic International Commission. ARCIC I concluded 10 years of dialogue with the publication in 1982 of its *Final Report*[1], and the same year Pope John Paul II paid his historic visit to England, which included a service in Canterbury Cathedral in which he and Archbishop Robert Runcie knelt side by side in prayer.

So we have come a long way in the last 30 years. And most Christians would surely prefer to see Pope and Archbishop praying together than hurling anathemas at one another. But does this mean that the issues, for which our English Reformers were willing to die a horrible death at the stake, have been settled? You certainly would not think so if you read *Observations*, the comment on the *Final Report* produced by the Vatican's Sacred Congregation for the Doctrine of the Faith[2].

Evangelical Anglicans have given a guarded welcome to ARCIC's *Final Report*. It contains much that is good. We applaud its concern for truth (confessing that there are 'essential matters where it considers that doctrine admits no divergence'), its resolve to get behind sixteenth century debates to the real issues at stake, and its complete freedom from rancour. At the same time, it contains (inspite of its 'Elucidations') some serious ambiguities, omissions, and weaknesses.[3] It is greatly to be hoped that ARCIC II will remedy these.

In the light of this contemporary dialogue between Anglicans and Roman Catholics, I have found it most refreshing to re-read *Masters of the English Reformation*. Three characteristics of our Reformers impress me most.

The first is *their convinced commitment to the Bible*. They believed and taught, and incorporated in the Church of England's formularies, both the *sufficiency* of Scripture for salvation (extra-biblical beliefs being permitted as pious private opinions, if Scripture does not prohibit them, but not required) and the *supremacy* of Scripture (all human opinions and ecclesiastical traditions being subordinate to it, as our Lord himself insisted in debate with the Pharisees).

The English Reformation may be said to have begun in the White Horse Inn in Cambridge, where from 1519 a group met in secret to study the Greek Testament which Erasmus had published three years previously. It was this that Tyndale translated into English, determined (as he put it) that the ploughboy should know the Scriptures better than the Pope.

And once the Bible was available to the people in the vernacular, the leaders of the Reformation urged the clergy to expound it to their people. So from the time of the second Prayer Book onwards (1552), the symbol of office presented to the newly ordained presbyter was no longer the chalice but the Bible.

There can be no continuing reformation of the church without a return to the Bible. Yet of the four 'Agreed Statements' of ARCIC I the two on 'Authority' are the weakest; they contain no clear affirmation of the supreme authority of Scripture and therefore of the need to reform our traditions accordingly. How can solid progress towards reunion be made without this? Evangelical Anglicans stand by the Open Letter which a hundred of us addressed in 1977 to the Anglican Episcopate. 'We are obliged to press the question', we wrote, 'whether the non-reformed Churches are yet sufficiently ready to test all their traditions of teaching and practice by Holy Scripture, as we know we are bound to test ours, in order to correct what the theology of the Bible will not justify'[4].

The second characteristic of the English Reformers which impresses me is *their clear convictions about the way of salvation*. This was because they not only found it plainly set out in Scripture, but had also experienced it themselves personally. For example, Marcus Loane tells the moving story of 'little Bilney' who, having tried unsuccessfully to find salvation through penance, 'at last . . . heard speak of Jesus' and 'chanced upon this sentence of St Paul (O most sweet and comfortable sentence to my soul!)' that 'Christ Jesus came into the world to save sinners'. Immediately his 'bruised bones leaped for joy'. Then Bilney led Latimer to Christ, and then Latimer became the popular preacher of the Reformation, proclaiming with wit, eloquence and homely illustrations the biblical gospel of justification by grace alone through faith alone.

This gospel of free grace came then to be enshrined in the Book of Common Prayer. For, as Cranmer wrote about Justification in his 'Homily on Salvation' (1547): 'This faith the holy Scripture teacheth: this is the strong rock and foundation of Christian religion: this doctrine all old and ancient authors of Christ's church do approve: ......this whosoever denieth is not to be counted for a true Christian man . . .'.

The English Reformers were also resolved, being consistent theologians, that their doctrines of Justification and of the Lord's Supper should be compatible with one another. They strenuously denied transubstantiation ('the change is not in the nature, but the dignity' – Latimer), the real presence of Christ in the elements ('his true body is truly present to them that truly receive him, but spiritually' – Cranmer), and the notion that the mass could be a propitiatory sacrifice (for then 'doth this sacrament take upon it the office of Christ's passion, whereby it might follow that Christ died in vain' – Ridley). They were also consistent (as we should be) in their vocabulary, believing that the presbyter is a minister serving a sacramental supper from a table, not a priest offering a sacrifice on an altar.

Do we not need to contend in our day for the same gospel of justification by God's free grace? I am persuaded that we do, for there is widespread ignorance of it. Many Anglican congregations do not know it, for many clergy do not preach it. One sometimes wonders if Latimer's candle, which he claimed at the stake to be lighting in England, has almost gone out. It is a disaster that ARCIC I produced no statement on either salvation in general or justification in particular. We are assured that ARCIC II will remedy this. May it be so. It is small wonder that ARCIC's statements on Eucharist and Priesthood are muddled; for a clear doctrine of ministry and sacraments is impossible without a clear doctrine of salvation.

The third impressive characteristic of the English Reformers is *their zeal for the glory of Christ*. Of their zeal and courage there is no doubt. They spoke their minds without fear, and were prepared to suffer for it. They had to endure exile, vilification, forfeiture of office and goods, prison and death. Cranmer had to bear two and a half years in prison, alone, tormented by an inner conflict of loyalties and by the cat and mouse game which his captors played with him. It is true that he temporarily recanted. For, though a heroic figure, he was also a man of flesh and blood. But he later repented of his recantation.

What was the secret of the courage and devotion of these men? Why did they feel so strongly about their theological convictions? It was zeal for the glory of Christ. The reason they repudiated the medieval doctrine of the Mass as propitiatory is that they saw it as 'a great derogation of the merits of Christ's passion' and 'prejudicial and derogatory to Christ's blood'.

The same zeal should motivate evangelical Anglicans today. We need to repent of all bigotry, and be ready patiently and openly to listen to Roman Catholics in our dialogue with them, in order to understand them and with them to explore new ways of grappling with old issues. We need also to repent of partisanship, as if our first loyalty were to the evangelical party in the church. It most emphatically is not. Our loyalty is to Christ. And it is only when we perceive a doctrine to be incompatible with the unique perfections of his person and work that we can be expected with vehemence to oppose it.

I am glad and grateful that Hodders have brought out this new edition of *Masters of the English Reformation*. Sir Marcus Loane writes as both a historian and a theologian. His thumbnail sketches of Bilney, Tyndale, Latimer, Ridley and Cranmer are well documented. He also brings out the theological issues at stake. Yet he is no detached scholar; the fire of truth burns hotly within him. And although he will not appreciate being likened to the Reformers he here describes, yet I consider that he has had to suffer a certain isolation as a result of his faithfulness. At the Lambeth Conference of 1958, which he attended as the representative of Archbishop Mowll (who was unwell), he bravely spoke up against popular but false doctrines of priesthood and sacrifice in liturgical revision, and at the Lambeth Conference of 1978 he pleaded publicly that ARCIC should be asked to add to its agenda a consideration of Justification by Faith. He was listened to with impatience and without due respect.

In 1982 he retired, after a distinguished ministry as Archbishop of Sydney and Primate of Australia. The republication of this book is a fitting tribute to his evangelical leadership. If ARCIC II can produce an agreed statement on Justification, which magnifies the free grace of God and the

Masters of the English Reformation

unique glory of Christ, I am sure that nothing could bring Marcus Loane greater joy and thanksgiving.

February 1983

End Notes

1 *The Final Report* of the Anglican–Roman Catholic International Commission was published jointly by CTS and SPCK in 1982
2 *Observations* (CTS 1982)
3 See *Evangelical Anglicans and the ARCIC Final Report* – an Assessment and Critique, produced by the Church of England Evangelical Council (Grove Books 1982)
4 The 'Open Letter' of Anglican Evangelicals is included in its exposition entitled *Across the Divide* by R T Beckwith, G E Duffield and J I Packer (Lyttleton Press 1977)

CONTENTS

THOMAS BILNEY

*Fellow of Trinity Hall,
Cambridge*

c. 1495–1531

"It was to a copy of this New Testament (the *Novum Testamentum* brought out by Erasmus in 1519), read by a single devout student, that the origin of the Reformation movement in the University (of Cambridge) may be traced."

R. DEMAUS, *Hugh Latimer, A Biography*, p. 22.

THOMAS BILNEY WAS BORN ABOUT the year 1495, either in the village of East Bilney or in Norwich itself. Nothing is now known with regard to his home or childhood. There are in fact many gaps in the whole biography. Foxe was obliged to skim over the first half of his life with a very light touch, and we are left with a sense of elusive mystery as to many details in his career. It is clear that both by nature and by choice he was a lover of books, and he must have been a ready learner from his childhood. It was in the order of things that such a lad, in due course, should be sent up to Cambridge, and we find that he was enrolled as a resident in Trinity Hall. We cannot now fix the exact year in which his studies began, but it must have been while Cambridge was still humming with the excitement which clung to the name of Erasmus. Bilney settled down to detailed study in Law and made rapid progress in both branches of the subject. This was still the age when education in Civil and Canon Law was in the hands of the two Universities, while a training in Common Law such as Sir Thomas More received was confined to the inns of court in London. But the only dates or events in the life of Bilney known to us in these years are his ordination to the priesthood and his graduation in Law. In 1519, he was ordained by the Bishop of Ely to the title of St. Bartholomew's Priory, Smithfield; and in 1520, he obtained his degree as a Bachelor of Law in the University of Cambridge. He became a Fellow of Trinity Hall apparently in the same year, and one or two traditions of his Fellowship have been preserved by Foxe. It was believed that he never slept for more than four hours a night, and he could not abide the sound either of swearing or of singing. He would protest to his pupils as he returned from church that the "dainty singing" of the clerks was no more than a profane mockery of God. Thomas Thirlby, who was to stand so high in the eyes of Mary Tudor as well as of Thomas Cranmer, lodged in rooms below Bilney on the same staircase, and would often drive poor Bilney to his knees in spiritual protest as the sound of his flute drifted upstairs. "He would resort strait to his prayer."[1]

But great events had been brewing in the cauldron of those years in Europe. In the winter months of 1514, Erasmus had finally left Cambridge; and before the summer of 1515 was over, he was on his way to Basle, where his two great works were in the press. In March 1516, the first edition of his *Novum Instrumentum* appeared and was shortly followed by his edition of the *Works of Jerome*. In 1516, Zwingli made his famous appeal to the supreme authority of the Scriptures; and in 1517, Luther nailed his *Theses* to the door of the church in Wittenberg. There was a great trade in books and theses, and the name of Luther began to seep through the walls of silence into England. In March 1519, a new edition of the *Novum Instrumentum* was issued from Froben's press, but with an altered title as the *Novum Testamentum*. In 1520, Henry VIII was once more at war with France, while Luther dared to burn the Papal Bull; and in 1521, Henry published his famous book against Luther, while Luther himself braved the Diet of Worms. But as yet the sense of stir in the New Learning and the Reformation had made no great impact upon life or thought in Cambridge. It was perhaps in 1516 that William Tyndale had transferred his studies from Oxford to Cambridge, but he was then no more than a quiet and obscure scholar. Then in 1517, a certain Peter de Valence defied the Pope, Leo X, who had authorised fresh Indulgences in Cambridge; but the storm died down as soon as he was declared excommunicate. Yet this affair was only one symptom of a ferment which could not be contained. Cambridge, like all the world, was in a state of flux. Luther's works were being smuggled into England through the Eastern Counties and were read in secret by many a student. They were proscribed by law, but remained in circulation. Rooms were searched, books were seized, until at length, in May 1521, they were burnt at a great public bonfire in the heart of Cambridge. But an outbreak of plague occurred, and the Michaelmas Term was delayed, and the hand of authority was stayed, for there was no time to persecute heretics in the heat of local troubles.

Meanwhile, what of Bilney? He may have had neither time

[1] *John Foxe*, Vol. IV, p. 621.

nor inclination to read the signs which were being inscribed by the Divine finger on the walls of Europe. Nevertheless, it was during these years that he passed through the great experience which made him a new man in Christ Jesus. Our knowledge is meagre, but there is one vital remark in his own words which helps us to connect this great change with a fixed time and event. He had perhaps been too absorbed in his studies and his ordination to give much thought to the rise of the New Learning, and yet he had felt for some time in a vague and indefinite kind of way the emptiness of the religion in which he had been born and bred. His soul was sick and he longed for health, but nowhere could he find it. He went to the priests for guidance, but they could only send him to broken cisterns which mocked his thirst. No words could be stronger or more scathing than the tremendous indictment which he drew up some years later, speaking from the depths of his own experience. The priests might call themselves pastors, but they were in fact wolves, "which seek no other thing of their flock but the milk, wool, and fell, leaving both their own souls, and the souls of their flock unto the devil."[1] He spoke with a vehemence which was quite out of the common, but which shows in proportion how much he had suffered: "These are they, these I say, most reverend father, are they who under the pretence of persecuting heretics follow their own licentious lives. . . . These men do not find pasture, for they never teach and draw others after them, that they should enter by Christ who alone is the door whereby we must come unto the Father; but set before the people another way, persuading them to come unto God through good works, oftentimes speaking nothing at all of Christ; thereby seeking rather their own gain and lucre than the salvation of souls: in this point being worse than those who upon Christ (being the foundation) do build wood, hay and straw. These men confess that they know Christ, but by their deeds they deny Him."[2]

Just what Bilney had to endure in the way of inner torment is told in a valuable letter which he wrote in Latin to Tunstall of London. He was oppressed by the burden of sin, but knew not how to find relief. He was like the woman who spent all that she had on her misguided physicians, and yet only grew worse. "I

[1] *John Foxe*, Vol. IV, p. 634.   [2] Ibid., pp. 634, 635.

also, miserable sinner, . . . before I could come unto Christ, had even likewise spent all that I had upon those ignorant physicians." He knelt at the feet of unlearned confessors (indoctos confessionum auditores) and told out all his sins: "so that there was but small force of strength left in me (who of nature was but weak), small store of money, and very little wit or understanding." His confessors prescribed for him various penances: now fastings, now vigils, then payment for Masses, then purchase of pardons. He had carried out in detail all that was thus required, yet he found no consolation. From time to time a doubt would cross his mind, only to be sternly repressed; and it was long before he could allow himself to see that in all these matters, "they sought rather their own gain than the salvation" of a sick and languishing penitent.[1] His third letter contains a short passage in which he undoubtedly refers to his own pre-converted experience, and which asserts that the mediaeval style of preaching was all to beat down and not to build up. "But here," he wrote, "whether Christ have been a long time heard, I know not, for that I have not heard all the preachers of England; and if I had heard them, yet till it was within this year or two, I could not sufficiently judge of them. But this I dare be bold to affirm, that as many as I have heard of late preach (I speak even of the most famous), they have preached such repentance that if I had heard such preachers in times past, I should utterly have been in despair."[2] All his spiritual travail, his fasts, vigils, Masses, pardons, were done without Christ, and only carried him yet further out of the way. He was neither eased nor relieved beneath the sharp pressure of his goaded conscience, and he was borne down by the load of sin until he felt as though his soul must needs be crushed.

But God's time was at hand, and the words which tell of it are ever memorable: "At last I heard speak of Jesus, even then, when the New Testament was first set forth by Erasmus."[3] We do not know who the friends were who thus spoke of Jesus; they may have been students of the works of Luther who were in touch with the latest books from Europe. But their conversation in the schools at Cambridge meant as much to Bilney as the conversation of those godly women was to mean for Bunyan in the streets of Bedford. They told him of the New Testament

[1] *John Foxe*, Vol. IV, p. 635.   [2] Ibid., p. 640.   [3] Ibid., p. 635.

which had been brought out by Erasmus, furnished with the Greek text in one column and a Latin version in the other. It was in March 1516 that the *Novum Instrumentum* had first come from the press; and, in June, John Colet wrote from England with news of its welcome: "The volumes of your new edition of it are here both eagerly bought and everywhere read. . . . Go on, Erasmus. As you have given us the New Testament in Latin, illustrate it by your expositions, and give us your commentary most at length on the Gospels."[1] But in Cambridge there was opposition, and Erasmus wrote to his friend Boville about a formal decree which had been issued to forbid any attempt to bring the book within College precincts, "by horse or by boat, on wheels or on foot".[2] Nevertheless, in March 1519, he brought out the *Novum Testamentum*, and it is clear from the Latin original of his letter that this was the version of the New Testament to which Bilney referred. (Sed tandem de Jesu audiebam, nimirum tum, cum novum Testamentum primum ab Erasmo aederetur[3]). Men were full of praise for the style of its Latin, and it was the beauty of the Latin rather than the teaching of the book which at first captivated Bilney. "Being allured rather by the Latin than by the Word of God (for at that time I knew not what it meant), I bought it even by the providence of God." But the hand of God was behind it all, and the very first time when he sat down to read, a light divine shone through his soul. "And at the first reading, as I well remember, I chanced upon this sentence of St. Paul (O most sweet and comfortable sentence to my soul!), 'It is a true saying and worthy of all men to be embraced, that Christ Jesus came into the world to save sinners; of whom I am the chief' (I Tim. 1:15)."[4] (O mihi suavissimam Pauli sententiam[5].)

These words were just what he needed. They seemed to stand out in letters of light; they were to haunt his mind like a strain of purest music. He could not tell what had happened, except that he was now filled with comfort and strength whereas he had been bruised and almost in despair. "This one sentence," he wrote, "through God's instruction and inward working, which I did not then perceive (Deo intus in corde meo, quod tunc fieri ignorabam, docente), did so exhilarate my heart, being before wounded

[1] Seebohm, pp. 395, 396.
[2] Ibid., p. 399.
[3] *John Foxe*, Vol. IV, p. 633.
[4] Ibid., p. 635.
[5] Ibid., p. 633.

with the guilt of my sins, and being almost in despair, that immediately I felt a marvellous comfort and quietness, insomuch that my bruised bones leaped for joy."[1] It was as if a fresh wind had begun to blow through the lanes of his soul, as if a new day had begun to dawn in the hour of greatest darkness. Bilney had grasped the great Pauline doctrine of Justification *Sola Fide* and had learnt to renounce all hope in the fancied merit of his own works. This one verse of Scripture led him to the discovery that all Scripture is most sweet and wholesome, and he began to read it with much prayer for a steady increase of faith. He would review the vows of his recent ordination in the light of this great discovery, and would return to his duties with the quickened footsteps of new inspiration. "At last," he told Tunstall, "I desired nothing more than that I, being so comforted by Him, might be strengthened by His Holy Spirit and grace from above, that I might teach the wicked His ways which are mercy and truth; and that the wicked might be converted unto Him by me who sometime also was wicked."[2] Bilney did not break away from the Church, even though he saw her sins with clear-eyed reality; nor did he grasp the full stretch of Reformation theology, even though he felt its power with increased understanding. But he was the first of Cambridge scholars whose name is known to us to take his stand for the Reformation, and he was the central figure in a new school of Evangelical life and witness in the University.

Bilney was by nature shy and gentle, but this new light could not be hid. "There was never a more innocent and upright man in all England than he was",[3] so Foxe declared; and his guileless sincerity soon began to attract his friends to share his faith in Christ. He now knew no Law but Scripture and no Master but Christ, and there was in his heart what Foxe calls "an incredible desire" to lead others into a like joyful experience.[4] And his labours were not in vain; quite a remarkable group of men were either won or strengthened by means of his loving witness. There were Thomas Arthur of Trinity Hall and St. John's College, and John Thixtill of Pembroke Hall. Then there was George Stafford, who had become a Reader in Divinity and was widely

---

[1] *John Foxe*, Vol. IV, p. 635, cp. p. 633.   [2] Ibid., pp. 635, 636.
[3] Ibid., p. 619.   [4] Ibid., p. 620.

admired for his blameless life and learning. And there was John Lambert, who had read the Classics while at Cambridge and had become "a mass priest in Norfolk".[1] Then in 1522, Matthew Parker was enrolled in Corpus Christi, and was strongly drawn to Bilney. There would be a strong link between them at once as sons of Norwich, and they may have known each other in their native city. Parker soon heard of the new and better way of faith through Bilney and was soon numbered among them that believe. Bilney and his friends then turned their thoughts to Robert Barnes, who returned from the Louvain in 1523 to become the Prior and Master of the Augustines in the Peasmarket. Barnes had won for himself no mean name in Cambridge as one who was mighty in the Scriptures and quite fearless in his preaching; and yet he was still blind to the full truth of the Gospel message of grace. But Barnes was the doctor who had to put Stafford through the oral test of disputation for his Divinity degree, and, to the great consternation of Barnes and the other unenlightened divines, he proved himself more than able to hold his ground. This wrought such a sense of need in Barnes that Bilney was soon able to lead him to a clear faith in Christ as Saviour.[2] Such men were all noble converts, found and won for Christ through Bilney, whose heart never ceased to yearn for those who were still out of the way.

Thus to Bilney must be ascribed the first human impulse in the Reformation movement in the schools of Cambridge, and the Reformation itself had its cradle in the meetings which were held at the White Horse Inn. This inn was just across the street from the gates of Corpus Christi, and stood on a block of land which belonged to St. Catherine's. There was a small postern door which opened on to Milne Street, or Queens' Lane as it is to-day, and this allowed men to slip in without too much ado. The inn came to be known in more hostile quarters by the nickname of "Germany", a reference to the Lutheran interests of those who met behind its doors. Bilney was the leading spirit in the group of friends who used to thread their way down Milne Street in the dusk of evening, and an impressive group it was. Thomas Arthur and John Thixtill, Robert Barnes and George Stafford, Matthew Parker and John Lambert, came

[1] *John Foxe*, Vol. IV, p. 620.   [2] Ibid., Vol. V, p. 415.

night after night for new light and inspiration. There were others as well, who had begun to share the new sunrise and were glad to meet with Bilney and his friends at the White Horse Inn. There were Richard Smith and William Paget of Trinity Hall; there were Edward Crome and Nicholas Shaxton of Gonville Hall; there were John Rogers of Pembroke and Miles Coverdale of the House of which Barnes was the Prior; and to all these perhaps we may add the names of William Tyndale, who had come from Oxford to Cambridge in 1516, and of John Frith of King's, who was to leave Cambridge for Oxford in 1525. They were men of all years, Fellows, Doctors, masters, students, but all intent on the study of the *Novum Testamentum*, men of vision to whom "thoughts of reform still came as by fire and lightning".[1] They met in the shelter of the White Horse Inn as so long before others had met in the seclusion of the Catacombs, and the recovered loveliness of personal devotion and Christian fellowship bound them in heart and mind with bands of gold. It was the glad morning of the Reformation, still too early to see the dark shadows that all too soon would fall. "So oft", said one of the younger members as in after years he looked back upon those days, "so oft as I was in their company, methought I was . . . quietly placed in the new glorious Jerusalem."[2]

But quite the most famous convert to be won by Bilney was still outside the fold. Hugh Latimer had become a Fellow of Clare in 1510 and a Master of Arts in 1514. His name then drops right out of view until 1522, when it appears in the Proctor's records as one of twelve preachers who were licensed to preach in all parts of the realm. In the same year he was chosen to carry the silver cross for the University in all official processions, "which", in the words of Ralph Morice, "no man had to do but such an one as in sanctimony of life excelled other."[3] Then in 1523, Wolsey declined to start a fresh inquiry with regard to heretics in the schools at Cambridge, and George Stafford was thus free to give a course of public lectures to large crowds of eager students on the text of Holy Scripture. But Latimer's "popish

---

[1] Edith Weir Perry, *Under Four Tudors, being the True Story of Matthew Parker and Margaret*, p. 38.

[2] Thomas Becon, *The Catechism with other Pieces* (Parker Society), p. 426.

[3] Hugh Latimer, *Sermons and Remains*, p. xxvii.

zeal could in no case abide in those days good master Stafford, reader of the divinity lectures in Cambridge; most spitefully railing against him, and willing the youth of Cambridge in no wise to believe him".[1] Then in 1524, his name appears in the list of certain Masters of Arts who had taken their first Divinity degree, and he had then reached an age when there would seem no great risk of a change in his way of thought. Yet his mind was still far from ease, and the rise of controversy made him sigh at times for the peace of the cloister. But it was the custom for those who had taken a degree in Divinity on their graduation to deliver an oration before the University on some aspect of their studies. Latimer determined, with the zeal of one who was full of strong indignation at the spread of Reformation Truth in Cambridge circles, to press home the attack. He left Stafford for a much more illustrious adversary and set out to castigate Melancthon, who had lately impugned the School Doctors and had dared to maintain that their teaching must be brought to the test of Holy Writ. It was a strong and most intemperate declamation, too strong indeed to ring quite true. It would seem that there was something in the preacher's manner, perhaps in the tone of certain remarks, which showed that this was zeal without knowledge; nay more, zeal that knew no peace or comfort within.

But there was one who heard Latimer's oration, almost hidden in the crowd on account of his diminutive stature, and to him the secret disharmony in the preacher's heart was clearly disclosed. This was Bilney, and to his quick insight it was plain that he stood in the presence of a man who was now caught in the same web in which his own soul had once been tangled. Foxe tells us that he was "stricken with a brotherly pity towards him, and bethought by what means he might best win this zealous ignorant brother to the true knowledge of Christ".[2] His heart went out to him as one who was still in error in spite of his rugged honesty and his homely eloquence, and he longed to win him for Christ. He was only Little Bilney, and would never do any great service for God; but let him win the soul of that one man, and what great things would he do in His Name? Therefore, after a short delay, he sought out the preacher in his study and begged him for the love of God to hear his confession. There was Bilney,

[1] *John Foxe*, Vol. VII, p. 437. [2] Ibid., p. 438.

with his pale face and his wasted features and his perfect sincerity, asking him to shrive his soul; what could it all mean? Latimer did not understand all at once, but he could never forget that scene. "Bilney . . . desired me for God's sake to hear his confession", so he recalled in his first sermon before the Duchess of Suffolk; "I did so; and to say the truth, by his confession I learned more than before in many years."[1] Latimer thought to hear a confession of sin and would listen without mistrust; but there can be no doubt as to what the tenor of that confession must have been. Bilney would tell him with touching simplicity his own story of conflict and anguish, how he had gone about seeking health and healing for a soul that was sick. He would tell how he had once been bruised and broken at the hands of those Church physicians whom Latimer would commend, and how at last he had been healed as he had read the New Testament which Latimer would denounce. And would he not draw that little Book out of his pocket, and let it fall open at the words which he had read so often: "It is a true saying, and worthy of all men to be embraced, that Christ Jesus came into the world to save sinners."

The great preacher was thus taken by storm. He had heard the voice of the Holy Ghost as well as the voice of Bilney, and he could not resist. That quiet story of a long and painful conflict, that clear testimony to the pardon and peace which the Gospel had brought, told out in the solemn stillness of his study, awoke in his heart new thoughts and feelings which were too deep for words. Bilney had brought him a revelation of the Grace of God such as he had never heard before; it was like a Divine Secret which he had been trying for years in vain to grasp. It was not the penitent but the confessor to whom the Word of God came in absolution that day, for the change was instant and decisive. His first act no doubt would be to procure that Book which he had so despised, and the clouds and darkness soon passed away in the sunlight of God's presence. He would gladly recall that hour to the end of his life and could hardly speak of Bilney without the accent of divine animation. "Master Bilney, or rather Saint Bilney, . . . was the instrument whereby God called me to knowledge; for I may thank him, next to God, for that know-

[1] Hugh Latimer, *Sermons*, p. 334.

ledge that I have in the Word of God."[1] He forsook his studies
in the Schoolmen and found a new authority in the Scriptures.
He joined in the meetings which were held in the White Horse
Inn, and he sought out Stafford to ask his pardon for the rude
attack which he had made a year before.[2] And with Bilney, there
sprang up a close and lasting friendship, and this was "much
noted of many" in Cambridge.[3] They used to walk almost daily
in the lanes or fields near Cambridge, and Castle Hill where they
were most often seen was long to be known as Heretics' Hill.[4]
Would that we were able to learn something of the conversation
which would make their hearts burn within; for may we not
think that Jesus Himself drew near and went with them?

Latimer's conversion must have taken place in spring or
summer 1524, and for about two years he and Bilney remained
free to walk and converse in peace. Bilney was now more than
ever a man whose heart was on fire with the love of Christ, and
day by day he gave himself to the task of seeking out the poor and
outcast. He went to the lazar cots to tend the lepers, to wrap them
in clean sheets and to supply their needs, above all, to tell them of
Christ; he went to the prison-cells in search of sinners, to win
their trust and to cheer them in their distress, above all, to lead
them to Christ. Bilney soon took Latimer with him as his companion on these errands in the name of mercy and so taught him
how to help them that were in need and to feed the hungry for
the sake of Jesus.[5] Those were days which lived in Latimer's
memory. "Now after I had been acquainted with him," he said,
"I went with him to visit the prisoners in the Tower at Cambridge; for he was ever visiting prisoners and sick folk. So we
went together, and exhorted them as well as were able to do;
moving them to patience, and to acknowledge their faults."[6]
They took a close personal interest in the case of one poor woman
who was accused, wrongly as they believed, of the murder of her
own child; they not only procured for her the king's pardon but
were able, as well, to set her free with her conscience at rest.[7]
There was also the wife of an officer who had been cast into

[1] Hugh Latimer, *Sermons,* p. 334.   [2] *John Foxe*, Vol. VII, p. 438.
[3] Ibid., p. 452.   [4] Ibid., p. 452.
[5] Ibid., p. 452.   [6] Hugh Latimer, *Sermons*, p. 335.
[7] Ibid., *Sermons*, pp. 335, 336.

prison for the sin of adultery; but the daily conversation which she had with Bilney brought her to such true repentance and sincerity of faith that in after life she was quite ready to die for the Christ she had found.[1] We can hardly fail to love the picture of this beautiful ministry in the poorest parts of Cambridge or to believe that they have long since heard the glad voice of welcome: "Come, ye blessed of my Father, . . . For I was an hungred, and ye gave me meat: I was thirsty, and ye gave me drink: I was a stranger, and ye took me in: naked, and ye clothed me: I was sick, and ye visited me: I was in prison, and ye came unto me. . . . Inasmuch as ye have done it unto one of the least of these my brethren, ye have done it unto me" (Matt. 25: 34–40).

Meanwhile, the train had been unconsciously prepared for the spread of Bilney's teaching into new fields. As early as 1518, Wolsey had armed himself with the authority of a Papal Bull for reformation of the monasteries. He had used its power to suppress twenty-one monastic houses and had seized their wealth to provide the funds necessary for the establishment of a new and magnificent college which was to bear his name in the heart of Oxford. Cardinal College, or Christ Church as it was to become, was the greatest academic foundation of the age, and the Imperial Ambassador, Eustace Chapuys, wrote that almost every stone was blazoned with the arms of Wolsey.[2] His plans for the College were nearing completion by the end of 1524, and he spared no pains in his search for young men of mark and learning whom he could install as its first canons. Wolsey's agents found in Cambridge some eight or ten choice young scholars who were amenable to his offer, and a few months later they were transferred from the banks of the Cam to the new foundation in Oxford. Among them were Richard Cox and John Clark, John Frith and John Fryer, Godfrey Harman and Henry Sumner, William Betts, Goodman and Radley. They were chosen for their academic ability, and no thought was given to their spiritual affinities. Yet they had all been more or less convinced of the truth of Bilney's teaching, and they found in Oxford a field where they could plant the new ideas which they had reaped from the study of the Scriptures. But, in 1528, an explosion of heresy took place which caused profound dismay to the Oxford authorities.

[1] *John Foxe*, Vol. IV, p. 621. [2] A. F. Pollard, *Wolsey*, p. 217.

Rigorous inquiry traced it back to Wolsey's men from Cambridge, and the warden of New College complained that they had tarred "the most towardly young men in the University".[1] "Would God", so the warden wrote with reference to the Cardinal, "Would God my Lord's Grace had never been motioned to call Clark nor any other Cambridge man into his College. We were clear, without blot or suspicion, till they came; and some of them long time hath had a shrewd name."[2] John Clark died in prison, but John Frith was released, and the light continued to spread.

But the year in which the Cambridge scholars were transferred to Oxford was a year of sunshine before the storm. There was still no open conflict with Church authorities, no sign of real alarm at the progress of the Reformed teaching. Thus in July 1525, the Bishop of Ely allowed Bilney to take out a licence to preach anywhere in his Diocese, for as yet no serious misgiving had been aroused. But those who were preachers as well as doers of the Word were to find that fearless preaching in those days was no light burden, for the Bishop of Ely soon began to feel that he had not been strict enough in his general attitude. Loud and constant complaints began to pour into his ears concerning Latimer's preaching, and at length he came up to hear and to judge for himself when he had to preach in Great St. Mary's. Latimer was then forbidden to preach any further either in the See of Ely or in any Cambridge pulpit over which the Bishop had the final control. Then on Christmas Eve, Barnes preached a sermon in which he launched the most reckless attack, full of personal violence, on the whole Bench of Bishops, and on Wolsey as the Cardinal-Archbishop of York in particular. He was at once accused before the Vice-Chancellor of heresy and sedition and was required to recant or to abide the consequences. In February 1526, he was taken up to London under arrest and was cited before Wolsey at Westminster. He was urged to submit, but he stood firm and was therefore sent to the Fleet prison. But the Bishops wrought on his fears, threatened him with burning, and at last got him to recant. At daylight on Sunday the 12th, he was marched through the streets to St. Paul's, a faggot on his shoulder, and was forced to recant and seek absolution before the eyes of

[1] J. F. Mozley, *William Tyndale*, p. 120.   [2] Demaus, p. 39.

half London. He was then sent back to prison during Wolsey's pleasure. But that single sermon, more marked by hot language than by honest proclamation of the Gospel, had plunged Cambridge into weeks of controversy, and that recantation was to prove an unfortunate precedent which seems to have cast its own kind of spell over the path which the friends of Reform were called to tread.

Bilney and Latimer must have been compromised by the conduct of Barnes and the uproar which had ensued. They had refrained in their sermons from all attack on the Bishops, but they were known to be preaching doctrines which bordered on Lutheran heresy. We do not know what took place in Cambridge after the trial of Barnes, but it would seem that they were both seized and sent to London to stand their trial before Wolsey. But the Legate was by no means prone to drastic forms of persecution, and he seems at that time to have been in his most genial frame of mind. Ralph Morice has preserved quite a racy account of his interview with Hugh Latimer, and the result was more favourable than the best of prophets could have foretold. Wolsey seems to have been impressed with his wit and candour, and he was soon dismissed with a licence from the Legate himself which would give him authority to preach in all parts of England.[1] But Ralph Morice does not mention Bilney, and our knowledge of what happened in his case is not so precise. He fared lightly compared with Barnes, but he did not escape so well as Latimer. Our knowledge is meagre, and is based on the words of Sir Thomas More with regard to his trial in 1527: "This man had also been before that (i.e. before 1527) accused unto the greatest prelate in this realm, who for his tender favour borne to the University did not proceed far in the matter against him; but accepting his denial with a corporal oath that he should from that time forth be no setter forth of heresies, but in his preachings and readings impugn them, dismissed him very benignly; and of his liberal bounty gave him also money for his costs."[2] The truth of this account is borne out by certain features of the trial in 1527, and it conforms to the general impression of Wolsey's lenience. He gave Latimer a licence to preach; he gave Bilney money to pay his costs. But

[1] Latimer, *Sermons and Remains*, pp. xxx, xxxi.
[2] *Sir Thomas More: Works*, Vol. II, p. 193.

whereas Latimer went out quite free, Bilney was bound over by
an oath as to his future preaching. He was neither punished nor
required to recant; but he had to promise that he would cease to
preach Reformed doctrine, and that he would instead impugn it
as far as he could.

It was more than sad that Bilney should have taken an oath
which he could not in good conscience observe. In the spring of
1527, he suddenly overcame his natural nervousness and left
Cambridge for an itinerant course of preaching in the Eastern
Counties. Thomas Arthur was his companion on this enterprise,
and he taught in town and country through the See of Norwich,
where he had been brought up. It is still on record that he preached
at Christ Church, Ipswich, where he dared to say that the cowl of
St. Francis, wrapped round a dead body, had no power to take
away sin.[1] To be buried in a friar's habit, together with letters of
enrolment in a monastic order, was thought a sure way to obtain
deliverance from eternal condemnation. Thus King John was
buried in a monk's cowl; and Piers Ploughman describes a friar
as wheedling a poor man out of his money by saying that:

"St. Francis himself shall fold thee in his cope,
And present thee to the Trinity, and pray for thy sins."

Bilney's tilt at this superstition led to a curious dialogue with a
Franciscan Friar named John Brusierd; and the details have been
preserved by Foxe in a copy of the Latin account drawn up by the
Friar himself. "Whereas you said that none of the Saints do make
intercession for us, nor obtain for us anything," said the Friar,
"you have perilously blasphemed the efficacy of the whole
church, consecrated with the precious blood of Christ." Bilney's
reply was based on the words of Scripture: "If there be but one
Mediator of God and men, the Man Christ Jesus, where is our
blessed Lady? Where are then St. Paul and other saints?" This led
to an altercation on the subject of saint worship and on the Pope
as Anti-Christ. When the Friar claimed that signs and wonders
were in favour of the authority of Rome, Bilney answered:
"These wonders which they call miracles be wrought daily in the
church, not by the power of God as many think, but by the
illusion of Satan . . . to make them put their faith in our Lady,

[1] *John Foxe*, Vol. IV, p. 627.

and in other Saints, and not in God alone, to Whom be honour and glory for ever." The Friar could hardly contain his rage. "But that I believe and know that God and all His Saints will take everlasting revengement upon thee, I would surely with these nails of mine be thy death."[1]

We are hardly surprised to learn that twice he was dragged out of the pulpit in that church at Ipswich.[2] But he was not to be deterred, and he moved down from the Eastern Counties to preach in and around London. We need not imagine that the statements drawn up for his accusation do full justice to his teaching, but they contain clear proof of the Scriptural genesis of his doctrine. He was outright in his condemnation of image worship and adoration of the Virgin and of the Saints; he was fearless in his declarations on the folly of pilgrimage and the falsehood of miracles. He would have it "that the Pope hath not the keys that Peter had, except he follow Peter in his living", and "that man is so imperfect of himself that he can in no wise merit by his own deeds."[3] But his preaching was not all negative; he strove above all to proclaim to his hearers that great doctrine of the mediation of Christ which had brought light and peace to his own soul. His own words to Tunstall make it plain that his one supreme object was to preach Christ: "Whom with my whole power I do teach and set forth, being made for us by God His Father our wisdom, righteousness, sanctification, and redemption."[4] There were many friends of Reformed teaching among the clergy of London, and we find him in the parish church of Willesden where he urged the people to put away their gods of silver and gold: for, he said, "Jews and Saracens would have become Christian men long ago, had it not been for the idolatry of Christian men in offering of candles, wax, and money, to stocks and stones."[5] At length Whitsun week brought him to the church of St. Magnus, where he spoke most strongly against image worship, and the intercession of Saints, and the authority of Popes: "These five hundred years there hath been no good Pope, and in all the times past we can find but fifty: for they have neither preached nor lived well nor conformably to their dignity; wherefore till now they have borne the keys of simony. Against them, good

---

[1] *John Foxe*, Vol. IV, pp. 628: 631. [2] Ibid., p. 627.
[3] Ibid., p. 627. [4] Ibid., p. 636. [5] Ibid., p. 627.

people!"[1] And in particular, he spoke against "the new idolatrous rood newly erected, before it was gilded".[2] This was too much! Both Bilney and Arthur were seized and thrown into the Bishop of London's coal-house until they could be transferred to the Tower.

On November 27th, 1527, the Lord Cardinal Wolsey and Archbishop Warham, the Bishops of London and Ely, and a number of other Bishops and Divines, processed to the Chapter House at Westminster. Bilney and Arthur were summoned before them to answer certain questions, and their ordeal began. It would seem that Wolsey at once recognised in Bilney the man who had been brought before him as Latimer's companion hardly more than twelve months before. His very first questions, therefore, were to ask him whether he had taught in public or in private any of the Lutheran heresies which the Church had condemned, and then, whether it was not true that he had sworn on oath neither to preach nor to defend those false opinions anywhere. Bilney had to admit that he had taken such an oath; but he argued that the oath had not been administered "judicially" (*judicialiter*).[3] He meant that he did not regard it as binding on his conscience, because he had been forced to swear the oath in a private interrogation, and not with the judicial formula of a law-court. This was a poor quibble for a man of Bilney's standing, and we are not surprised that it only irritated Wolsey. Bilney was then required to swear again, and to swear that he would "answer plainly, . . . and that he should do it without any craft, qualifying, or leaving out any part of the truth."[4] This was indeed a most grievous reproach to his integrity, and this second oath was meant to humiliate as well as to correct. Wolsey then turned his eyes upon Arthur. He was also required to take this oath, and was then asked whether he had not once told Sir Thomas More that in the Sacrament of the Altar there was not the very Body of Christ. But this was just a brief preliminary examination, and the two men were told that they might have until noon to deliberate and to frame a written statement. After midday, Wolsey and the Bishops returned to the Chapter and swore in the men who were to witness against Bilney. But the case had hardly begun when

[1] *John Foxe*, Vol. IV, p. 627.   [2] Ibid., p. 621.
[3] Gilbert Burnet, *The History of the Reformation*, Vol. I, p. 53.
[4] *John Foxe*, Vol. IV, p. 622.

the Legate, "because he was otherwise occupied",[1] perhaps because he thought two such troublesome heretics too mean to take up so much time, adjourned the case and left it in the hands of the Bishop of London and the other Bishops who were present.

Bilney thus found himself sent back to his prison quarters, and five more days were to elapse before he was summoned for a further hearing. He had heard the Legate's last words to the Bishops, charging them to proceed against all men and all writings which were favourable to the spread of Lutheran heresies; and he had heard Wolsey tell them that they were to compel those who were found guilty to a solemn abjuration by law, or else that they were to give them up to the arm of the State for suitable punishment. But fresh hope sprang up in his heart when he knew that Cuthbert Tunstall, the Bishop of London, was to conduct the trial, for he believed that he would be mild and considerate. He wrote him a series of five letters in the naïve belief that a simple record of his spiritual experience would touch his heart and guide him in judgment. Tunstall had these letters copied out with scrupulous honesty for his episcopal register, and Foxe in turn transcribed three of them from Latin into English for his own narrative. This is the sole literary composition which has come down to us from the hand of Bilney,[2] and they excel in an honest sincerity and an artless pathos which might have been enough to melt a heart of stone. The first of the series is of particular value, for it throws up the blinds and lets us see through the windows into his own hidden experience; it makes us the hearers of his confession just as he had once made Latimer, and we are told how he came out of great conflict into peace with God through the Word of Truth. Perhaps it was Bilney's hope that Tunstall would be no less impressed than that other in his room at Cambridge; perhaps Tunstall's heart would answer to that written testimony so that he would also awake beneath the mystic touch of God the Holy Ghost. "I rejoice," he wrote, "that I have now happened upon such a judge, and with all my heart give thanks unto God Who ruleth all things."[3]

In the second letter which Foxe preserves, he set out to reply to those "who like Malchus, having their right ear cut off, only

[1] *John Foxe*, Vol. IV, p. 622.
[2] But see two more letters in Appendix to Vol. IV of J. Pratt's Edition of John Foxe.   [3] Ibid., p. 634.

bring their left ear to sermons". Was it true that he had maintained that the Gospel had not been preached in real sincerity for
some time past? He would write down what he had learned of
God through Christ in the Scriptures and show how the doctors,
even of great name and renown, did not teach on this wise in
their sermons. "Therefore I do confess that I have often been
afraid that Christ hath not been purely preached now a long time;
for who hath been now for a long season offended through
him?"[1] This was his great argument; where was the offence of
the Cross? "But now, to pass over many things whereby I am
moved to fear that the Word of God hath not been purely
preached, this is not the least argument, that they that come, and
are sent, and endeavour themselves to preach Christ truly, are evil
spoken of for His Name."[2] Bilney had some written questions,
drawn up by the Bishop, before him as he wrote. "Now you do
look that I should show unto you at large (as you write) how that
they ought sincerely to preach, to the better edifying hereafter of
your flock. Here I confess I was afraid you had spoken in some
derision, until I well perceived that you had written it with your
own hand. Then again I began to doubt for what intent Tunstall
should require that of Bilney: an old soldier, of a young beginner;
the chief pastor of London, of a poor silly sheep. But for what
intent soever you did it, I trust it was of a good mind; and albeit
that I am weak of body, yet, through the grace of Christ given
unto me, I will attempt this matter, although it do far pass my
power."[3] But he postponed this to his third letter, and closed
with the touching request: "I would to God you would give
me leave privately to talk with you, that I might speak freely
that which I have learned in the Holy Scriptures for the consolation of my conscience; which if you will do, I trust you shall not
repent you. All things shall be submitted unto your judgment;
who, except I be utterly deceived, will not break the reed that is
bruised and put out the flax that is smoking; but rather, if I shall
be found in any error as indeed I am a man, you, as spiritual, shall
restore me through the spirit of gentleness."[4]

His third letter came to a close with the renewed request for a
personal interview, such as he had once had with Latimer: "The

[1] *John Foxe*, Vol. IV, p. 636. [2] Ibid., p. 637.
[3] Ibid., p. 638. [4] Ibid., p. 638.

want of paper will not suffer me to write any more, and I had rather to speak it in private talk unto yourself: whereunto if you would admit me, I trust you shall not repent you thereof: and unto me, Christ I take to my witness, it would be a great comfort, in Whom I wish you with all your flock heartily well to fare. Your prisoner, and humble beadman unto God for you, Thomas Bilney."[1] But that was not to be. The Bishop of London, with the Bishops of Ely and Rochester, met in the house of the Bishop of Norwich, and resumed the hearing against Arthur. They swore in those who were to bear witness, and then cross-examined him in the light of their statements. Arthur was warned on no account to disclose the details of that cross-examination, and was sent back to his prison quarters. On December 2nd, they met again in the same house, and swore in a second group of men who were to witness against Bilney. Some were laymen; two were divines of the Franciscan Order; one was the Chief Provincial of the Friar-preachers for all England. Was it at all probable that a man like Cuthbert Tunstall, a warm friend of Erasmus, would let monks and friars, condemn one who owed his soul to the *Novum Testamentum*? But they were not ready to hear Bilney's case yet, and he must have been sent away so that Arthur might be summoned again. Him they charged with eight Articles of heresy, three of which he denied, while the other five he confessed. He was forced to repudiate these as heretical, and to submit himself to the judgment of the Bishops. We lose sight of Thomas Arthur at this point, but Bilney was brought back the next day. "I desire you that you will remember me," he had written, "that by your aid I may be brought before the tribunal seat of my Lord Cardinal; before whom I had rather stand than before any of his deputies."[2] But he was brought before the same Bishops, and he firmly resolved to stand his ground. Tunstall then produced the letters in his presence, and bound the notaries with an oath to make and keep a faithful copy of them. The trial then proceeded, and he was examined on no less than thirty-four counts of heresy.[3]

Bilney's answers to most of the questions seem to have been acceptable, and his Letters prove that he could defend himself on the others with no little ability. It is clear from a calm study of the

[1] *John Foxe*, Vol. IV, p. 641.   [2] Ibid., p. 638.
[3] *Sir Thomas More: Works*, Vol. II, pp. 12, 13, 193.

points which he would admit that he had no thought of separating from the Church like Luther, and that he was still far from the full light of the Reformation on some major issues. But his partial assent to some questions and his qualified replies to others show that his mind was still moving into the light. Thus he did not doubt that many of the Pope's laws were both wise and necessary, but how could he determine what his attitude should be to those of which he was ignorant? Or he agreed that the true Church cannot err since it is the whole congregation of God's elect, but how could men point out that Church with their finger when it is known to God alone? There were other questions on which he was suspect because of his unorthodox reply. He would allow the use of an image as a "liber laicorum", but he declared that it was not heretical for a man to believe "that our Lady remained not always a Virgin". He was convinced that "it is best that the people should have the Lord's Prayer and the Apostles' Creed in English, so that the devotion might the more be furthered by the understanding thereof: and also that thereby they might be the more prompt and expert in the articles of their faith, of which it is to be feared, a great number are ignorant." But in reply to the question whether the whole Scripture should be in English rather than Latin, "he did partly doubt; notwithstanding he wished that the Gospels and Epistles of the day might be read in English." He was quite clear on one leading question: "As touching pardons, he said that as they be used, and have too long been, it were better that they should be restrained, than that they should be any longer used as they have been, to the injury of Christ's Passion". We must regret that we have no answer to some of the questions, and the final question was most significant: "Whether that thou, Thomas Bilney, being cited upon heresy to appear before my Lord Cardinal, and before the day of thy appearance, not having made thy purgation as to those points that thou was cited upon, hast preached openly in divers churches of the City and Diocese of London, without sufficient license from the Bishop or any other?"[1]

On December 4th, Tunstall and his colleagues resumed the trial in the Chapter House at Westminster. Bilney was first solemnly exhorted to abjure and recant, but he simply replied

[1] *John Foxe*, Vol. IV, pp. 624: 626.

that he would stand to his conscience. Then the Depositions of those who had been asked to bear witness, the Articles of Inquiry, and his Answers were read aloud, and a remarkable struggle at once ensued. Tunstall, who was neither harsh nor sanguinary, had no desire to proceed to extremities with a man like Bilney; perhaps he had observed signs of weakness and now thought to exploit his fears. If he were to acquit Bilney, he might embroil himself with the Legate or the other Bishops; but if Bilney would now recant, he could at least protect his life. Therefore he urged him to deliberate in his own mind whether he would return to the Church and its faith, and sent him out of the room to reflect alone. But he only replied on his return: "Fiat iustitia et iudicium in nomine Domini." Tunstall tried still further to change his mind, but he remained steadfast, saying: "Haec est dies quam fecit Dominus: exultemus et laetemur in ea." At length, Tunstall, on the advice of the other Bishops, put off his cap, crossed his forehead and breast, and addressed himself to Master Bilney: "I by the consent and counsel of my brethren here present, do pronounce thee, Thomas Bilney, who hast been accused of divers articles, to be convicted of heresy; and for the rest of the sentence, we take deliberation till to-morrow."[1] It was a surprising situation. Bilney would no doubt have in mind the case of Barnes and his sorry failure, and the reproach which this had brought upon the Name of Christ; he would also have in mind the promise he had himself made to Wolsey a year before, and his troubled conscience, and the necessity which had compelled him to go out and preach. It was his great desire not to be found faithless, and yet how was he to resist in that time of ordeal? He was repeatedly given time to reflect, and the sentence itself was thrown into suspense at the vital moment. What would happen in the morning?

The morning found Bilney once more in the presence of the Bishops. He was asked by Tunstall if he would now revoke his errors and return to the fold of the Church. Bilney said that he had never separated from the Church as was thus implied, and that for one hostile witness, he was ready to call thirty men of honest life who would speak in his favour. But the Bishop told him that it was too late to call fresh witness, and he urged him

[1] *Iohn Foxe*, Vol. IV, p. 631.

again to abjure his errors. Then he dismissed him to consult his friends, and the case was adjourned until one o'clock the same day. The old question was at once put to him when the trial was resumed, but was met by the same request as he had made in the morning to call further witness. This was refused, and he was asked again if he would return to the Church; but he replied as before, "and other answer he would give none."[1] Tunstall sent him outside so that he could consult with the other Bishops; but when he was recalled, he still returned the same answer. Tunstall told him flatly that he could not call fresh witness, and asked if he would now abjure; but the answer was No. Nevertheless, Bilney asked for time to consult his friends "in whom his trust was", and "required space till the next morrow" to deliberate with himself.[2] Tunstall hesitated, afraid that he meant to appeal, but at length gave him two nights of respite. Therefore on Saturday, December 7th, at nine o'clock in the morning, Tunstall asked him once more if he would now return to the Church and revoke all the errors for which he stood condemned. These two nights, and their dreams, the long suspense and fear of the unknown, had done their work. Bilney's answer was that on the advice of his friends he would now submit, praying that they would deal gently with him in his abjuration and his penance. Tunstall handed him the form of abjuration which had been drawn up in advance, and he read it through in private. Then he was required to read it aloud and to subscribe his name. Tunstall at last spoke the words of absolution, but for penance required him to bear a faggot next day and to lie in prison until such time as it might please Wolsey to set him free.

Thus on Sunday, December 8th, he stood where Barnes had stood nearly two years before, in front of St. Paul's Cross, with his head bare and a faggot on his shoulder, and his conscience torn with shame and remorse, while he listened to a sermon which would exult at the Church's triumph over him as a reclaimed heretic; and then he was led back to his place of imprisonment and to the solitude of his own thoughts. This was a grave failure on the part of Bilney, and it could have been small comfort for him to know that he was not alone. No one had yet withstood the hour of trial or faced danger without flinching, and for men

[1] *John Foxe*, Vol. IV, p. 632.   [2] Ibid., p. 632.

like Barnes and Bilney to lose courage and then deny their faith was a grievous blow to the cause. Nothing in the early records of the English Reformation is so pitiful or so pathetic as the many recantations made by men who were in honest search for truth, and the fact is that Episcopal Registers for those years are full of abjurations which make painful reading. It is probable that the relative lenience of Wolsey and Tunstall was more dangerous by far to the progress of the Reformation than the bloody crusade of Sir Thomas More and Bishop Stokesley who were soon to succeed them in office. Death at the stake threw a lustre over the cause for which men died, while a public recantation cast a shadow over the truths which had thus been disowned. But not only would these recantations pain and perplex those who looked on; they would reflect the bewilderment and uncertainty which so often possessed the men who were involved. The time had yet to come when the issues between the old mediaeval way of worship and the new light of the Reformation were plain and clear, and it was not easy when men had to clarify convictions to the point where they were willing to die for them. Bilney did all that was in his power to insist that he had not broken away from the Church in which he had been ordained; he was not like Luther who had gone right outside its pale and who thundered for its reform from an external vantage-point. Bilney was a conservative student, and it was no light thing for him to face death at the hands of his fellow churchmen. The iron had yet to enter into his soul.

Nevertheless, Bilney stands in the place of honour at the head of the English Reformation. There had been a noble movement in the fourteenth century with John Wycliffe and the Lollards, but it was quite distinct from the Reformation in the sixteenth century. There had also been a reform movement which had begun with John Colet at Oxford in 1497, and it was this movement which had inspired the *Novum Instrumentum* in 1516. But John Colet died in honour as a dignitary of the Church in 1519, whereas Bilney was to die at the stake as an outcast from his Church and Orders. Bilney was not the man to take the lead or to burst forth like an English Luther; his work was done in the private school of friendship or in hours of conversation behind the closed doors of the White Horse Inn. Once he had found peace and comfort for his own soul, he could not help talking to his friends of the great discovery which he had made. He had gone through a long and a painful conflict of mind and soul just as Luther had done; he had by fasts and by self-mortification sought peace, and sought in vain. He owed his soul to a verse of Scripture which it had pleased God to illuminate, just as Luther owed his, and not Luther himself held more tenaciously to the great truth of the Righteousness which is of God by faith. "With all my whole power," he told Tunstall, "I teach that all men should . . . hunger and thirst for that righteousness."[1] Or he quotes another great Pauline word (1 Cor. 2:2) with the glowing exclamation: "O voice of a true Evangelist!"[2] But he was as gentle as Luther was rugged, and he was slow to lift his voice against the Church of his fathers. He was at home with his friends in Cambridge, but he never thought to appear before the eye of all England. It would be in spite of himself should he ever appear as a public figure, and it was long before his place could be clearly seen or rightly assessed. Bilney doubtless had no idea whereunto that seed-time would grow, but in quiet and imperceptible ways, it was to grow unto harvest. And the time of harvest which brought forth the Reformation of the Church in England must be traced back to the simple goodness and the loving witness of Bilney in Cambridge.

Foxe has etched his likeness with the features of a beautiful character, one which the Church can ill afford to lose. "This godly man, being a bachelor of law, was but of a little stature and very slender of body, and of a strait and temperate diet, given to good letters, and very fervent and studious in the Scriptures, as appeared by his sermons; his converting of sinners; his preaching at the lazar cots, wrapping them in sheets, helping them to what they wanted, if they would convert to Christ; laborious and painful to the desperates; a preacher to the prisoners and comfortless; a great doer in Cambridge, and a great preacher in Suffolk and Norfolk; and at last in London he preached many notable sermons."[3] And as if this were not enough, Foxe goes on a little later to add: "Concerning his diet which we spake of, it was so strait that for the space of a year and a half, he took commonly but one meal a day; so that if he were disposed to sup, he would keep his

[1] *John Foxe*, Vol. IV, p. 636.   [2] Ibid., p. 639.   [3] Ibid., p. 620.

commons; and likewise his supper, if he were disposed to dine; and would bear it to some prison where he used commonly to frequent, and to exhort such as were infamed or imprisoned for evil life."[1] We can all feel the charm in this sketch of Little Bilney, the gentle scholar, the loving servant, frail and diminutive in health and in stature, the slave of a severe diet, content with but one meal a day, never spending more than four hours in sleep, absorbed in prayer and in reading of the Scriptures, who gave himself with an ascetic devotion to the works of Christian charity. From the moment when there had been born in him a living faith through the Word of God, he had spent his time and abilities like the Master Himself as a doer of good. It is very pleasant to find in that age of strong and strident personalities one whom the love of Christ had so constrained, and who was as pleased to talk with the poor and the leper as with fellow-scholars at the White Horse Inn, if only "they would convert to Christ." We still see in Little Bilney one of the most lovable characters of the English Reformation.

Bilney won the hearts of his friends by his honest goodness, and he left an abiding impression on men like Hugh Latimer and Matthew Parker. There was both strength and weakness in his character; there is both charm and pathos in his narrative. A true scholar, a soul winner, "a great doer, a great preacher"[2]: these were marks of a man who must have been quite out of the common. The list of those whose lives were both touched and transformed by means of his witness in the schools of Cambridge is a noble testimony to his passion for souls. There were not a few who like him were to seal their faith by death at the stake: Barnes, and Lambert, and Latimer were all destined to lose their lives for the sake of that Christ to Whom Bilney had pointed them. Latimer could not recollect his name without speaking of him in terms aglow with reverence and affection. He could never forget how they had once conversed about the things of God in their daily walks in Cambridge, or how Bilney had taught him to visit those who were sick and in prison with words of love in the name of Jesus. His great debt to Bilney was still fresh in his mind towards the close of life, and found special mention in his talks with Ridley in their imprisonment.[3] His long letter to Sir

[1] *John Foxe*, Vol. IV, p. 621.　　[2] Ibid., p. 620.　　[3] *Ridley: Works*, p. 118.

Edward Baynton has an epitaph which is just as beautiful as that in *Foxe*: "I have known Bilney a great while," he wrote, "I think much better than ever did my Lord of London; for I have been his ghostly father many a time. And to tell you the truth, what I have thought always in him, I have known hitherto few such, so prompt and ready to do every man good after his power, both friend and foe; noisome wittingly to no man, and towards his enemy so charitable, so seeking to reconcile them as he did, I have known yet not many; and to be short, in sum, a very simple good soul, nothing fit or meet for this wretched world, whose blind fashion and miserable state (yea, far from Christ's doctrine) he could as evil bear, and would sorrow, lament, and bewail it, as much as any man that ever I knew."[1]

Latimer does no more than hint at his sound scholarship: "As for his singular learning, as well in Holy Scripture as in all other good letters, I will not speak of it."[2] The three letters which he wrote to Tunstall would be enough in the absence of all other literary remains to prove the strength and grasp of his spiritual insight or his mental capacity. After his death, friends in Cambridge treasured with the utmost care his copy of the Vulgate with its frequent notes in his handwriting down the margins. He seems to have acquired it in 1520, the year of its publication at Lyons; for the date 1520 is written in ink on the title-page, seemingly in his own handwriting. It is now lodged in the Library of Corpus Christi College, Cambridge; but, in 1940, the Rev. J. Y. Batley published a large number of the *Adversaria* for the benefit of students. These Adversaria or Animadversions consist of notes, of marked or underlined passages, of excisions and emendations; and they number 1852 in all. They show that he worked through the Old Testament from Genesis to Malachi; but at that point, the marginal notes come to an end. This was either because he meant to lay aside the Vulgate in favour of the Greek text in the *Novum Testamentum*, or else it was a result of his trial and imprisonment in 1527. A close study of this Vulgate helps us to see the real mind of Bilney and proves that he was a careful and painstaking student. His work was not meant for publication, and it is therefore a true index to his thinking. The notes suggest that his approach was inquiring rather than

---

[1] Latimer, *Sermons and Remains*, p. 330.   [2] Ibid., p. 330.

dogmatic; he was prepared to ask questions, but slow to pass judgment. But his Notes on Authority were bold in the extreme; he doubts, and cites the doubts of others. He did not say that the Church has erred, but he plainly states that the Church may err. And there is a very thoughtful comment in connection with Bildad's argument that a man cannot be justified before God. (Job 25:4). Batley renders it in English: "No one pure in the sight of God. We all might be condemned if God willed to enter into judgment with us. But O merciful Father, Who dost not impute as sin to us the impurity and sins of men Thy sons, if we have faith that our sins be remitted to us through our Lord Jesus Christ, Thy Son, Who has become to us justice, sanctification, and redemption."[1]

Sir Thomas More in his Dialogue Concerning Tyndale has much to say about Bilney, though he only refers to him with an indirect epithet as "that man ye wrote of."[2] He dealt with his trial at length on the ground that so many people thought that he had been wronged: "And they take for a great token . . . the proof . . . which men have had of him that he lived well, and was a good, honest, virtuous man, far from ambition and desire of worldly worship, chaste, humble, and charitable, free and liberal in almsdeeds, and a very goodly preacher, in whose devout sermons the people were greatly edified."[3] He was forced to admit that in his trial Bilney had proved very resolute; indeed he went on to maintain that his abjuration was very imperfect.[4] Bilney had, in fact, stood like a rock through the first stage of his trial and had refused to be shaken by the terrors which lay before him as a heretic. His fall must be largely ascribed to the friends whom he was given leave to consult, for they bent their strength to persuade him not to stake his life on an issue of faith against the Church and her judgment. But those friends quite failed to see that Bilney fallen would be Little Bilney no more, and the repercussions of his fall were long felt as a signal warning to those who came after. Tyndale's letter to John Frith in 1533, while he lay in prison subject to the pressures which had beset Bilney, had this in mind: "Fear not the threatening, neither be overcome of sweet words, with which twain the hypocrites shall assail you.

[1] J. Y. Batley, pp. 38, 39.   [2] *Sir Thomas More: Works*, Vol. II, p. 6.
[3] Ibid., pp. 6, 7.   [4] Ibid., pp. 195: 202.

Neither let the persuasions of worldly wisdom bear rule in your heart; no, though they be your friends that counsel you. Let Bilney be a warning to you. Let not their vizor beguile your eyes. Let not your body faint. He that endureth to the end shall be saved."[1] So, too, Hugh Latimer in his Seventh Sermon before Edward VI in 1549 referred to it: "Here is a good lesson for you, my friends; if ever you come in danger, in durance, in prison for God's quarrel . . . as he (Bilney) did for purgatory-matters, and put to bear a fagot for preaching the true Word of God against pilgrimage and such like matters, I will advise you first and above all things, to abjure all your friends, all your friendships; leave not one unabjured. It is they that shall undo you, and not your enemies. It was his very friends that brought Bilney to it."[2]

We do not know how long Bilney had to remain in prison after his recantation; it may have been twelve months or more. Latimer's phrase, "a whole year after", is not quite so definite as a point of reference as we might wish.[3] He was at length released and at once made his way back to Cambridge. But his recantation was so great a burden on his conscience that he was close to the point of total despair. He was harassed by an acute sense of remorse, and the peace which had once been his strength had now fled. His friends could not console him, and Scripture itself seemed to utter no voice at all except that of condemnation. Latimer feelingly referred to that awful sorrow in one of his Sermons before Edward VI in 1549: "I knew a man myself, Bilney, Little Bilney, that blessed martyr of God, what time he had borne his fagot and was come again to Cambridge, had such conflicts within himself . . . that his friends were afraid to let him be alone: they were fain to be with him day and night and comforted him as they could, but no comforts would serve."[4] When they tried to cheer him with the comfortable words of Scripture, he shrank away as though they had tried to transfix him with a sword. Always strict and sparing in such points as sleep and food, he could now hardly bear to eat at all for sorrow. He could find no comfort even in the intimate fellowship of a companion like Hugh Latimer, and the older man tried in vain to bring him new heart and new hope. In an Advent sermon in 1552, Latimer

[1] William Tyndale, *Works*, Vol. I, p. LIX.   [2] Latimer, *Sermons*, p. 222.
[3] Latimer, *Sermons and Remains*, p. 51.   [4] Latimer, *Sermons*, p. 222.

looked back again in sad reverie: "That same Master Bilney . . . was induced and persuaded by his friends to bear a fagot at the time when the Cardinal was aloft and bore the swing. Now when that same Bilney came to Cambridge again, a whole year after, he was in such an anguish and agony so that nothing did him good, neither eating nor drinking, nor any other communication of God's Word; for he thought that all the whole Scriptures were against him, and sounded to his condemnation. So that I many a time communed with him, for I was familiarly acquainted with him; but all things whatsoever any man could allege to his comfort seemed unto him to make against him."[1]

It is not clear how long Bilney laboured under this great burden of sorrow and remorse. "The space almost of two years" to which Foxe refers may be correct, if we reckon it from the date of his abjuration at the close of 1527.[2] "Yet for all that," so said Latimer, "afterwards he came again"[3]; "he was revived."[4] It would seem that Latimer encouraged him to walk once more on Heretics' Hill, deep in conversation about the things of God, and to resume his old pastoral ministry to the sick, to the poor, and to them that were in prison. The God of Hope and Peace began to build up the disconsolate Bilney once more, and there came to birth in his soul a strong and settled resolution that he would yet redeem his fall and seal his faith for the glory of God. There were major events on foot in the world at large which would help to stir his soul. It was during the year 1529 that George Stafford died from the plague which had driven so many away from Cambridge, while he was still labouring for the conversion of a priest who was plague-stricken. Then came Wolsey's fall from power and pre-eminence, and Sir Thomas More took his place as the Lord Chancellor. The full story could not be told, and all kinds of rumour filled the country. On Sunday, December 19th, Latimer preached his famous Sermon on The Card, and Cambridge was set by the ears with strife and debate. Buckenham preached his Sermon on The Dice in reply, and the Vice-Chancellor had to caution Father Hugh to avoid "such things in the pulpit as had been in controversy between him and others".[5]

[1] Latimer, *Sermons and Remains*, pp. 51, 52. [2] *John Foxe*, Vol. IV, p. 642
[3] Latimer, *Sermons and Remains*, p. 52. [4] Latimer, *Sermons*, p. 222.
[5] Demaus, p. 70.

The year 1530 kept the popular excitement at white heat with news of Wolsey's death and rumours of the King's Cause. The mild-natured Tunstall was transferred to Durham, and the far more violent Stokesley was nominated for London; and fresh measures for suppression of heresy kept the friends of reform in a state of constant uncertainty. Latimer left Cambridge in the summer months of 1530, and a sense of common danger drew the old White Horse Inn friends still more closely together. But those days of danger had at last put mettle into Bilney's soul, and the hour was now at hand when he was to confess his faith before the eyes of all England.

Bilney's resolution had grown up in secret in his own heart; he would obey that still small voice which was so insistent, so compelling, in its summons. He would ignore the risks which lay before him and would go out to proclaim the Truth which he had twice in his weakness denied. "He, by God's grace and good counsel, came at length to some quiet of conscience, being fully resolved to give over his life for the confession of that truth which before he had renounced."[1] So one evening in the early days of 1531, he took his leave of the few friends who were still in Cambridge, with the moving words of St. Paul that he must go up to Jerusalem and that they would see his face no more. It was then ten o'clock at night, and soon afterwards he left Trinity Hall, and the gate closed behind him for the last time. His manner of going was like his whole career; it was a perilous venture "in darkness and loneliness".[2] He made his way into Norfolk, where at first he spoke in private to those whom he knew as brethren, and in particular to an anchoress in Norwich whom he had led to Christ. Then he began to preach in the fields and meadows, bearing constant testimony to the Faith which he had before abjured. He had with him copies of Tyndale's *New Testament* and *The Obedience of a Christian Man*, books which had been proscribed and which prove, if proof be needed, the true bent of his heart. On March 3rd, Stokesley proposed to Convocation certain articles of accusation against Latimer, Bilney, and Crome, on the ground of heretical preaching in the See of London. Crome was seized and forced to recant, but the other two were beyond his reach. Nevertheless Bilney must have travelled south from

[1] *John Foxe*, Vol. IV, p. 642.   [2] Batley, p. 10.

Norfolk, for he was in Greenwich six weeks before the date of his arrest;[1] and Latimer was in Kent and London in mid-summer, preaching in the teeth of Stokesley's opposition. Did Latimer on this journey meet and converse for the last time with his Father-in-God? We do not know. Little Bilney, "setting forward on his journey toward the celestial Jerusalem",[2] returned to his native heath in Norfolk and was suddenly arrested and thrown into prison until a writ could be secured for his burning.

Richard Nix, Bishop of Norwich, was old and blind, bitterly hostile to Tyndale's *New Testament* and angrily resolved on the burning of heretics. But while he was waiting for Sir Thomas More's writ, he sent a succession of friars and doctors to see Bilney lest he should die in a state of damnable heresy. Friars from four Orders, Grey Friars, White Friars, Black Friars, Augustinian Friars, were engaged in constant debate with him; but one at least, Dr. Call, a Provincial of the Grey Friars, was in the end "somewhat reclaimed" for the Gospel through his testimony.[3] Bilney had now exposed himself to the extreme penalty of the law as a relapsed heretic, and the case against him was very simple. When the application for a writ to burn him was laid before the Lord Chancellor, he is supposed to have replied: "Go your ways and burn him first; and then afterwards come to me for a bill of my hand."[4] The writ was soon procured, the trial was short and summary, and he was condemned as a relapsed heretic. Foxe says that "the whole sum of his preaching" had been "chiefly against idolatry, invocation of saints, vain worship of images, false trust to men's merits, and such other gross points of religion as seemed prejudicial and derogatory to the blood of our Saviour Jesus Christ. As touching the Mass and Sacrament of the Altar, as he never varied from himself, so like-wise he never differed therein from the most gross Catholics."[5] This helps us to see just how far he had gone in the path of the Reformation, and how far he still had to go. Conscience, taught by Scripture, drove him into revolt against certain aspects of Church teaching, but he had not renounced the Church or its authority in the way that the men who came after him were to do. Thus before the sentence could be pronounced at his trial by

---

[1] Demaus, p. 105 n. [2] *John Foxe*, Vol. IV, p. 642.
[3] Ibid., p. 642. [4] Ibid., p. 650. [5] Ibid., p. 649.

the judge spiritual, Bilney made an appeal to the King as Supreme Head of the Church. This meant that the Mayor of Norwich had to decide whether he was bound in duty to treat him as the King's prisoner, and so withdraw him from the Bishop's jurisdiction.[1] The Mayor seems to have been disposed to take action accordingly; but the appeal was soon dismissed, perhaps on the ground that the new title had yet to be confirmed by Parliament.

But this appeal had its repercussions long after Bilney's death. On the Sunday after Michaelmas, the Mayor summoned to the council chambers all who had been present at his burning and asked for their signatures to a certificate as to his death, which he could then produce if he should find himself questioned in Parliament. He read aloud his own account of the execution, but one alderman asserted that it failed to refer to a bill of recantation. It was said that Bilney had read this bill while in prison and had confirmed it at the stake. But a dispute at once broke out as to whether this were the case, and this dispute in due time came before Sir Thomas More. It would seem that this was at the bottom of the attack which he launched on Bilney in his Preface to the Confutation of Tyndale's Answer: "But yet was God so gracious Lord unto him that he was finally so fully converted unto Christ and His true Catholic faith, that not only at the fire, as well in words as in writing, but also many days before, he had revoked, abhorred, and detested such heresies as he before had holden; which notwithstanding, there lacked not some that were very sorry for it, of whom some said, and some wrote out of Norwich to London, that he had not revoked his heresies at all, but still had abiden by them. And such as were not ashamed thus to say and write, being afterwards examined thereupon, saw the contrary so plainly proved in their faces by such as at his execution stood by him while he read his revocation himself, that they had in conclusion nothing else to say, but that he read his revocation so softly that they could not hear it."[2] Indeed, there were other places in his writings where Sir Thomas More made the same kind of statement with regard to Bilney: that he revoked his heresies before his death and was properly penitent; that he received absolution, and at his own request, though not without hesitation on the part of the Chancellor of the Diocese, he was

[1] Gairdner, p. 401.   [2] See Gairdner, p. 404, n.

allowed to receive the Sacrament; and that at the stake he read his recantation.[1] "And how is this proved?" asks John Foxe. "By three or four mighty arguments, as big as mill-posts fetched out of Utopia."[2] We have to ask ourselves whether, in fact, the Lord Chancellor did fail to state sober realities and did "juggle with truth".[3]

John Foxe himself was never so partial in his statement of facts as Sir Thomas More, for the Lord Chancellor knew that his own credit was at stake. He would argue, not only on behalf of the Church and its cause, but also in defence of his own name and the course of action he had pursued. His Dialogue was published in June 1529, before he became Lord Chancellor; his Confutation appeared in 1533, while he still held that high office. It was in the former that he discussed Bilney in an anonymous spirit as "the man ye wrote of", and dealt at length with his trial before Tunstall in 1527; it was in the latter that he spoke of Bilney by name and dealt with his trial and execution in 1531. The first book was relatively mild and moderate in tone, although he made it clear that heretics were fit only to burn, whether at the stake or in hell. But the second work was far more violent, and nothing could have shown more plainly what the leaders of the Reformation had to anticipate than its language with regard to persecution. More worked hand-in-glove with Stokesley in "God's great cause", and it was all to the good if he could turn the dispute with the Mayor of Norwich to his own advantage. This alone were reason enough why we should hear John Foxe in his indignant defence of Bilney: "A strange matter, that he who two years before had lain in such a burning hell of despair for his first abjuration, and could find no other comfort but only in returning to the same doctrine again which before he had denied, utterly resigning himself over to death, and taking his leave of his friends, and setting his face with Christ purposely to go to Jerusalem, voluntarily there to fall into the hands of the Scribes and Pharisees for that doctrine's sake, should now so soon, even at the first brunt, give over to the contrary doctrine again! It is not likely."[4] Even were it true that Bilney had done what Sir Thomas More had said in other respects, and there is no proof but

[1] Gairdner, p. 400.   [2] *John Foxe*, Vol. IV, p. 643.
[3] Ibid., p. 644.   [4] Ibid., p. 643.

More's own word, even if he had knelt down and asked for absolution, or if he had heard Mass and received the Sacrament, it would not prove that he had read or signed a fresh recantation. "Ah, Master More," wrote Foxe, "for all your powder of experience, do ye think to cast such a mist before men's eyes that we can not see how you juggle with truth!"[1]

But Foxe was less concerned with More himself than with those who might read his books, and, with an eye to them, he examined that paragraph in The Confutation so as to show up its fatal weakness. "Bilney was heard, and yet not heard," he wrote; "he spake softly, and yet not softly! Some said he did recant; some said he did not recant. Over and besides, how will this be answered, that forasmuch as the said Bilney (as he saith) revoked many days before his burning, and the same was known to him at London, then how chanced the same could not be as well known to them of Norwich? who, (as his own story affirmeth) knew nothing thereof before the day of his execution; then, seeing a certain bill in his hand, which some said was a bill of his revocation, others heard it not."[2] But John Foxe did more than contest Sir Thomas More's statement with a negative attitude; he was able to call on the testimony of men who had known Bilney or had seen him die. There were men of Norwich, men who were still alive and whom he had taken pains to consult: these men had been present at the death of Bilney and had neither themselves heard him recant nor yet ever heard tell of his recantation. Nor was that all. "Forasmuch as Bilney was a Cambridge man, and the first framer of that University in the knowledge of Christ, and was burned at Norwich, being not very far distant from Cambridge; there is no doubt but that amongst so many friends as he had in that University, some went thither to hear and see him. Of these, one was Thomas Allen, then Fellow of Pembroke Hall, who returning the same time from Bilney's burning, declared to Dr. Turner, Dean of Wells, being yet alive, that the said Bilney took his death most patiently, and suffered most constantly, without any recantation for the doctrine which he before had professed."[3] And then he adds: "But what need I to spend time about witness, when one Master Latimer may stand for a thousand?"[4] What then did Latimer have to say?

[1] *John Foxe*, Vol. IV, p. 644.   [2] Ibid., p. 645.   [3] Ibid., p. 651.   [4] Ibid., p. 651.

"God endued him with such strength and perfectness of faith, that he not only confessed his faith, the Gospel of our Saviour Jesus Christ, but also suffered his body to be burnt for that same Gospel's sake."[1] Thus it becomes certain that Sir Thomas More had succumbed to falsehood and slander in his attack upon Bilney; and the final refutation of that slander is an account of his death which was drawn up by Matthew Parker and which forms the basis of the following narrative.

Before the year 1531 came to a close, Richard Bayfield and John Tewkesbury were both to perish at the stake. But the foremost of the Reformation Evangelists, the first among the Fellows of Cambridge, to lay down his life was Little Bilney. The Friars and Doctors all took their part in his degradation from the priesthood after his trial, and he was then handed over to the City Sheriffs so that the Law might take its course. One of the two sheriffs was an old friend, Thomas Necton; he was helpless to stay the Law, but he could not bear in conscience to attend the execution. But he did make things more comfortable for him than they had been in the Guildhall, and it must have strengthened Bilney to know that his friends were at hand. Matthew Parker had come down from Cambridge to be near him in his supreme ordeal and was no doubt in the small group of friends who were allowed to spend the last evening with him. They were surprised to find that he could still refresh himself with a calm and cheerful spirit; nor did courage fail as the end drew near. Someone tried to console him with the trite remark that though the fire would be hot and painful to the body, yet the Spirit of God might well cool it to his everlasting comfort. But he knew in sober reality what God could do, even for one who had been so weak and fearful; and he forthwith put his finger into the flame of a candle, and held it there until it had burnt down to the first joint. "I feel by experience," he said, "and have known it long by philosophy, that fire by God's ordinance is naturally hot: but yet I am persuaded by God's holy Word, and by the experience of some spoken of in the same, that in the flame they felt no heat, and in the fire they felt no consumption: and I constantly believe that howsoever the stubble of this my body shall be wasted by it, yet my soul and spirit shall be purged thereby: a pain for the time,

[1] Latimer, *Sermons and Remains*, p. 52.

whereon notwithstanding followeth joy unspeakable." Then he went on to quote words which in his Vulgate had been marked with his pen in the margin: "Fear not: for I have redeemed thee, I have called thee by thy name; thou art mine. When thou passest through the waters, I will be with thee; and through the rivers, they shall not overflow thee: when thou walkest through the fire, thou shalt not be burned; neither shall the flame kindle upon thee. For I am the Lord thy God, the Holy One of Israel, thy Saviour" (Is. 43:1-3). And no wonder that the comfort of those words was never taken from them that heard them as long as they lived.[1]

The next morning was the Saturday appointed for his execution, but the true date is no longer certain. Was it March 10th, as in Foxe's "Kalender"? Or was it St. Magnus' Day, August 19th, as in Foxe's Narrative? The leading argument for an early date is the fact that "August 16th" is stamped on the copy of what was called "Bilney's Book", an account of the last scenes, which the Mayor of Norwich sent on to the Duke of Norfolk. At all events, on that fatal day in March or August 1531, while still in his early thirties, he was led out to the place for burning by men armed with glaves and halberds. It was "without the city gate"[2]: would he not take comfort as he went forth, bearing reproach, in the recollection that this was like Him Who also had to suffer "without the gate"? (Heb. 13:12). When he emerged from his prison quarters at the Guildhall, one of his friends drew near "and prayed him in God's behalf to be constant, and to take his death as patiently as he could".[3] Was this Matthew Parker, who had come from Cambridge on purpose to strengthen his hands, if that might be? And Bilney was able to make reply with quiet face and mild voice: "Ye see when the mariner is entered his ship to sail on the troublous sea, how he for a while is tossed in the billows of the same; but yet in hope that he shall once come to the quiet haven, he beareth in better comfort the perils which he feeleth: so am I now toward this sailing; and whatsoever storms I shall feel, yet shortly after shall my ship be in the haven, as I doubt not thereof, by the Grace of God, desiring you to help me with your prayers to the same effect."[4] On his way through

[1] *John Foxe*, Vol. IV, p. 653. [2] Ibid. p. 653.
[3] Ibid., p. 654. [4] Ibid., p. 654.

the streets, he gave alms to many by the hand of a friend: this was no doubt Dr. Warner of Winterton who was allowed to go with him for the sake of "ghostly comfort".[1] Bilney was dressed in a layman's gown, with the sleeves hanging down and with the arms out: "his hair being piteously mangled at his degradation; a little single body in person, but always of a good upright countenance."[2] So they came to the place where the stake had been set up in a large hollow called the Lollards' Pit, just beneath St. Leonard's Hill; it was indeed circled with hills, and was chosen so that people could look on with ease.

While the fire was being prepared, he stood and spoke to the people. "Good people," he began, "I am come hither to die; . . . and that ye may testify that I depart out of this present life as a true Christian man, in a right belief towards Almighty God, I will rehearse unto you in a fast faith the articles of my creed."[3] Then he rehearsed the Creed, often lifting both eyes and hands up to heaven, and in all, speaking with great reverence. He then put off his gown, and went up to the stake, and knelt on the ledge on which he was soon to stand, and gave himself to prayer. Those who looked on saw him praying "with such earnest elevation of his eyes and hands to heaven, and in so good and quiet behaviour, that he seemed not much to consider the terror of his death".[4] At last he was heard to recite a Psalm and to repeat one verse in a spirit of deep meditation three times over: "And enter not into judgment with thy servant; for in thy sight shall no man living be justified" (Ps. 143:2). He then took off his jacket and doublet and stood on the ledge in underclothing only as the chain was bound round his waist. Dr. Warner came to bid him farewell but could hardly speak for weeping. Bilney saw him, and "did most gently smile"; and spoke a few words of thanks and encouragement: "O Master Doctor, feed your flock, feed your flock; that when the Lord cometh, He may find you so doing. Farewell, good Master Doctor, and pray for me."[5] Warner could not reply for grief, nor bear to stay; he went his way, "sobbing and weeping".[6] Then the Friars who had taken part in his trial came and begged that he would exonerate them in the eyes of the people who might blame them for his death and withdraw their

---

[1] *John Foxe*, Vol. IV, p. 654.　　[2] Ibid., p. 654.　　[3] Ibid., p. 654.
[4] Ibid., p. 654.　　[5] Ibid., p. 655.　　[6] Ibid., p. 655.

alms. Bilney seized the chance to forgive while bound to the stake, even as his Master forgave when nailed to the Cross, saying with a loud voice: "I pray you good people, be never the worse to these men for my sake, as though they should be the authors of my death; it was not they!"[1] But while Dr. Warner could not bear to stay to the end, Matthew Parker remained until all was over. He had watched that slow and sombre progress from the city and had marvelled at his calm and patient bearing. Now he watched them pile the reeds and faggots round his body and set the reeds on fire. They blazed up in his face, causing untold pain and distress, while he held up his hands or beat upon his breast, crying sometimes "Jesus!", sometimes "Credo!" Then a strong wind blew the flame right away from his body, so that he stood awhile out of reach from the fire. Two or three times the flame was blown aside before the wood was set alight; but then, at last, the fire began to burn in strength. He did not long survive, and his body soon fell forward upon the chain. One of the guards used his halberd to knock out the staple in the stake behind him and allowed his body to fall into the midst of the burning faggots. Little Bilney had not escaped from death by fire, but those who had eyes to see may have seen that he was not alone: there was One like unto the Son of Man Who stood by him in the heat of dying and went with him through the gate of glory.

[1] *John Foxe*, Vol. IV, p. 655.

BIBLIOGRAPHY

STEPHEN CATTLEY, *The Acts and Monuments of John Foxe* (8 Vols.), 1841

HUGH LATIMER, *Sermons* (Parker Society Edition), 1844

HUGH LATIMER, *Sermons and Remains* (Parker Society Edition), 1845

WILLIAM EDWARD CAMPBELL, *The English works of Sir Thomas More* (7 Vols.), 1931

JAMES GAIRDNER, *Lollardy and the Reformation in England* (3 Vols.), 1908

J. B. MULLINGER, *The University of Cambridge, From the Earliest Times to the Royal Injunctions of 1535*, 1873

ROBERT DEMAUS, *Hugh Latimer: A Biography*, 1881

J. Y. BATLEY, *On a Reformer's Latin Bible, being an Essay on the Adversaria in the Vulgate of Thomas Bilney*, 1940

FREDERIC SEEBOHM, *The Oxford Reformers: John Colet, Erasmus, and Thomas More*, 1911

GILBERT BURNET, *The History of the Reformation of the Church of England* (Edited by Edward Nares in 4 Vols.)

WILLIAM TYNDALE

*Magdalen Hall, Oxford;
and Cambridge*

c. 1490–1536

"The true father of the English Bible is William Tyndale," whose "genius shows itself in the fact that he was able to couch his translations in a language perfectly understanded of the people, and yet full of beauty and of dignity".—SIR FREDERIC KENYON, *Our Bible and the Ancient Manuscripts*, pp. 211, 217.

WILLIAM TYNDALE WAS BORN some time between the years 1490 and 1495, little more than a century after the death of John Wycliffe. The facts of his early life are shrouded in the mists of uncertainty, but Foxe tells us that he was born "about the borders of Wales"[1]; and it would seem that the Cotswolds and the Severn were the playground of his boyhood. He sprang from a house of yeoman farmers, and his kinsfolk were men of good standing in the Western Counties. His father and mother are quite unknown to the annals which have come down to us, but each of his brothers, John and Edward, was to feel the spiritual magnetism of the Reformation literature. No records now remain of his schooldays or the kind of education which he must have received, but there is one suggestive allusion in his own works which still deserves mention: "Except my memory fail me, and that I have forgotten what I read when I was a child, thou shalt find in the English Chronicle how that King Athelstane caused the Holy Scripture to be translated into the tongue that then was in England."[2] He seems to have confused Athelstane with Alfred, but the recollection is a valuable sidelight on his boyhood. It is our one glimpse of the lad, evidently fond of reading, storing his mind with such items of history, artlessly disclosing his life's master passion. But he grew up in a county where he would see the Church at the lowest ebb of spiritual vitality, for each parish priest did that which was right in his own eyes. The County of Gloucester was the most neglected Archdeaconry in the most neglected Diocese in all England. It was still part of the See of Worcester which had been farmed out to foreign prelates who had never so much as set foot in the realm, and which could boast six mitred abbots who held seats in the House of Lords. But the common clergy were bogged in a mire of superstition which was nowhere surpassed in the length and breadth of England. "God it knoweth," wrote Tyndale, with regard to the priests of his own county, "there are a full

---

[1] *John Foxe*, Vol. V, p. 114.   [2] *Works*, Vol. I, p. 149.

ignorant sort, which have seen no more Latin than that they read in their portresses and missals."[1]

But the tale of appalling ignorance on the borders of Wales was just the worst of a series of tales which could be told of clergy throughout the realm. Thus in 1530, Tyndale himself bluntly affirmed that there were some twenty thousand priests in England, who could not so much as translate a plain clause from the Pater Noster into simple English.[2] The Convocation of Canterbury had refused to allow any man to translate any part of Scripture into the English tongue, and the Bible was an unknown book to priests and laymen alike. Knowledge of the Scriptures would have perished from the land but for the forbidden translations which the Lollards read in secret. But the tidal waves of common feeling had been sapping the walls of the mediaeval fortress of Church life for many a year, and the voice of protest was now growing in volume and in frequency. It might be true that the Lollard Movement had been suppressed, true too that the Wycliffe Bible had been proscribed: but John Purvey had once preached in Bristol, and the Lollards had been strongly entrenched in the west of England. We can hardly doubt that distant echoes of that stirring movement would reach the ears of the youthful Tyndale in the Vale of Berkeley. They would perhaps touch the chords of reality in his own mind even in the days before he had become aware of God's purpose in life for him. But that forbidden purpose was at work in his heart as he pondered the zeal of a king like Alfred, or the struggle of men like the Lollards. It was slowly to take shape in the form of a resolution to turn the Book of books into the kind of speech which the common people could read and understand. This was the grand motive behind all that he sought to do; it ran through his life and work like a thread of gold. There was little perhaps in the English Reformation so fine as the deliberate forgetfulness of self and the entire consecration of life which he brought to this task for God.

Foxe tells us that Tyndale was "brought up from a child in the University of Oxford".[3] The voice of an unvaried tradition claims that he was enrolled as a student in Magdalen Hall, and we may fix the date of his entry about the year 1505. Tyndale himself

---

[1] *Works*, Vol. I, p. 394.   [2] Ibid., Vol. III, p. 75.
[3] *John Foxe*, Vol. V, pp. 114, 115.

held no brief in favour of the course of study prescribed; a few trenchant lines were enough to sum up his protest against the method of training men for the Church. "In the Universities," he wrote, "they have ordained that no man shall look on the Scripture until he be noselled in heathen learning eight or nine years, and armed with false principles with which he is clean shut out of the understanding of the Scripture."[1] Logic was the essence of Arts, and the course left no room for the study of the Scriptures. It was a course which might foster sharpness of wit and much mental agility, but which could impart no spiritual fire and no real reverence for the truth. Things were little better when men passed from Arts to Theology, for even in Theology, the true purpose of the Scriptures had been buried out of sight in dismal oblivion. "Theology," so said Erasmus, "once venerable and full of majesty, had become almost dumb, poor, and in rags."[2] Yet there were signs that it would not always be so, signs that the dawn of a new day was not far off. A few English scholars such as Colet and Grocyn and Linacre had been to Italy and had brought back a good report of the Renaissance in art and culture. The New Learning had found a voice in the halls of Oxford in the last years of the fifteenth century, and the Greek and Latin Classics had been held up for the admiration of the younger students in place of the mediaeval Schoolmen. Thus in 1496, John Colet had given the first of his famous lectures on the Pauline Epistles. It was his great desire to let the text speak for itself and to avoid the trammels of tradition. This was a bold innovation, but for ten years it was maintained with far-reaching results in the study of the Scriptures.

Thus, while Tyndale's normal course of study was in "the scholastic treadmill"[3] of those syllogisms with which Scotists and Thomists loved to confound each other, he would also have his share in the joy of that awakening which was inspired by John Colet and the friends of the New Learning. Colet himself is thought to have been a resident in Magdalen Hall, until his appointment as Dean of St. Paul's in 1505.[4] Tyndale may have entered the Hall just in time to get to know him, certainly in time to fall under the spell of his influence. In July 1512, he graduated

---

[1] *Works*, Vol. II, p. 291.   [2] Demaus, p. 23.   [3] Mozley, p. 23.
[4] Seebohm, *The Oxford Reformers*, p. 138, n.

as a Bachelor of Arts, and in July 1515, he secured his Master's degree. It is just possible that his ordination took place in June 1514, at Whitborne, by the Bishop of Hereford, but the details are by no means certain.[1] He is silent as to his own spiritual thought and experience during these years, but there can be little doubt that they were years of transition from mediaeval teaching to Reformation doctrines. Certain it is that he grew and increased in his knowledge of the Scriptures as well as of Logic and the Classics. Foxe says that he was so drawn to Scripture that he began to expound it in private to the Fellows and students of Magdalen Hall.[2] The ray of light which had thus shone into his soul was pure and sweet, and his progress in the path of light was far more rapid than with many of his contemporaries. He was quite free from the hesitation which they felt at cutting adrift from doctrine or practice which was only enforced by long custom. He brought all his beliefs to the touchstone of the Scriptures, and he did this with far more care than most of the early friends of Reform in England. This meant that there was a clearness and a boldness in his thoughts and statements from the very outset of his public career which proved beyond doubt that he had not lost his head to the whim of the hour. We may add that his strong sense of freedom from the bonds of traditional authority is in itself a clear witness to the strength and vigour of his intellect. And Foxe makes it plain that his whole revolt from Church and tradition was due to the discovery of a higher secret for a life of faith and holiness: "His manners also and conversation . . . were such that all they that knew him, reputed and esteemed him to be a man of most virtuous disposition, and of life unspotted."[3]

Tyndale at length transferred his studies from Oxford to the sister schools of Cambridge, where, says Foxe, "he made his abode a certain space."[4] This could hardly have been before the year 1516; it may have been even later. Masters of Arts had to teach for a full year, at least, in the schools, and the "certain space" at Cambridge is in contrast with his "long continuance" at Oxford. We do not know where he lodged in Cambridge, nor why he made the change; but we know that Cambridge had now displaced Oxford as the leading centre of new light and letters.

[1] Mozley, p. 21, n. [2] *John Foxe*, Vol. V, p. 115.
[3] Ibid., p. 115. [4] Ibid., p. 115.

Cambridge was less exposed to the outbursts of violence and bigotry which had disturbed life at Oxford from time to time, and it offered a more tranquil environment for the student who wished to grapple with the problems of the New Learning. The residence of Erasmus at Queens' and the impact of his teaching between the years 1511 and 1514 were still a force to be reckoned with in Cambridge circles. Tyndale found his guiding star in the great Dutchman, until he fell in with Martin Luther and began to follow the light of a brighter luminary. Meanwhile, he versed himself in the words of Erasmus, and it may have been from him that he first caught the idea of a translation of the New Testament. At all events, his sojourn at Cambridge served a higher purpose than just to fill out his knowledge of the Classics. Foxe tells us, in fact, that he was "further ripened in the knowledge of God's Word".[1] This is confirmed by Sir Thomas More, who observed in the *Dialogue* of 1529 that Tyndale had been well known "before he went over the sea for a man of right good living, studious, and well learned in Scripture".[2] More was in close touch with both seats of learning and would get his reports direct from Oxford and Cambridge. He goes on to say that Tyndale "was very well liked and did great good with preaching"[3]; and this is of more than cursory interest, even though we have no details. Preaching had been allowed to fall into shameful neglect, and his later writings never fail to reproach the priests on this account.

There are very few facts available to guide us as to the circumstances in which he was "further ripened" in the Scriptures. But in 1519, Thomas Bilney bought a copy of the *Novum Testamentum* and was soon led to trust in Christ and Christ alone for the saving pardon of all his sins. This great discovery could not be hid, and the result was that a small circle of like-minded men grew up round Bilney in the very heart of Cambridge. They soon began to meet in the White Horse Inn where they could strengthen their faith in the earnest study of the *Novum Testamentum*. We do not know when those meetings first came into being, but there is good reason to think that it was while Tyndale still lingered in Cambridge. It is pleasant to think that he may have been an early member of that little circle which would include some who were to play a chief part in the epic struggle of the English

[1] *John Foxe*, Vol. V, p. 115.   [2] *Sir Thomas More*, Vol. II, p. 7.   [3] Ibid., p. 7.

Reformation. It was also about this time that John Frith came up to Cambridge and was soon known as one in whom God had planted rare gifts of mind and a singular love for learning. "At last," says Foxe, "he fell into knowledge and acquaintance with William Tyndale, through whose instructions he first received into his heart the seed of the Gospel and sincere godliness."[1] Where heart meets heart in the apprehension of truth, a few months may be long enough to forge links of close and lasting friendship: so it was in the case of John Frith and William Tyndale. Thus, in bonds of friendship with the men who met at the White Horse Inn, himself a scholar of no ordinary ability and conscious of the highest aspirations, Tyndale might have found a congenial sphere of work in Cambridge. But in 1520, he would mark the lavish pomp and splendour of Wolsey's visit to Cambridge; and in 1521, he would note the bitter spleen and rancour of John Fisher's sermon at the public burning of Luther's works. Late in that year, or early in 1522, he left Cambridge, choosing the discipline and adventure of life rather than the world of books and learning, and he took a post as tutor to the children of Sir John Walsh of Gloucestershire.

Sir John Walsh and his wife, Anne Poyntz, dwelt in the Manor House of Little Sodbury, out on the slopes of the Cotswolds which were so well known to Tyndale. The tender age of the children gave their tutor ample time for private reading in his room at the back of the house, where he would look out against the hill. The manor house itself was a welcome resort for the local gentry and the parish clergy, and much would pass before Tyndale's eyes to stir him into fresh thought and new activity. He sat with Sir John Walsh at his table, where he dined with Deans and Abbots and Archdeacons, and he often heard them discuss the New Learning or the views of men like Luther and Erasmus. But when table talk turned on the Scriptures, Tyndale would speak his own mind with perfect frankness. He would often differ from such dignitaries, and he always offered them the simple words of Scripture as his reason for the hope that was now in him. It was disconcerting for these accredited leaders of the Church to be brought back to the text of the Scriptures by a humble tutor. Wealthy clerics and lordly abbots, whose learning

[1] *John Foxe*, Vol. V, p. 4.

was now rusty from long disuse, would fret at the very mention of the odious heresies which had sprung from Martin Luther, and they would writhe at the shrewd and determined arguments of an obscure scholar. They soon grew tired of such disputes and formed a grudge against Tyndale. It was in his own self-defence that he prepared his first piece of translation, having chosen the once famous work of Erasmus called the *Enchiridion Militis Christiani*, or the *Manual of a Christian Soldier*. He did not send it to the press, but gave it to his hosts to read. This they did in private and were convinced. "The doctorly prelates were no more so often called to the house, neither had they the cheer and countenance when they came as before they had," wrote Foxe; "which thing they marking, and well perceiving, and supposing no less but it came by the means of Master Tyndale, refrained themselves, and at last utterly withdrew, and came no more there."[1]

It seems that the manuscript of this translation passed from hand to hand in London, until it was consigned to the flames with other papers when he was denounced as a heretic. But he had scored his first success in the lists of controversy and had gained the favour of Sir John Walsh and his Lady. Neither did he confine himself to reading and debate at home; he soon became active as a preacher in the open air at near-by hamlets. But Little Sodbury was not more than fifteen miles from Bristol which was then the second city of all England. He soon began to repair to Bristol as John Purvey had long since done, and to preach to the crowds on the College Green just in front of the Augustinian Convent. This was a bold challenge to the priests and friars who still felt sore from their discomfiture at his master's table, and his conduct would come under fire from the bar of the ale-house where they could mouth their threats without fear or contradiction.[2] "These blind and rude priests," as John Foxe declared, "raged and railed against him."[3] They would not preach themselves nor yet would they allow others to preach. They soon hatched a plot which was meant to wreck his whole career, and a charge of heresy was brought against him before the Chancellor. Tyndale was kept in the dark as to the nature of the accusation, "so that he by the way,

---

[1] *John Foxe*, Vol. V, p. 116.   [2] *Works*, Vol. I, p. 394.
[3] *John Foxe*, Vol. V, p. 116.

in going thitherwards, cried in his mind heartily to God, to give him strength fast to stand in the truth of His word."[1] But the accusers who had laid their charge in private remained in the background, and it was the Chancellor who would confront Tyndale. "He threatened me grievously," Tyndale recalled in after years, "and reviled me, and rated me as though I had been a dog, and laid to my charge (things) whereof there could be none accuser brought forth."[2] But he vindicated himself with such ability that he left the court a free man, neither branded as a heretic nor fettered by an oath of abjuration. But he could not ignore the red lights of warning; he could only anticipate danger and death if he were to persist in his opposition to the local clergy.

Tyndale knew that the priests would soon return to the attack and that neither Sir John Walsh nor any other friend could shield him should he once fall into their hands. It would have been just as foreign to his nature to seek refuge in a qualified reticence as it would have been to make terms with an ignorant bigotry. The whole affair would give rise to serious reflection. He had derived his own faith from that Book which was honoured as the perfect standard of Truth, and he found that it was confirmed by the authority of ancient fathers and modern scholars alike. Why then did it cause such offence? Was this sense of offence confined to the local clergy? This raised wider questions: were the ruling authorities of the Church in opposition to the plain law of the Scriptures? He knew neither what to think nor how to reply to such problems as they began to force themselves upon his mind. It was in this strait that he sought advice from the humanist, William Latimer, the friend of Sir Thomas More and Erasmus, who had taught at Oxford while he was in residence at Magdalen Hall. Tyndale sought his advice as an old friend and venerable divine, and his doubts were resolved in a single sentence. "Do you not know," the old man said, "that the Pope is very Antichrist, whom the Scripture speaketh of? But beware what you say; for if you shall be perceived to be of that opinion, it will cost you your life."[3] This was the truth in the form of a kindly caution, but his hearer was not the man to trim his sails for fear of things future. He owed his own enlightenment to the study of the Scriptures,

---

[1] *John Foxe*, Vol. V, p. 116.   [2] *Works*, Vol. I, p. 395.
[3] *John Foxe*, Vol. V, p. 117.

and he was now convinced that the root cause of the ills of the Church was the fact that men did not know that Word which was able to save their souls. The one thing to open the eyes of the people would be to give them the Bible in their own tongue. "I perceived by experience," he wrote, "how that it was impossible to establish the lay people in any truth, except the Scripture were plainly laid before their eyes in their mother tongue."[1]

He was ahead of most men in that age in his vision and his grasp of reality, for as yet the Reformation had not produced any vernacular version of the Scriptures. Such an undertaking would be quite as novel and at least as adventurous as the voyage of Sebastian Cabot from near-by Bristol in search of the unknown beyond the seas. But the idea took firm hold of his mind, and his leisure hours were absorbed in new fields of study. He knew that John Wycliffe had based his work on the Latin Vulgate which had been drawn up by Jerome a thousand years before; but he saw quite plainly that his work must be based on the Greek text of the *Novum Instrumentum* of 1516 or the *Novum Testamentum* of 1519. He could hardly know that Martin Luther was even then engaged in the preparation of his German New Testament from the same text; but he was in fact to do for England just what Luther was doing for Germany. Foxe tells us that it was at this time that he fell into dispute with a certain man who boldly affirmed that men would be better without the laws of God than they would be without those of the Pope. Tyndale's reply showed that the die had now been cast beyond recall. "I defy the Pope and all his laws," he said; "If God spare my life, ere many years pass, I will cause a boy that driveth the plough shall know more of the Scriptures than thou dost."[2] This saying has become famous. But it proves that he was immersed in the works of Erasmus, for it was the echo of a remark which he had read in the Paraclesis, or the Preface, to the *Novum Instrumentum*. This had expressed the hope that the farmer as he followed the plough and the weaver as he sat at the loom would cheer themselves with the songs of Scripture.[3] But it was clear that he could not hope to carry out his plans in the home of Sir

[1] *Works*, Vol. I, p. 394. [2] *John Foxe*, Vol. V, p. 117.
[3] Seebohm, *The Oxford Reformers*, p. 327.

John Walsh. "I perceive," he told his patron, "that I shall not be suffered to tarry long here in this country."[1] But he was not dismayed. His heart was built of oak, and in July 1523, he left the Manor House at Little Sodbury to set out for London.

Tyndale had grown up far from the crowded life of London, and he only knew by report of the doings of the metropolis. Now he was to see for himself something of the guile and intrigue of Henry's statesmen, something also of the pride and practice of Wolsey's prelates. His keen eyes would observe what was going on all around, and he could not suppress his own mental protest. "And so remained he in London the space almost of a year," wrote Foxe, "beholding and marking with himself the course of the world, and especially the demeanour of the preachers, how they boasted themselves, and set up their authority and kingdom; beholding also the pomp of the prelates, with other things more, which greatly misliked him."[2] But he had come in the hope that he would receive help from Cuthbert Tunstall, the Bishop of London, who had won the praise of Erasmus as a friend of learning. He thought that the Bishop would be willing to act as his patron and would perhaps allow him to reside in his Palace while he pursued his plans for an English version of the *Novum Testamentum*. "I gat me to London," he wrote, "and through the acquaintance of my master (Sir John Walsh) came to Sir Harry Guildford, the King's Grace's Controller, . . . and desired him to speak unto my Lord of London for me; which he also did, as he showed me, and willed me to write an epistle to my Lord, and to go to him myself."[3] But for some time, Tunstall was out of reach; affairs of State left him scant time for an unknown scholar from the country. Tyndale began to preach at St. Dunstan's in the West during this time of delay, and so became the guest of a godly merchant, Humphrey Monmouth. But when he was at length received by the Bishop, his hopes were dashed at once. Tunstall was urbane and cultured, the friend of Sir Thomas More and Warham, but a smooth and courtly prelate who had little to share with the spiritual enthusiasm of a man like Tyndale. It is clear that Tunstall felt an instant dislike for

[1] *John Foxe*, Vol. V, p. 117.
[2] Ibid., p. 118; cp. *Works*, Vol. I, p. 396.
[3] *Works*, Vol. I, p. 395.

Tyndale, and Tyndale an equal distrust for Tunstall. Tunstall had no wish to risk his name and reputation in the hands of this young hothead; Tyndale was chilled to the bone by the cold reserve in the words of the great Churchman. "My Lord answered me," he recalled in after years, "his house was full; he had more than he could well find (provide for)."[1]

Time could never erase from his mind the bitter disappointment of this rebuff. But it was an experience which taught him to seek his comfort in the Scriptures alone; thus it helped to prepare him for the task on which his heart was set. It would not be in the learned leisure of a bishop's palace, but amid the constant perils of a lonely exile that he was to hammer out his English Version.[2] He now had to think out afresh how to get that episcopal approbation which was imperative if he were to carry out his work in London without risk from the law. He still had a friend in Humphrey Monmouth, and he remained in his house while he took stock of the situation. It was at his table that he met so many of the leading merchants who were to help in later years at Antwerp. It was in his study that he first pored over the thick tomes of Martin Luther, who had begun to oust the great Dutchman from first place in his heart. Tyndale did not waste those months in London, though the details which have come down to us are so meagre. He was known as a hard student and a man of frugal habits, whose life and walk were such as to commend his high purpose as the servant of God. No foe ever tried to deny the fact of his learning, and no slur has ever adhered to his personal character. It was perhaps during these months that he conferred with John Frith on the need to give men the Word of God in their own speech so that they read it for themselves.[3] It was also during these months that he reached the sorrowful conclusion that he would have to leave his own country if that need were ever to be supplied. "I . . . understood at the last," he wrote, "not only that there was no room in my Lord of London's palace to translate the New Testament, but also that there was no place to do it in all England."[4] The one alternative would be to go abroad as a voluntary exile, so that he could employ the free printing presses of the Reformed

[1] *Works*, Vol. I, p. 396.
[2] Demaus, pp. 76, 77.
[3] *John Foxe*, Vol. V, p. 118.
[4] *Works*, Vol. I, p. 396.

countries. Therefore in May 1524, he left his books in the home of Humphrey Monmouth and took ship for Hamburg, little knowing that he would never again set foot in England.

Hamburg was a bustling city, immersed in the trade and commerce which would pass through its docks as one of the leading ports of Germany. But it was no city for a man like Tyndale, who was in search of the leisure which his studies required. But his movements are lost in the mists of obscurity, and there are few enough facts to guide us. Foxe says that "he took his journey into the further parts of Germany, as into Saxony, where he had conference with Luther and other learned men in those quarters".[1] It is almost certain that he settled down in Wittenberg and went on with his work in its congenial environment for some nine or ten months. He had none of the aids which now seem so essential for the work of translation; grammars and lexicons were still few in number, thin in content, difficult to get, expensive to buy. He had no choice in the matter of the text which he would employ; he was confined to the *Novum Instrumentum* which had been reprinted as the *Novum Testamentum* with an improved text in 1519 and again in 1522. He had to base his work upon this text, and he compared his English translation with the Latin translation by Erasmus; then he compared it with that of Jerome in the Latin Vulgate, and with that of Luther in the German vernacular. He had to learn German before he could consult Luther; he had no friend with whom he could discuss questions of idiom. But his work was complete within the year, and he was in Hamburg by the spring of 1525. Thence he made his way to Cologne as a city which could boast more than one printing house with business links in England. Plans were made to print three thousand copies in the form of quarto volumes, which were to be enriched with a prologue and with marginal notations. The type was set up in secret as far as the letter K in the signature of the sheets for the first Gospel; then the secret leaked out. Drunken printers spilt the story over their cups, and the Senate of the city at once ordered the work to stop.

Tyndale barely had time to snatch up the printed sheets and flee by the Rhine to the City of Worms. There is but a single

[1] *John Foxe*, Vol. V, p. 119; cp. *Sir Thomas More*, Vol. II, pp. 209, 315.

fragment of this Cologne edition still in existence, and it shows that the tone of the prologue and the glosses was in a strong Lutheran direction. They were simple comments on the meaning of the text, and they were quite free from the biting satire of the glosses in later editions. His choice of Worms as the new scene for his labours was not without reason, for in recent months the city had swung over to the Reformation. Here the type was set up again, without fear of interference from priests or magistrates, and six thousand copies of the English New Testament had been printed by the spring of 1526. There are but two copies of this book still extant, and they are in the form of an octavo production. There were only a few minor alterations in the text of the book, but it left out the long prologue and the glosses which had been part of the work at Cologne. It gave the plain text of Scripture, without note or comment, but there was a short and moving address to the reader at the close of the book. No doubt it was reduced from a quarto volume to an octavo production owing to the change of printers and the pressure of time. Tyndale had in fact lost time as well as money in the Cologne venture, and it was plain wisdom to print the text and get it off his hands at once before his foes could strike again. Thus the spring saw thousands of New Testaments on their way to England, smuggled through the Customs in bales of cloth, in sacks of flour, in barrels and cases of every kind. German merchants had built up a large trade in the prohibited literature of the Reformation, and their English agents had worked out a skilful system by means of which such books were sold in the country towns and in the Universities. Tyndale's New Testament did not want for buyers who were willing to risk discovery, and Foxe informs us that "it can not be spoken what a door of light they opened to the eyes of the whole English nation".[1]

Tyndale had been glad to avail himself of the current versions in Latin and German, but the solid basis of his own work was the Greek text itself. He was in debt both to Luther and Erasmus in a hundred details, but his version was marked by a sturdy independence in its plan as a whole. He was as good a Greek student as were his guides, and he frankly differed from them or chose between them on all sorts of points. His judgment was correct to a

[1] *John Foxe*, Vol. V, p. 119.

remarkable degree, and the Revised Version has re-instated a large number of his disputed renderings. His agreement or divergence was the free and unfettered choice of a sound and scholarly mind; he dealt with the text as one who passed an original judgment on each fragment of the work without fear or bias of any kind. Thus his work could stand on its own merit by the tests of truth and accuracy, and it outshone all its competitors as a piece of literature.[1] One proof of the superlative value of his work was the fact that the Authorised Version was so largely drawn up in the ipsissima verba of his translation. Tyndale did what Luther had done and spoke straight to the heart of the common people; he broke away from the stilted jargon of the Schoolmen and wrote in the homely language to which plain men will most quickly respond. If the message of the Scriptures is not foreign to the heart, its language should not be foreign to the ear. There were occasions when he chose to paraphrase the text rather than be artificial, and he would not weary the reader through monotony when he could cheer him by the use of some variation. Froude not only confessed that our Authorised Version owes an enormous debt to Tyndale, but he summed up his thoughts on the English Bible with a remarkable tribute: "The peculiar genius . . . which breathes through it, the mingled tenderness and majesty, the Saxon simplicity, the preternatural grandeur, unequalled, unapproached in the attempted improvements of modern scholars, all are here, and bear the impress of the mind of one man—William Tyndale."[2]

His work cannot be too highly valued from the point of view of English literature, for it marked an epoch in the development of a worthy prose style. Prose was still an unformed art of writing among men of letters, and they did not yet know that their mother tongue was capable of such artistry. English prose had never yet been used for any major literary undertaking, and most men of letters were apt to look on it as an unpolished means of expression. Tyndale had now shown how fine and flexible it was as an instrument in the hand of a skilled craftsman; it was rich in variety and unlimited in capacity. In strength and simplicity, in awe and solemnity, in music and rhythm, in pathos and feeling, in graceful narrative, in cogent argument, he proved that

[1] Mozley, pp. 87: 89.   [2] See Demaus, p. 132.

it had no need to yield to any other form of language. His own style was often rugged, but his sense of cadence was superb. He was simple and homely, and yet he was majestic and sonorous. His flair for the right word never seemed to fail him, and his text is rich in the kind of phrase which haunts the mind with a lasting sense of beauty. He could use an obvious word without seeming commonplace; he could coin an eloquent phrase without seeming obtrusive. Some of the most familiar quotations in the Authorised Version come direct from Tyndale, and so many of its finest chapters bear the impress of his style and diction. His work has been revised under the eyes of so many scholars with modern aids and superior texts, and men who have been by no means over-friendly to him have had it in their power to oust it from its place in the English Bible: but it holds its pre-eminence in spite of time and change, and his original wording is still retained in those parts of Scripture which are chiefly treasured in mind and heart.[1] The broad stamp of Tyndale's work cannot be effaced from the two great English Versions of 1611 and 1881; yet the reader is so little conscious of such a fact that he never gives it a thought. It was Tyndale's glory that he made the Bible speak for God to the hearts of the common people, while he remained wholly anonymous.

Tyndale remained in Worms for some twelve months, and the Battle of the Book was soon in full swing. Little is known of his private movements, but he was safe enough while the secret of his authorship was preserved. He was "like one of the ancient prophets whom men seldom saw, whose way of life was little known, but whose voice seemed to pervade all the nation".[2] He had left his own land as an obscure student who felt himself driven into voluntary exile; but his heart was across the water, and his words were being scattered throughout the country. It would only be a matter of time before the prelates and the statesmen were forced to see in him the most dangerous opponent who had as yet entered the lists to do combat with the mediaeval system. Meanwhile he gave up his leisure to the study of Hebrew, and he spent the summer in his dealings with merchants. He would repair to the spring and autumn fairs at Frankfort which was then the centre of the book trade. There he would meet merchants

[1] Demaus, p. 132.   [2] Ibid., p. 140.

from England and Antwerp through whom he could arrange for the rapid transport of his precious volumes by the North Sea. There are few more moving stories than the saga which tells how the books were smuggled into England in spite of the vigilant watch of bishops and magistrates. They were bought and sold in secret for months before they came under the eyes of the authorities. They were passed from hand to hand with loving caution by those who were eager for true reform. There was no name on the title page to disclose Tyndale's identity, and it won an instant welcome on the ground of its own merit. But as summer wore on, its wide circulation seems to have become known to the authorities, who then had to decide on their course of action. It was soon brought under Wolsey's notice, and he arranged a conclave of prelates in his London palace to determine their policy. Tunstall was more concerned than most of the Bishops because London was the major field of distribution. Thus he urged a course of stringent prohibition, and the Bishops agreed that all copies of the book should be seized and burnt.

Accordingly in October 1526, Tunstall ordered his Archdeacons to call in all copies of the *New Testament* within thirty days, on pain of excommunication and suspicion of heresy. He had resolved to make known his disapproval by one of those displays of which the age was so fond, and late in the same month or early in November, there was a huge bonfire at Paul's Cross in London. Tunstall preached a sermon in which Tyndale's work was denounced as replete with error and heresy; then the condemned book was flung into the flames and burnt to ashes. This was endorsed by the Archbishop of Canterbury who drew up a letter for the Bishops of the Province urging them to adopt the same course of action. But it had small effect. Tunstall's lament that the Book was spreading in large numbers throughout his See is the best proof that the merchants had sold their wares successfully, and the spectacular conflagration at Paul's Cross could not check the flow of books for which there was such a ready market. There had been a pirate reprint of three thousand copies, carried out in Antwerp, and some of these copies were in England by the middle of that same November. But the printer was placed under arrest, and some hundreds of copies were destroyed before they could cross the Channel. But men were not to be lightly deterred when they could see easy profits, and at least four unauthorised reprints took place within the next few years. This meant that some thirteen thousand copies, or more, were thrown into circulation. We do not know how the authorities solved the problem of its undisclosed authorship, but by the close of the year it had been traced to Tyndale. He had by then added to his offence by the publication of his *Prologue to the Epistle to The Romans*, and they began to plot revenge. But he was not unacquainted with the trend of affairs at home, for the fame of Tunstall's doings at Paul's Cross had spread far and wide throughout Europe on the wings of rumour. "In burning the New Testament, they did none other thing than that I looked for," Tyndale observed; and clear foresight led him to add: "No more shall they do, if they burn me also."[1]

The years 1527 and 1528 were a critical period in the life of Tyndale, as well as in the history of his *New Testament*. The Archbishop of Canterbury was making huge efforts to buy up and destroy all the copies which his agents abroad could track down and locate. In November 1527, Thomas Bilney was placed under arrest and was brought to London to stand his trial before Wolsey. But the conduct of the trial was left to Tunstall, and it seems to have brought to his notice the clue to the distribution of the *New Testament*. Doctor Ferman of Honey Lane was examined as a witness on behalf of Bilney, and his cross-examination disclosed the fact that his curate, Thomas Garret, had sold a large number of these *New Testaments* to "divers scholars in Oxford".[2] Thus in 1528, a fresh search took place in Oxford, and it was soon found that Wolsey's new and splendid College was, in fact, the home of a group of these scholars. Pitiful confessions were wrung from the weaker brethren, and the whole scheme for the circulation of these books came to light. Clark, and Frith, and others, were thrown into prison, where some died and some were forced to abjure. Tunstall set in motion a great new drive against Lollards and Lutherans, and the city prisons were soon choked with suspects. All this imposed no mean restraint on the circulation of the *New Testament*, and an energetic campaign was launched against Tyndale as well. Wolsey had been stung by recent attacks on his own name and now resolved to secure Tyndale's arrest

[1] *Works*, Vol. I, pp. 43, 44.   [2] *John Foxe*, Vol. V, p. 421.

and extradition. But it was one thing to issue orders to have him seized, and quite another to seize him or even run him to earth. He must have left Worms during the year 1527, but our knowledge of his movements is still cloaked with uncertainty. He is supposed to have spent some time at Marburg, and we may take it that he did at least visit the seat of the Landgrave of Hesse. Marburg was not far from Frankfort where he used to repair to the great fairs, and it would have much to attract him as one of the new centres of the Reformation light and learning.

There he would meet Francis Lambert, the Reformer, and Herman Buschius, the Humanist, who had come as Professors to the University which had only just been founded in May 1527. There he would meet the young Scot, Patrick Hamilton, who was to sail for home in the autumn and to die in the flames at St. Andrews in February 1528. There, too, he may have met John Frith and Barnes who both fled from England at the close of 1527, and from them he would learn at first hand the course of events across the sea. No one could have told him more clearly all that had so lately occurred at Oxford and Cambridge. He would hear of Henry's plans for the great Divorce, and of Wolsey's schemes for the Pope's consent. He would learn of Bilney's trial and faggot-bearing through the streets of London; he would hear of Tunstall's threats and fulminations at the expense of the Lollards. He would receive details of the circulation of the *New Testament*, and the opposition from the Bench of Bishops. Such news was not lost on Tyndale; it seems to have stirred up the depths of his being. It was not in Frankfort nor in Marburg that his days were to lie; he could spare such cities no more time than measures for his safety required. Antwerp is the only city with which his name is linked in a consistent tradition after his stay in Worms, and, as early as in 1528, he seems to have chosen it as the base for his future activities. It was a strong centre from the viewpoint of large printing houses, and it was close to the English market. He could arrange for the transport of his books to England, and he could keep abreast of home affairs. He might retire from the city and go into hiding from time to time when safety required it, but he always returned to the post of danger. Other men like Barnes and Rogers and Coverdale withdrew into the safe retreats which were to be found in Lutheran Germany, but he hovered by the narrow sea which cut him off from England. His heart was in England, and his exile was only for his country's sake.[1] But it was from this time that his strictures began to cut with a new edge, and their sharpness was made clear in two works which he published in the course of this year.

In May 1528, Tyndale published the *Parable of The Wicked Mammon*, the first of his works to bear his name on the title-page. It was really a short treatise on the Doctrine of Justification by Faith, but it shows up his deep chagrin at the treatment meted out to his *New Testament*. The book borrows a large section from Luther's work on the same Parable, and it expounds all those texts which were so often cited as in opposition to his teaching. It was meant as an aid to the proper understanding of the Doctrines of Grace, and it soon had a wide circulation. More than one-third of those who came from the County of Essex and were accused before the Bishop of London between the years 1530 and 1532 were found to have possessed copies of *The Mammon*, and Sir Thomas More declared that many had been beguiled by its teaching. It stirred his ire not a little. "Never," he cried in his preface to *The Confutation*, "never was there made a more foolish frantic book!"[2] But in October, it was followed by *The Obedience of a Christian Man*, the longest and most elaborate of all his works. It was a great contribution to the Reformation controversy, and it ranks with the *New Testament* as the book by which he was most widely known in his own lifetime. This book took up the charge that the Reformation was out to fan into flame the popular discontent of which reigning princes were so afraid. The Peasants' War of 1524 in Germany had made this a burning question, and the persecution of his friends in England helped to lend a sharper note to Tyndale's treatment of it. He ranged over a wide field of controversy and struck at the evils which were rampant in Church life with unsparing directness. But there was more than scathing denunciation; there was a note of lofty enthusiasm. He not only pointed out with drastic clearness what was wrong; he went on with equal plainness to point out how to set it right. His remedy for the crisis in Church and State was to assert the supremacy of Holy Writ in all matters of faith, and the

[1] Mozley, p. 153.   [2] See Tyndale, *Works*, Vol. I, p. 36.

supremacy of Civil Law in all matters of discipline. He was thus the first man to bring forward those two great truths which were like twin pillars of iron in the fabric of the English Reformation.

Tyndale loved his Bible and longed for the common sense which lies at the root of all its teaching; and he loved his country and grieved for the common man who was so often robbed and misgoverned. His case for truth, argued out on such lines, so sweeping in application, so searching in comprehension, set out with rare force of expression, brought home with rare skill in argument, at once took root in the minds of English readers. *The Obedience of a Christian Man* won more support for the Reformation and gave more offence to the authorities than most books of the age. Thomas Bilney left Cambridge in 1531 to go up once more, as he said, to his Jerusalem, and he carried with him copies of Tyndale's *New Testament* and *The Obedience of A Christian Man*.[1] Richard Bayfield, a monk from Bury St. Edmund's, was won for the Reformation by his reading of *The Wicked Mammon* and *The Obedience of A Christian Man*, and went abroad as an agent for the purchase of such books for England.[2] James Bainham, a member of the Middle Temple, was flogged and racked until he agreed to recant; but it left such a scar on his conscience that he could find no rest of heart until he had confessed his fall and had asked the forgiveness of all his friends. Therefore, he went to St. Austin's Church with the *New Testament* in his hand and *The Obedience of A Christian Man* near his heart, and there with tears, he told what he had done, praying friends to beware of his weakness and to forgive him his failure.[3] And the book which meant so much to Bilney and Bayfield and Bainham also found an entrance into the court of Anne Boleyn and of Henry VIII. It was Anne who induced the king to read it for himself, and she marked out certain sections with her finger-nail for personal interest. Henry read it with no little satisfaction. "This," he cried, "is a book for me and for all kings to read!"[4] It fell into his hands at a timely moment, for he was about to take the reins of government out of Wolsey's control. It was indeed a book suited for him to read as he began to rule with an iron rod in his own name. "Whereas," wrote Brynklow

[1] *John Foxe*, Vol. IV, p. 642.   [2] Ibid., p. 681.
[3] Ibid., p. 702.   [4] A. F. Pollard, *Wolsey*, p. 229.

in 1543 of Tyndale and certain others, "the king was before but a shadow of a king, or at the most but half a king, now he doth wholly reign through their preaching, writing, and suffering."[1]

Tyndale had made up his mind to supplement his work on the New Testament with a translation of the Old Testament, and this absorbed all his time and strength in the months at hand. He had begun to learn Hebrew some years before, and as early as in 1526, Buschius had told Spalatin of his progress. "He is so skilled in seven languages," he wrote, "Hebrew, Greek, Latin, Italian, Spanish, English, French, that whichever he spoke, you would suppose it his native tongue."[2] Tyndale had been at work on his translation in 1527 and may have completed the first draft before the end of 1528. But the Regent had launched a search for him in the Low Countries during the month of June, and there were yet others on his trail from Frankfort to Antwerp by the end of September. He was denounced in court as a rebel and heretic in January 1529, and a fresh hunt was planned within the next few weeks. Antwerp had thus become too hot for his safety, and to attempt to print his book there would have been suicidal. His thoughts turned to Hamburg, where a new press had just begun to turn out books, and where he had loyal friends of long standing. Hamburg had just taken a stand for the Reformation, and he would be out of danger once he were in that great northern city. Therefore, early in 1529, he left Antwerp to sail round the coast for Hamburg; and then Foxe takes up the story. "At what time Tyndale had translated the fifth Book of Moses called Deuteronomy, minding to print the same at Hamburg, he sailed thitherward; where by the way, upon the coast of Holland, he suffered shipwreck, by which he lost all his books, writings, and copies, and so was compelled to begin all again anew, to his hindrance and doubling of his labours. Thus having lost by that ship both money, his copies, and his time, he came in another ship to Hamburg, where at his appointment, Master Coverdale tarried for him, and helped him in the translating of the whole Five Books of Moses from Easter till December."[3] This story has often been brushed aside as a fable, but the incidentals which Foxe mentions all bear the stamp of truth. Tyndale must have known Miles Coverdale while at Cambridge and would be glad

[1] A. F. Pollard, *Wolsey,* p. 359. [2] Demaus, p. 128. [3] *John Foxe,* Vol. V, p. 120.

to meet him at Hamburg. It was true that Coverdale knew no Greek or Hebrew, but he could render constant help in comparing versions and correcting copies; and it may be safely assumed that his later years in London would give John Foxe ample means to confirm his story in detail.[1]

Thus it seems that Tyndale must have spent the latter half of 1529 in a re-translation of the Books of Moses with the help of Coverdale at Hamburg; then he sailed for Antwerp once more since the danger had blown away, while Coverdale travelled up the Rhine to carry on as a schoolmaster. It was in the early months of 1530 that his Translation of the Pentateuch was struck off from the press, and six copies of this primary edition have been preserved. There was a preface to the whole volume and a prologue to each book in detail, and these introductions are a real proof of his genuine modesty. He had no thought for his own name or fame; all his pains were spent to secure the best possible translation. Any scholar was welcome to correct or supplant his versions, if he could bring to the task a better knowledge of the Greek and Hebrew originals. He had prepared a series of marginal notes, one hundred and eight all told; not one had been borrowed from the work of Luther, but they were like enough in boldness and vigour.[2] His *New Testament* had been fiercely denounced in spite of its moderation, and the result was that these notes went much further in sharpness and asperity. He had based his translation of the Pentateuch on at least four older versions; he had begun with the Hebrew, and had compared it with the Greek Septuagint, and the Latin Vulgate, and the German Bible which had been brought out by Martin Luther. Hebrew had been almost unknown in Western Europe until some fifty years before, but he had caught its genius and mastered its idiom as well as any scholar of his age. His own judgment was called into frequent play as he chose between older authorities, and the soundness of his instinct for the correct reading puts the question of his knowledge of the language beyond all doubt. His translation was carried out with the freedom of a strong confidence in his own scholarship, and his diction, always clear and precise, rose at times to heights of sacred beauty. He coined words such as "the passover" and "the mercy seat" for the Old Testament just as he had coined words like "long-suffering" and "tender mercies" for the New Testament, and his version of the Books of Moses has thus enriched the whole stream of sacred literature with word pictures which will never grow old.[1]

Do we wonder what else transpired for good or ill during the year 1529? There is quite a romantic tradition, which has come down to us through Halle's Chronicle. The Bishop of London is thought to have been in Antwerp for a short time in the month of August while Tyndale was also in the city. Tunstall was on his way home to England after the Treaty of Cambrai, and was anxious to try his hand at the game of buying up large stocks of prohibited literature. Halle says that an English merchant by the name of Augustine Packington went to Tunstall with an offer to buy up all unsold copies of Tyndale's *Testament*, if he were supplied with ready cash. Tunstall thought that he had God by the toe, and gave him an open order. But the merchant then went straight to Tyndale and told him of the plan. Tyndale saw that the books would be destroyed by fire, but that all the world would cry out at the burning of God's own Word. He saw as well that the purchase money would not only release him from his debts but would also provide a large enough surplus to correct and reprint the book at once. Thus the bargain was made. Tunstall had the books, and Tyndale had the money, and there was no great loss of time before newly printed *Testaments* began to pour across the Channel "thick and threefold".[2] But this story has lost nothing in the telling, and it will not stand the test of proof in detail. Tyndale may have left Hamburg for a brief visit to Antwerp in August, but it is not likely that he would have on hand many unsold copies of his *New Testament*. Perhaps Tunstall did buy up a number of the pirate reprints; perhaps Tyndale would throw in some superfluous copies of *The Wicked Mammon* and *The Obedience of A Christian Man*.[3] At all events in May 1530, Tunstall held a second conflagration at Paul's Cross in London, and there was another holocaust of books and *Testaments*. It was in the same month that the King in the Star Chamber, before his lords spiritual and temporal, signed a proclamation which denounced *The Wicked Mammon* and *The Obedience of A Christian*

[1] Mozley, pp. 176, 177.   [2] Ibid., pp. 147, 148.
[3] Ibid, pp. 149, 150.

Man, and which enjoined the immediate surrender of all copies of the English Bible. This measure was ascribed to the arch-influence of the prelates, and the year was not out before Hugh Latimer had addressed his appeal direct to the King's Grace. "They have made it treason to your noble Grace," he wrote, "to have the Scripture in English!"[1] But we cannot be sure how far Tunstall really did help to clear Tyndale's debts in Antwerp, for no less than five years were to elapse before he could bring out a fresh edition of the *New Testament*.

Meanwhile it was clear that further efforts were to be launched to stamp out the Reform movement. Wolsey's fall from power, in October 1529, meant that the Church courts were released from his legatine incubus, and so regained their statutory powers under the old Lollard acts of Henry IV and of Henry V. Wolsey was replaced as Lord Chancellor by Sir Thomas More, and Tunstall was followed as Bishop of London by John Stokesley. But Sir Thomas More and Stokesley were the kind of men from whom the friends of Reform could expect no mercy. Tyndale read the signs from afar, and the latter months of 1530 saw the sternest of all his works in print. *The Practice of Prelates* voiced a scathing accusation against the pride and power that were rife in the Church. This had indeed been the object of his thought and observation for ten years past; his own exile and the persecution of his friends had only strengthened his views. Now he gave full vent to all the pent-up indignation of his exile, and his words burst on their readers with the thundering emphasis which was wont to mark the tremendous indictments of the Hebrew prophets.[2] The shameless greed, the sordid wealth, the subtle intrigues, the selfish wrangles, and the alternate policies of high-handed tyranny and base-hearted flattery wrapped up with the rule of Popes and Prelates, were all set down in the darkest colours until at length he took up the story of his own times. Wolsey, he lashed under such titles as "Thomas Wolfsee" and "Caiaphas the Cardinal".[3] Tunstall, he flayed as "that still Saturn, the imaginer of all mischief", "a ducking hypocrite, made to dissemble".[4] Sir Thomas More was scorned as "the Proctor of Purgatory", and the Bishops were mocked as "blind

[1] Latimer, *Sermons and Remains*, p. 299.   [2] Demaus, p. 250.
[3] *Works*, Vol. II, pp. 307, 333.   [4] Ibid., pp. 321, 337.

buzzards and shameless hypocrites".[1] He thought that the Divorce was a huge stratagem, meant to further Wolsey's own ends, and he closed the book with a strong appeal to King, Lords, and Commons to rise and save the realm. He was wrong in his views on the Divorce question, and they gave great offence to the King's party. *The Practice of Prelates* was marked out for attack in a placard set up by royal authority; but the placard only made men read it with the greater avidity, and it was soon withdrawn. But his mistake on the Divorce question was a relatively minor matter, and the book stands as a scathing rebuke of wrongs done by mediaeval churchmen.

Tyndale was still intent on the work of translation, and the Pentateuch was not his last contribution to the English Bible. In May 1531, he produced his version of the Prophet Jonah, which then seemed so pointed as a tract for the times. In 1534, he gave the world a few detached fragments of Old Testament translation, bound up with the second edition of his *New Testament*. No fresh work was published beyond this in his own lifetime, but there is an unvaried tradition that he left a version of the historical books from Joshua to Second Chronicles in the hands of his friend Rogers. It was not until the close of 1534 that John Rogers came to Antwerp, so that he could not have been in touch with Tyndale for more than a few months before his arrest and imprisonment. But he seems to have won a firm place in Tyndale's heart, and to have helped him in his last months of literary toil. To him Tyndale bequeathed the last stage of the work to which he had consecrated his life, and, in July 1537, he brought out his version of the English Bible under the pen-name of Thomas Matthew. Rogers had taken his version of the Pentateuch and of the New Testament almost without variation from William Tyndale, and had borrowed his version of the books from Ezra to Malachi as well as the Apocrypha direct from Miles Coverdale. But while this shows us how Rogers came by the great body of his material, it still leaves the problem as to the source from which all the historical books from Joshua to the Chronicles had been derived. This is just the section which is ascribed by the voice of unbroken tradition to the pen of Tyndale; it was rescued from the shades of oblivion by the hand of Rogers

[1] *Works*, Vol. II, pp. 335, 336.

after his death. Matthew's Bible was in fact a reprint of the work of Tyndale, and the gap from the Chronicles to the New Testament was filled in from Miles Coverdale. Thus the title-page bears the fictitious name of Thomas Matthew: but the initials J.R. for John Rogers are found at the foot of a Preface, and the initials W.T. for William Tyndale are found at the close of Malachi.[1]

This new version of the historical books bears all the marks of Tyndale's style and outlook, and a minute study of the text puts the whole question beyond shadow of doubt. There is the same sound and original scholarship, the same strong and independent attitude. It is translated directly from the Hebrew text, to which it adheres with more fidelity than did Luther, or the Vulgate, or the Septuagint. It sides with or against other versions with the same free judgment which marks his work elsewhere, and it carries on some of the distinctive renderings which are prominent in the *Pentateuch*. But the strongest proof of undoubted authorship lies in little idiosyncrasies or peculiarities, little habits and mannerisms, which are no less frequent in these historical books than in the Pentateuch or in the New Testament. Men may try to copy a difficult phrase or uncommon word, but no one would embark on an imitation of points like these. Thus it is not enough merely to say that there is no reason to doubt that he was the author; there is ample reason why the honest critic should boldly assert it. All the lines of witness converge in the same direction, and their common testimony is still further strengthened when we treat this version as a piece of literature. "There are the same bold touches, the same quaint turns of phrase which ... always awake our interest and pleasure. ... There is the same firm hand, the same simple and direct style, the same wonderful rhythm, the same noble dignity that rises with its theme."[2] The one problem which still remains is as to the time when Tyndale carried it out, and there are some who think that it was done during his imprisonment in Vilvorde. There might have been little trouble in getting the necessary books and materials in some prisons; but in Vilvorde, he could scarcely secure clothes or lighting from the authorities. Mozley observes that the idea of the heroic prisoner, toiling through long winter nights at his trans-

[1] Mozley, p. 180.   [2] Ibid., pp. 184, 185.

lation of the Old Testament, would be so grand if it were true that a man like Poyntz could not fail to pass it on to Foxe. But though Foxe does refer to some papers written out in Vilvorde, he gives no hint that one of these prison papers was a translation manuscript.[1] We can only say that Tyndale's version of the historical books must belong to the last year or two of his freedom, and it comes down to us as his latest effort to break new ground for the English Bible.

But there had been a change in the trend 'of English affairs, and the result was that Cromwell had now conceived a plan to win Tyndale over to the King's cause. Cromwell thought that he might find in him an ally whose pen could be used to promote a moderate policy of reform. Henry plainly thought of him as still in need of pardon, but he allowed Cromwell to try out his ideas. The task was placed in the hands of Stephen Vaughan, a merchant in Antwerp and King's Factor in the Netherlands. The year 1531 would be almost a blank page in Tyndale's story were it not for Vaughan's labours. "It is unlikely to get Tyndale into England when he daily heareth so many things from thence which feareth him," wrote Vaughan on January 26th. ". . . The man is of a greater knowledge than the King's Highness doth take him for. . . . Would God he were in England!"[2] Cromwell did not mean to deceive him with false hopes; but he knew too well the empty value of safe conducts. The Lord Chancellor had called him "the Captain of our English heretics",[3] and he was not likely to leave the realm alive if he made the venture. But on April 17th, Vaughan had a talk with him, and he declared: "If for my pains therein taken, if for my poverty, if for mine exile out of my natural country, and bitter absence from my friends, if for my hunger, my thirst, my cold, the great danger wherewith I am everywhere compassed, and finally, if for innumerable other hard and sharp fightings which I endure, not yet feeling their asperity, by reason I hoped with my labours to do honour to God, true service to my prince, and pleasure to his commons; how is it that his Grace, this considering, may either by himself think, or by the persuasions of others be brought to think, that in this doing, I should not show a pure mind, a true and incorrupt zeal and

[1] Mozley, pp. 336, 337; *John Foxe*, Vol. V, p. 128.
[2] Demaus, p. 292.   [3] See Mozley, p. 191.

affection to his Grace?"[1] But Vaughan's despatch breaks off in the middle of a sentence, and it has been thought that Henry, perhaps enraged at its praise for Tyndale, may have torn it in two. The king would have Tyndale return as a penitent or a prodigal to whom he might extend mercy; not as one more orthodox than all his bishops, one who had been driven into unmerited exile! Cromwell was forced to pen a stiff reply in which Vaughan was taken to task; but he added his own post-script, to hint that Vaughan should still persist in his efforts. Vaughan met him again in May, and heard him vow that he would write no more if the king would but grant a bare text of Scripture to be put in the hands of the people. They met again in June, but this was the last time; Vaughan went back to England within a few weeks, and did not return till the autumn. It was too late by then to win Tyndale, for home affairs had changed once more and were worse than ever.

The whole face of England had grown darker as the summer months wore away, and no one could mistake signs of the times which were spelt out in the blood-red letters of fire. Either in March or in August, Bilney suffered at the stake in Norwich; in December, Bayfield perished in the flames at Newgate and Tewkesbury at Smithfield. "There should have been more burned by a great many than there have been within this seven year last passed," wrote Sir Thomas More at this time; "the lack whereof I fear me will make more burned within this seven year next coming than else should have needed to have been burned in seven score."[2] Cromwell's failure to win Tyndale through Vaughan's diplomacy stirred the king in the last part of 1531 to instruct his ambassador at the Imperial Court to demand his surrender from Charles V; but Charles refused. Henry then ordered his servants to seize Tyndale by force, to kidnap him, and ship him home for trial. The Lord Chancellor had now begun to examine his prisoners with regard to Tyndale, and to ask close questions about his habits and doings. Tyndale would hear of this, and he knew that safety was best assured by caution and obscurity. Thus he lurked in or near Antwerp, looking out with wary eyes

[1] Demaus, p. 297.
[2] Sir Thomas More: Confutation of Tyndale. (See Tyndale, *Works*, Vol. III, p. 97, n.)

and moving on when danger began to loom across his path. Henry's ambassador spent large sums of money in bribes, but could not run Tyndale to earth. In June 1532, he returned to England without success. But in April, Bainham had been burnt at Smithfield, and he was the fifth to suffer within the last few months. Worse was to come, for in July, John Frith paid a visit to England and fell into the hands of his enemies. In October, he was placed in the Tower, where he received a letter from Tyndale charged with tenderest affection. At length he was condemned, and in July 1533 was bound back to back with a young Kentish martyr to die in the flames at Smithfield. Tyndale was well aware of his danger and wrote him a second letter, although it may never have come into his hands. John Frith was his dearest friend and convert, one whose life had been marked by great beauty and rare ability, and he poured out his heart in words that were meant to cheer and strengthen him for that last ordeal by fire. "Let not your body faint," he wrote; "he that endureth to the end shall be saved. If the pain be above your strength, remember, Whatsoever ye shall ask in My Name, I will give it you. And pray to your Father in that Name, and He shall ease your pain, or shorten it. The Lord of peace, of hope, and of faith be with you. Amen."[1]

These years were marked by the famous literary duel which was fought between Sir Thomas More and Tyndale; a duel which was memorable both on account of the character of the authors and the magnitude of the issues at stake. Tunstall was in despair at his failure to put down the *New Testament* by brow-beating the book-sellers; and in March 1528, he asked More to take up the case and to write in defence of the traditional theology. He could not have made a better choice from his point of view; there was no subtler wit in the realm, no wiser son in the Church. Sir Thomas More was a man of charm and culture, a friend of truth and learning; if he could not defend the Church, nothing but the rack and the stake remained. Tunstall did not indict Tyndale by name, but Sir Thomas was too shrewd not to see that he was still chief and captain of the English Reformation. He had found a foeman worthy of sword and steel, and to confute Tyndale was to become his great object in life. He put out a

[1] *John Foxe*, Vol. V, p. 132.

thousand and more folio pages within five or six years, and he
returned to the attack time and again when he thought that he
had driven him from the field. In June 1529, he brought out his
first work, *A Dialogue*, of one hundred and eighty closely printed
pages. He ranged over the whole field of controversy and used
all his literary art to press the attack on men whom he despised
as an illiterate rabble. It was bound to inflict damage on the
Reformation if not answered at once, and the gauntlet had been
flung with special vigour at the feet of Tyndale. He was singled
out by name as the chief spokesman of the English Reformation,
and he could not avoid the summons to combat. He had to take
up the challenge, or own by his silence that there was no reply to
make. Thus in July 1531, he published his *Answer*, and so entered
the lists with the greatest lay warrior then in England. Tyndale
lacked the literary skill and the artistic grace of his opponent, but
he was more than his match in factual argument. He was strongest
just where More was weakest, for he grappled at once with the
major issues at stake. Sir Thomas had skirted round the moral
failures of the old Church, but the *Answer* struck hard at the sin
and wickedness of the age. He brushed sophistries and subtleties
aside to deal with facts as they were, and his style, plain, terse,
vigorous, workmanlike, matched his hard common sense.[1]

Tyndale's *Answer* proved that he was equal to the combat, and
he remained master of the field on many points in dispute: he had
roughly squashed More's quibbles and had boldly maintained the
cause of the Reformation. Thus just as Sir Thomas had left
Tyndale with no alternative but to reply, Tyndale had now left
More with no alternative but to return to the attack. He was
immersed in his duties as Lord Chancellor, but he set out at once
to deal with his opponent. By May 1532, he had published the
first three books of his *Confutation*, a work which was to swell
to the length of nine books before he called a halt. It was composed on such a scale that he had not advanced beyond the first
thirty pages of *The Answer* when the first three books were
published in a folio volume of three hundred and sixty pages.[2]
But Tyndale ignored *The Confutation*, and turned away from
such controversy to a new task altogether. In September 1531,
he published an *Exposition of the First Epistle of St. John*, and a

[1] Mozley, pp. 218: 221.   [2] *Works*, Vol. III, p. 2.

year or two later, he published an *Exposition of The Sermon on The Mount*. He felt that the English Bible should be backed up with an explanation of the text which would be free from all the fads and fancies of the Schoolmen. Both works have real merit in their grasp of truth and breadth of mind, and they were of far greater service than a further bout of controversy with Sir Thomas More could ever have been. But More could not leave him alone, and this controversy became the chief occupation of his leisure moments. It was pursued in his *Apology* which came out in 1533, and he followed it yet further in two more works before his life came to an end. The length to which he ran in self-defence marks the extent of his failure, for *The Confutation* was ten times the length of the book it was written to meet. Brevity may be the soul of wit; it is also the essence of retort. More had been the friend of Colet and Erasmus, and a disciple of the New Learning; but his reputation suffered a grave reverse in this controversy. He had lavished contempt on the man he opposed, while he had failed to prove his own tenets; and all this served to fix Tyndale in the public eye and to win applause for the skill and courage with which he had met and foiled his great assailant. The only gains from the controversy were gains for the Reformation.[1]

In 1534, Tyndale found a lodging in the famous English House at Antwerp which had been set apart some sixty years before for the use of merchant adventurers. His host at the House was Thomas Poyntz, a distant kinsman of Lady Walsh, and he rejoiced in some of the rights and immunities of the merchant classes. For some two years, Tyndale had had to turn aside from his life's work on the English Bible to plunge into controversy or to take up exposition. Now he returned with all his strength to the tasks of revision and of translation, and, in November 1534, he brought out his second edition of the New Testament. There had been at least four pirate reprints of the Worms edition, but no further issue had been put out by his authority or under his supervision. He had prepared the Worms version in times of great difficulty, and he knew that there was much room for improvement. He had spoken about the faith which God had brought to birth in his own soul through the Scriptures in his *Answer* to More, and

[1] Demaus, pp. 261: 286; Mozley, pp. 212: 238.

he had then declared his one supreme desire on behalf of others. "And I bow the knees of my heart unto God night and day that He will show it all other men; and I suffer all that I can to be a servant to open their eyes."[1] He had written about the text of the version at Worms and the pains which he had taken in his letter to Frith, and he had then maintained his own integrity of conduct and purpose: "I call God to record against the day we shall appear before our Lord Jesus to give a reckoning of our doings that I never altered one syllable of God's Word against my conscience; nor would this day if all that is in the earth, whether it be pleasure, honour, or riches, might be given me."[2] That was still his spirit as he sent forth this new edition from Antwerp, and the Preface is a witness to his desires: "My part be not in Christ," he wrote, "if mine heart be not to follow and live according as I teach; and also if mine heart weep not night and day for mine own sin and other men's indifferently, beseeching God to convert us all, and to take His wrath from us, and to be merciful, as well to all other men as to mine own soul."[3]

The Worms version contained no more than the bare text, save for a short address to the reader by way of epilogue; now there was a Preface to the whole book, and a Prologue for each part, with glosses, tables, and marginal references. The Acts and The Revelation were the only two books for which Tyndale did not write a Prologue; but in the case of the other books, he borrowed quite freely from Luther. But he was not just an echo of the German scholar, and he would not confine his work to the narrow functions of translation. He would sometimes write in direct opposition, and he always tried to avoid those more reckless statements which made Luther a trial even to friends. Tyndale's glosses came from his own hand, and not from Luther; they were not meant to run a tilt against Rome so much as to throw light on the text.[4] They were a guide to the proper meaning and the moral lessons of the passage to which they were annexed, and they were much milder than the glosses in the Books of Moses. Westcott remarked that not even Bengel could have been more terse or pointed; there are perhaps no more sage and pithy

[1] *Works*, Vol. III, p. 192. [2] *John Foxe*, Vol. V, p. 134.
[3] Mozley p. 276. [4] *Works*, Vol. I, p. 468.

comments in the English language. But the dozen or so copies which still survive show that the chief glory of this version was in the text itself. He had worked out the whole translation de novo, and he had made some four thousand alterations. He not only based it again on the Greek text of Erasmus, but he brought his newer knowledge of the Hebrew background to bear on its problems. Perhaps half the changes were made with an eye to closer conformity with the original in grammar or meaning. Thus he made more use of particles, or he tightened up loose renderings; thus he reframed old lines of interpretation, or he rewrote whole texts in difficult cases. He took as much care to improve the style as he did to amend the sense of his version; he strove to throw light on what had been obscure, and give life to what had been inert. Roughnesses were ironed out, and weaknesses were smoothed away; and many an alteration helped to improve the ease and flow of cadence and rhythm.[1] One copy of this *New Testament* in the British Museum is an edition de luxe; it has the text only, printed on vellum, with illuminated capitals and woodcuts. The gold edges were once inscribed with three words now hardly legible, one on each face: Anna Regina Angliae. The Lady Anne Boleyn was then in the full blush of her queenly power and beauty, but not many months were to pass before her fall and doom. Did this Sacred Book bring solace to her saddened spirit before she placed her head upon the block?[2]

This second edition of the *New Testament* sold out with great rapidity, and he was soon at work again. He had indeed told his readers that if any faults came to light, he would shortly attend to them.[3] Thus he addressed himself at once to the details of revision and correction, and the last days of his freedom were passed at the chosen post of duty, toiling at the text of Scripture, watching the trend of home affairs. Daye's Folio describes how his leisure hours were absorbed in a simple round of holy living and kindly action which endeared him to all his friends in Antwerp. They knew him as "a man very frugal and spare of body, a great student, an earnest labourer in the setting forth of the Scriptures of God".[4] His simplicity and unselfishness in the tasks of life, his

[1] Mozley, pp. 285: 288.   [2] Ibid., pp. 289: 291.
[3] *Works*, Vol. I, p. 468.   [4] Mozley, p. 264.

sincerity and perseverance in the cause of truth, his energy of intellect, his diligence in translation, all mark him out as one of the noblest figures in the English Reformation. That he should have won the earnest support of men like Sir John Walsh, and Humphrey Monmouth, and Stephen Vaughan, is the clearest illustration of his private worth and friendship. That he should have won the veneration of men like John Frith, and John Rogers, and Miles Coverdale, is the finest testimony to his greatness of soul. Demaus rightly says that the one word which fits the life and work of Tyndale is the word heroic; his was an heroic character in the highest sense of the term.[1] His was the first voice raised in accents clear enough and loud enough to reach the ear and touch the heart of his people; his was, in fact, one of those great lives which form a kind of landmark in our national history. We feel instinctively that he was altogether out of the common, standing head and shoulders above most men in his own age. No mere scholar would have lived as he lived, toiled as he toiled, daring Churchmen and Statesmen, braving peril and exile, for the sake of God's Good News in England. The one grand aim of his life was to give England a version of the Scriptures in the language of the people, and for that high purpose, he had been quite content to bear the pains of privation and run the risks of martyrdom. So it was that within a month of the November edition of 1534, he had begun to print a new version, and early in 1535, his third and final edition of the *New Testament* made its appearance.[2]

This was his last piece of work on the New Testament, and it furnished clear proof of his continued care in detail. There were more than three hundred and fifty changes in this version, but the alterations were less radical than in the last edition. They brought the whole spirit of his text much closer to that of the original, and they gave a rhythm to its language which no English classic has yet excelled. But this was in no sense just a piece of literary labour; it was alight with the vital glow of his own incandescent spirit. The Word of God had now been cast into English speech by a man to whom that Word was no less than the breath of life. Thus he added to the obligations which his former efforts had laid upon England, and he proved that his skill in translation was

[1] Demaus, p. 484.   [2] Mozley, p. 292.

backed up by his strength in revision. "The one excellence which has so often been wanting to the perfection of a literary work, Tyndale possessed in the highest measure. He was master of what the poet calls 'the last and greatest art, the art to blot'; he was the beau-ideal of a translator, uniting consummate felicity in the first draft of his work with unwearied care in the subsequent revision of it."[1] Only four copies of this third edition still exist, and all four are imperfect; but for the next thirty years, there was a constant stream of reprints both in England and in the Low Countries. Only one year later, the year in which he met his death, the first volume of the Scriptures ever to be printed on English soil, in English speech, came from the King's own press; and that volume was a folio edition of his *New Testament*, prologues and all, with his own long proscribed name in full view on the title-page. "The king's heart is in the hand of the Lord, as the rivers of water: he turneth it whithersoever he will" (Prov. 21:1); the heart of this wayward king had now at last been turned to sanction the book he had so long opposed.[2] And a careful comparison of the extant copies of this final version shows that it was the text used by Rogers for his Matthew's Bible, which was published by royal licence in 1537 with a dedication to Henry himself. Then in 1539, the Great Bible was brought out by Cranmer, and an order was issued by Cromwell to the effect that a copy of this Bible should be placed in every parish church in England. The Great Bible was Coverdale's revision of Matthew's Bible, and so in large part was no more than a revised version of Tyndale's work. The tide was thus to turn within less than three years, and the English Bible was at last in the hands of the English people.

Tyndale had led a charmed life in spite of plots and perils during his ten years of exile; but an occasional ray of light from that great city which has no need of sun or moon had now begun to shine upon his path.[3] He had been kept through the years of battle until his work was done; but now when the heat of battle may have begun to pass, he fell as a victim to the sleepless hatred of a hidden enemy. While still engaged in his daily routine of translation and correction, he was caught in a mesh of guile and treachery. The plot was hatched by some unknown foe in England

[1] Demaus, p. 403.   [2] *Works*, Vol. I, p. lxxv.   [3] Smellie, p. 206.

and was carried out by Henry Phillips, an agent in Belgium. Phillips picked up Tyndale's trail in Antwerp and wormed his way into Tyndale's favour. Thomas Poyntz was filled with profound distrust, but he had come in the guise of a friend. He soon became Tyndale's guest at the meal table, and was shown the secret of his books and papers. At last, in May 1535, while Poyntz was out of the city, Phillips found means to lure Tyndale away from the safety of his quarters with the Merchant Adventurers. The hour had come when he should find himself betrayed at the hand of a friend. His fate was sealed when he walked straight into the arms of a band of soldiers whom Phillips had posted in a narrow alley. There was no hope of rescue or escape; there was nothing but the Castle of Vilvorde, the great State Prison of the Low Countries. Meanwhile trials for heresy in the Netherlands had been withdrawn from the jurisdiction of local magistrates, and were now placed in the hands of special commissioners. The Queen Regent, Mary of Hungary, would choose the men who were to try Tyndale, and we can draw a fair picture of the course of events from the well-known conduct of other such cases. The trial would be carried out in private from first to last; the prisoner would not appear in public at all until the commissioners were ready to pronounce the verdict. Long and weary months would drag by while he lay in the cells of Vilvorde and the law took its course. There, like John the Baptist in the dungeons of Fort Machaerus, he was forced to languish in loneliness and poverty, cut off from friends, from news, from books, shut up to walk with God through the valley of the shadow of death.

But his arrest, in May 1535, was in some sense a threat to the safety of the English merchants, and they tried to obtain redress on his behalf from the Court at Brussels. "Then incontinent," says Foxe, "by the help of English merchants, were letters sent in favour of Tyndale to the Court of Brussels."[1] But they could not deny that he was a heretic in the eyes of the law, and the laws against heresy had become more stringent than ever. Thomas Poyntz then made a noble effort to get Cromwell to bring pressure to bear upon the Low Countries, although he could hope for nothing except as a special favour. Cromwell was slow to move,

---

[1] *John Foxe*, Vol. V, p. 123.

for he knew that Henry was at odds with Charles V; the King had no love for Tyndale, and would hardly grieve to hear of his death. But in July, Cromwell's godson, Thomas Theobald, was in Antwerp and was able to glean something of Tyndale from Phillips himself. "I could not perceive . . . but that Tyndale shall die," he told Cranmer, "which he doth follow (urge) and procureth with all diligent endeavour, rejoicing much therein."[1] Late in August, Cromwell secured the King's consent to take action, and then composed letters to the Archbishop of Palermo and the Marquis of Bergen, who were leading members of the Council of Brabant. These letters reached Flanders before mid-September, asking for the release and extradition of Tyndale as a diplomatic favour. It was left to Poyntz to press the affair with the authorities, and he gave up the next few weeks to the task of winning Tyndale back to freedom. He spared no pains and shrank from no peril to save his friend, and at last he was told that he would be set free as the letters desired. Phillips was desperate; "he knew no other remedy but to accuse Poyntz."[2] Thus in November, Poyntz was himself seized and placed in custody, where he remained for some three months. He was in grave peril as the abettor of a heretic, but at last in February he made a clean escape. He was forced to flee from Antwerp, leaving behind his wife, his goods, and his business career. He was ruined from a human standpoint, but the lustre of his name will never grow dim while men honour deeds of sacrificial heroism. He had been the soul of all the attempts to save Tyndale; no other was willing to run the risk of life and goods which he had run. But his imprisonment was fatal for Tyndale; it had brought all active effort on his behalf to an utter standstill.

We know very little of his private affairs in those dark days, but Foxe tells us that his witness was as bright and true as ever. "Such was the power of his doctrine and the sincerity of his life," wrote Foxe, "that . . . . he converted his keeper, the keeper's daughter, and others of his household; also the rest that were with Tyndale conversant in the Castle reported of him that if he were not a good Christian man, they could not tell whom to trust."[3] But there is one letter, written out by his own hand in Latin, which still remains in the archives of the Council of Brabant,

[1] Mozley, p. 304.   [2] *John Foxe*, Vol. V, p. 124.   [3] Ibid., p. 127.

and it tells a story which no other words could repeat with such guileless pathos. It bears no date nor name of place, but there can be no doubt that it was sent from his prison cell to the Governor of the Castle in the winter months of 1535. "I beg your Lordship," he wrote, "and that by the Lord Jesus, that if I am to remain here through the winter, you will request the Commissary to have the kindness to send me from the goods of mine which he has, a warmer cap; for I suffer greatly from cold in the head, and am afflicted by a perpetual catarrh which is much increased in this cell; a warmer coat also, for this which I have is very thin; a piece of cloth too to patch my leggings. My overcoat is worn out; my shirts are also worn out. He has a woollen shirt, if he will be good enough to send it. I have also with him leggings of thicker cloth to put on above; he has also warmer night caps. And I ask to be allowed to have a lamp in the evening; it is indeed wearisome, sitting alone in the dark. But most of all I beg and beseech your clemency to be urgent with the Commissary that he will kindly permit me to have the Hebrew Bible, Hebrew grammar and Hebrew dictionary, that I may pass the time in that study. In return, may you obtain what you most desire, so only that it be for the salvation of your soul."[1] Strength and patience meet and mingle in this letter; it breathes the true spirit of dignity and endurance. He would neither cringe nor flatter for the sake of relief, but he would ask in terms that were frank and honourable. And the picture which it depicts of the lonely captive in his threadbare garments, "sitting cold and dark and solitary in the damp cells of Vilvorde during the long cheerless nights of winter, and earnestly soliciting the favour of light, and warm clothing, and above all, of books to solace him", reminds us how St. Paul sent for his cloke, his books, and his parchments, to cheer him in the damp and tedium of the Mamertine dungeons in Rome.[2]

Was his request allowed? Did he labour on with his translation of the Old Testament? We do not know; but there could have been no finer sequel to the story of the Venerable Bede, who came to the last words in St. John's Gospel as he approached the gate of death, than this sketch of Tyndale, in cold prison quarters, toiling bravely on to finish his task. But winter passed away, for

[1] Mozley, p. 334.   [2] Demaus, p. 477.

the end was not yet. The failure of Cromwell's appeal and the arrest of Poyntz meant that nothing could save him in the end; but in April, Stephen Vaughan wrote to Cromwell from the Low Countries with a final appeal for help. "If now you send me but your letter to the privy council (of Brabant)," he wrote, "I could deliver Tyndale from the fire, so it come by time, for else it will be too late."[1] Vaughan did not know that his efforts were now too late, his hopes too bright; Tyndale had been in the toils of formal trial and disputation for long enough, and the law had to run its course. The whole trial was carried out in writing, and months were spent in this paper debate between Tyndale and the theologians from the Louvain. The first step had been to frame a formal accusation, and then he would reply; and a series of such papers passed to and fro as his doctrines were brought up point by point for trial. Six years later, one of the three theologians, James Latomus, a Canon of Louvain and Doctor in Divinity, wrote of the case in a letter of the highest value. "When William Tyndale was in prison for Lutheranism," he said, "he wrote a book on the theme, Sola fides justificat apud Deum, Faith alone justifies before God; this he called his key to the healthy understanding of Sacred Scripture."[2] There was an answering book, or thesis, from the pen of Latomus, a reply by Tyndale, and two further answers from the Doctors of the Louvain. Tyndale was thus on trial for the great theme of the Reformation, and he prepared his statements with double care as one who was now exposed to the eyes of the world. But the written attack and his written defence were slow indeed, and it was not until summer that the trial came to its climax. Then, early in August 1536, he was condemned as a heretic, degraded from the priesthood, and delivered to the secular authorities for punishment. Two more months were allowed to pass; then on Friday, October 6th, he was led out to meet his death. He was bound to a stake with an iron chain round his waist, and a piece of hemp in a noose round his neck, and a pile of straw and faggots all round his feet. Foxe says that he lifted up his voice at the stake and cried aloud with great fervour: "Lord, open the King of England's eyes!"[3] And then, at a given signal, the rope was wrenched tight from behind and the faggots were lit with a torch to blaze up round the

[1] Mozley, p. 320.   [2] Ibid., p. 328.   [3] *John Foxe*, Vol. V, p. 127.

strangled body. Only one other brief report of that distant martyr pyre has come down to us; it is contained in a letter from John Hutton, written home to Cromwell two months later. "They speak much," so he wrote, "of the patient sufferance of Master Tyndale at the time of his execution."[1]

[1] Mozley, p. 342.

BIBLIOGRAPHY

STEPHEN CATTLEY, *The Acts and Monuments of John Foxe* (8 Vols.), 1841

WILLIAM TYNDALE, Doctrinal Treatises (Parker Society Edition: *Works*, Vol. I), 1848

WILLIAM TYNDALE, Expositions (Parker Society Edition: *Works*, Vol. II), 1849

WILLIAM TYNDALE, Answer to Sir Thomas More's Dialogue (Parker Society Edition: *Works*, Vol. III), 1850

WILLIAM EDWARD CAMPBELL, *The English Works of Sir Thomas More* (7 Vols.), 1931

ROBERT DEMAUS, *William Tyndale*, 1871

J. F. MOZLEY, *William Tyndale*, 1937

S. L. GREENSLADE, *The Work of William Tindale*, 1938

FREDERIC SEEBOHM, *The Oxford Reformers: John Colet, Erasmus, and Thomas More*, 1911

ALEXANDER SMELLIE, *The Reformation and Its Literature*, 1925

HUGH LATIMER

Fellow of Clare Hall,
Cambridge

c. 1485–1555

"His noble fame and virtuous renown is more known, not only in this realm of England, but also in foreign countries, among both learned and unlearned, than it can be hid. I for my part have known him before twenty years in the University of Cambridge, to whom next unto God I am specially bound to give most hearty thanks for the knowledge, if any I have, of God and of His most blessed Word."

—THOMAS BECON, *The Jewel of Joy* (*The Catechism with Other Pieces*, p. 424).

H̲UGH LATIMER WAS THE YOUNGEST
child in the family of a small country yeoman and was born at
Thurcastone in Leicestershire about the year 1485. Augustine
Bernher, his Swiss servant in later life, spoke of him as being
"above three score and seven years of age" in the reign of
Edward VI,[1] and he was commonly known as "old Father
Latimer" at the time of his last imprisonment.[2] These facts are
in favour of a year like 1485 as the year of his birth. To fix the
date at an earlier period would leave too large a part of his life
in total obscurity; to place it much later would be to break away
from the uniform tradition of those who knew him best during
his own lifetime.[3] Therefore, towards the close of the reign of
Richard III, perhaps when the rival armies were sweeping across
the Leicester Downs for the last fight in the Wars of the Roses,
Hugh Latimer was born on a little farm near Thurcastone and
was christened with his father's name in the old parish church.
The name of Latimer had not been uncommon in bygone days,
although nothing is known of the yeoman's line of descent. There
had been a powerful family of this name in Leicestershire two
hundred years before, wealthy knights and landlords, but they
appear to have died out even before the Wars of the Roses. The
Latimers of Thurcastone may have traced their descent in some
way from this once powerful family, but their fortunes had now
fallen and they were small country farmers. Foxe says that Hugh's
father was "a husbandman of right good estimation",[4] and Hugh
seems to have had older brothers as well as six sisters. But the
children could not have been very robust, and his brothers must
have died in childhood; for we gather that he was the only son
left to his parents after his fourth birthday, and he appears to
have suffered the loss of his mother while still in his boyhood.[5]
Perhaps he inherited a weakly constitution; certain it is that

[1] *Sermons*, p. 320. [2] Ridley, *Works*, p. 384. [3] Demaus, p. 4.
[4] *John Foxe*, Vol. VII, p. 437. [5] Ibid., Vol. VII, p. 437.

he often complained of his infirmities and found them a grievous burden in the years when he ought to have been in his prime.

Thurcastone was a peaceful village in the valley of the Soar at the foot of the Charnwood Hills, to the south of which one can see the county town of Leicester. This was country where the Lollard Movement had been cradled, and the Lutterworth Vicarage where John Wycliffe had once lived and laboured was no more than a day's journey away. There were only twenty-five families in the village of Thurcastone at the time of Latimer's martyrdom, and the population could have been little more than a hundred people all told, in his boyhood. The yeomen of England were the real strength of the country, and Latimer of Thurcastone was a true scion of his class. He knew them, and loved them, and spoke of them in terms of the highest honour. "For by yeomen's sons," he declared before Edward VI, "the faith of Christ is and hath been chiefly maintained."[1] We learn from a famous passage in this sermon that his yeoman father was the dominant influence in the formation of his character while in his teens. "My father was a yeoman, and had no lands of his own," he said; "only he had a farm of three or four pound by year at the uttermost, and hereupon he tilled so much as kept half a dozen men. He had walk for a hundred sheep, and my mother milked thirty kine. He was able, and did find the king a harness, with himself and his horse, while he came to the place that he should receive the king's wages. I can remember that I buckled his harness when he went unto Blackheath Field. He kept me to school, or else I had not been able to have preached before the King's Majesty now. He married my sisters with five pound, or twenty nobles apiece, so that he brought them up in godliness and fear of God. He kept hospitality for his poor neighbours, and some alms he gave to the poor. And all this he did of the said farm, where he that now hath it payeth sixteen pound by year or more, and is not able to do anything for his prince, for himself, nor for his children, or give a cup of drink to the poor."[2] The tang of the country clung to Latimer to the end of his life: the smell of the soil, the song of the plow, the life of the farm, have all been preserved in his sermons, and he never lost his large-hearted

[1] *Sermons*, p. 102.   [2] Ibid., p. 101.

sympathy for the humble tenant who had to toil for a living in the teeth of high rents and the policy of land enclosure.

The calm country routine was only once disturbed in his boyhood, and it still lived in his memory when he referred to those early days at Thurcastone. In June 1497, a large band of Cornish rebels marched across the southern counties and encamped at Blackheath prior to an attack on the Tower of London. Latimer's father was summoned to take the field under Henry VII, and the lad of twelve had helped to buckle on his armour before he set out for the war. But it was soon over, and his father would be home in time for harvest; and the winter evenings that year would be brightened up with tales of London and the rebels. This would be an added reason for the training which he gratefully acknowledged that he himself had been given. "In my time," he said, "my poor father was as diligent to teach me to shoot as to learn me any other thing; and so I think other men did their children: he taught me how to draw, how to lay my body in my bow, and not to draw with strength of arms as other nations do, but with strength of the body: I had my bows bought me according to my age and strength; as I increased in them, so my bows were made bigger and bigger; for men shall never shoot well except they be brought up in it: it is a goodly art, a wholesome kind of exercise, and much commended in physic."[1] England's archers had been her great asset in war, but archery was slowly becoming obsolete. It took time and trouble to train a good archer, and the cross-bow had been brought in to save trouble and time. But it was not nearly such a useful weapon in war, and, in 1512, a Parliamentary Statute laid down the use of the long-bow as a necessity. Latimer was trained in the old school; but his father discerned in him something more than brawn and muscle. He saw in him such a "ready, prompt, and sharp wit" that he sent him to "the common schools of his own country".[2] His own words bear witness to his father's anxiety for his education: "He kept me to school, or else I had not been able to have preached before the King's Majesty now."[3]

It must have been in the spring of 1506 that he entered Clare Hall to take up his studies in the schools of Cambridge. It was during the same spring that Henry VII and his mother, the

[1] *Sermons*, p. 197.   [2] *John Foxe*, Vol. VII, p. 437.   [3] *Sermons*, p. 101.

Countess of Richmond, came to visit Cambridge, and the Freshman at Clare would catch his first glimpse of regal splendour. He was trained in Aristotle and the Schoolmen, for the winds of the New Learning had not as yet begun to blow through the halls of Cambridge. Then in 1510, even before he had graduated, he was elected to a Fellowship at Clare, for he would have to keep twelve terms before his degree was conferred. The appointment of Erasmus as the Lady Margaret Professor just at the time when he took his degree and was ordained would mark a new epoch in the life of Cambridge; but he was slow to yield his mind to its refreshing influence. In 1514, he graduated as a Master of Arts, and became a Regent in the University. Nothing is known of his activities in the next years, but his letters in much later life prove that he never lost his zeal for the good name of Clare Hall.[1] Then in 1522, his name appears in the Proctors' Books as one of the Twelve Preachers licensed by the University to preach in all parts of the realm.[2] Perhaps it was in the same year that he became the cross-bearer for the University in all official processions. "For his gravity and years," wrote Ralph Morice in a graceful tribute, he was "preferred to the keeping of the University Cross."[3] Thus, when Henry VIII paid his famous visit to Cambridge in 1522 and was received with the magnificence which he loved, it fell to Latimer to bear the silver cross of the University before the King. He went on to take his degree as a Bachelor of Divinity, and this has been confirmed by an entry in the Proctors' Books in 1524: it links his name with those of George Stafford, Rogers, Thixtill, and certain other Masters of Arts who had taken their degrees in Divinity but had not paid the customary fees for some now unknown reason. We do not know whether he went on to take his Doctor's degree; the records are inconclusive. His name does not appear in the official Registers, and he was not treated as a Doctor in his trial at Oxford.[4] On the other hand, Sir Thomas More, in April 1534, spoke of him as "Master Doctor Latimer"[5]; and the deed for the Restoration of the Temporalities of the See of Worcester, in October 1535, described him as "Magistrum Hugonem Latymer sacrae Theologiae Professorem".[6]

[1] *Remains*, pp. 378, 382.　　[2] Ibid., p. 329.　　[3] Ibid., p. xxvii.
[4] *John Foxe*, Vol. VII, p. 540.　　[5] Demaus, p. 157.　　[6] Ibid., p. 171.

Latimer was a devout son of the Church, and he set his face resolutely against the New Learning and the friends of Reform. He had been schooled in Duns and in Peter Lombard, and he looked on the New Learning as a grievous sign of the times. "I understand no Greek," he told Weston at the Oxford Disputation; Greek he refused to learn while his mind was plastic, for to him it was the native language of heresy.[1] "All the Papists think themselves to be saved by the Law," he declared in later life; "and I myself have been of that dangerous and damnable opinion."[2] He was oppressed with such superstitious fears that he could never feel sure whether he had sufficiently mingled the wine with water for a Mass. "I remember how scrupulous I was in my time of blindness and ignorance," he wrote; "when I should say mass, I have put in water twice or thrice for failing; insomuch when I have been at my memento, I have had a grudge in my conscience, fearing that I had not put in water enough."[3] He was never as much at ease as he desired, and thoughts of death filled him with dread. When the storms of controversy began to break, he longed for the peaceful haven of a cloister. "I have thought in times past," he said, "that if I had been a friar and in a cowl, I could not have been damned nor afraid of death; and by occasion of the same, I have been minded many times to have been a friar."[4] But he entered the lists in the name of the Old Learning, for the innovations of George Stafford were more than he could bear. What was it that Stafford had so boldly ventured upon? He had dismissed the old text-books and had begun to expound the Scriptures from the Greek and Hebrew to large crowds of students. Latimer was dismayed to see how many students had left off the study of the Schoolmen for the reading of the Scriptures. He went and stood in the schools where Stafford gave his lectures and did all that lay in his power to urge students not to attend.[5] Nor was that all, for Ralph Morice declared that he "there most eloquently made to them an oration, dissuading them from this new-fangled kind of study of the Scriptures, and vehemently persuaded them to the study of the school authors".[6]

[1] *John Foxe*, Vol. VI, p. 504.
[2] *Remains*, p. 137.
[3] *Sermons*, p. 138.
[4] *Remains*, p. 332.
[5] *John Foxe*, Vol. IV, p. 656.
[6] *Remains*, p. xxvii.

Morice went on to say that this "he did not long before that he was so mercifully called to the contrary".[1] But there was one still more reckless step which he felt impelled to take, and his Oration when he graduated as a Bachelor of Divinity was a vehement attack on the works of Philip Melancthon. He was not to know that Thomas Bilney stood among his hearers; still less could he know that Bilney's heart was drawn out to him in a profound sense of love and longing. Bilney made up his mind to see him in private and to pour out the whole story of his own search for Truth with its final discovery of Christ. He found Latimer in his study, and begged him to hear his confession. Latimer must have known that Bilney was one of the Reformers, and he may have thought that he had come to confess and forsake his errors. But the mighty arrow of Truth from the long-bow of God's Word in Bilney's hand was about to pierce his heart. He was transfixed as he heard how God had dealt with Bilney, and he could do no less than fall at the feet of the same Divine Lord and Archer. Latimer was to recollect that moment of conquest to the end of his life; he could never forget how God had sent Bilney to him in his folly and pride. "Master Bilney . . . was the instrument whereby God called me to knowledge; for I may thank him next to God for that knowledge that I have in the Word of God. For I was as obstinate a Papist as any was in England, insomuch that when I should be made Bachelor of Divinity, my whole oration went against Philip Melancthon. . . . Bilney heard me at that time, and perceived that I was zealous without knowledge; and he came to me afterward in my study, and desired me for God's sake to hear his confession. I did so; and to say the truth, by his confession I learned more than before in many years."[2] He could never repay his debt to that gentle scholar who had so come to shrive his soul, and he referred to him both in sermons and in letters time and again to the end of his days.[3] Thus we hear him again in more general terms of reference describe this great change in his life's experience: "It were too long to tell you what blindness I have been in, and how long it were ere I could forsake such folly, it was so corporate in me: but by continual prayer, continual study of Scripture, and oft

[1] *Remains*, p. xxvii.   [2] *Sermons*, p. 334.
[3] Ibid., pp. 222, 334; *Remains*, pp. 51, 52, 330, 331.

communing with men of more right judgment, God hath delivered me."[1]

Latimer's conversion must have occurred in the spring or summer of 1524, and for two years he was unmolested as he walked with Bilney through the fields of Cambridge. He was still a priest of the Church in which he had been brought up and ordained, but he had now resolved to cast off the Schoolmen and the works of the Law for faith in Christ. Bilney soon taught him a better way to please God than by creeping to the Cross on Good Friday or lighting candles before the shrines of saints; he took him to visit the sick and to relieve those that were in prison, to teach the poor and to comfort those that were in trouble.[2] He had lost his desire for the safety of the cloister and had found a nobler calling to a life of energetic service among the haunts of men. Perhaps it was this strong practical emphasis on the ministry of true disciples which was to mould him so definitely as a preacher of the moral obligations of faith in Christ. There were many points of doctrine which he held as before, and his mind was to change slowly enough as the future unrolled. But Foxe says that he gave himself to the task of preaching, "spending his time partly in the Latin tongue among the learned, and partly amongst the simple people in his natural and vulgar language."[3] It was not until towards the close of 1525 that complaints about his preaching stirred the Bishop of Ely to action. He came up from Ely without warning to hear Latimer preach a Latin sermon in Great St. Mary's, and he entered the church just as he had fairly begun. But the preacher paused with admirable presence of mind while the splendid retinue was being seated. Then he declared that new hearers required a new sermon, and he began afresh on the Priesthood of Christ. The Bishop of Ely thanked him for his sermon and begged him to preach yet again in the same church against Luther and his doctrine. "My Lord," said Latimer, "I am not acquainted with the doctrine of Luther, nor are we permitted here to read his works; and therefore it were but a vain thing for me to refute his doctrine, not understanding what he hath written nor what opinion he holdeth." This was too shrewd for the Bishop's patience, and he rudely answered:

[1] *Remains*, p. 333.   [2] *Sermons*, p. 335.
[3] *John Foxe*, Vol. VII, p. 438.

"Well, well, Mr. Latimer, I perceive that you somewhat smell of the pan; you will repent this gear one day."[1]

Bishop West lost no time before hostilities opened. He preached against Latimer in Barnwell Abbey and formally inhibited him from preaching in any part of his Diocese or in any of the University pulpits. But this fulmination quite failed in its purpose since the monastery of the Austin Friars was exempt from episcopal jurisdiction, and the Prior, Robert Barnes, asked him to preach there the next Sunday morning. We know nothing of this sermon, but Barnes himself on the very same day preached a sermon in St. Edward's which caused a storm. Events followed each other in rapid sequence, and, in February 1526, Barnes was charged with heresy before the great Cardinal himself. His life was in immediate danger, and he only escaped after he had borne a faggot through the streets of London. This was a clear public sign of recantation, and it could not fail to react to the disadvantage of Bilney and Latimer. Cambridge had been racked with strident controversy for weeks, and the humiliation of Barnes seemed a favourable opportunity to take action against his friends. Bilney and Latimer were summoned to answer for their conduct before Wolsey, and Ralph Morice has left quite a racy account of the subsequent interview. A bell rang, and Latimer was summoned before the Cardinal. He told him that he had been a student of the Schoolmen and the Fathers. Wolsey at once asked two doctors who were present to test him with certain questions from Duns Scotus. "Latimer, being fresh then of memory, and not discontinued from study as those two doctors had been, answered very roundly; somewhat helping them to cite their own allegations rightly, where they had not truly nor perfectly alleged them."[2] Wolsey was pleased with his ripe and ready replies and asked frankly why the Bishop of Ely so misliked his preaching. Latimer then told him in detail of his sermon in Great St. Mary's, and assured him that he had preached no other doctrine than he had thus rehearsed. There was further conversation, and then Wolsey declared: "If the Bishop of Ely can not abide such doctrine as you have here repeated, you shall have my license, and shall preach it unto his beard, let him say what he will."[3] And so he was discharged, with an admonition to be

[1] *Remains*, pp. xxviii, xxix.   [2] Ibid., p. xxx.   [3] Ibid., p. xxxi.

96

cautious and with a licence from the Legate himself to preach in all parts of England.

It was confidently thought in Cambridge that he would be firmly silenced, but he returned to enter a pulpit, and produce his licence, and resume his preaching at once. Wolsey's authority would shield him from episcopal interference, and he slowly enlarged the scope of his preaching. Thomas Becon was a student during those years, and he has drawn up a valuable report of his sermons. Latimer was led to argue that the Scriptures ought to be read in the language of the people by priests and by laymen alike, and he hurled his rebukes at those clergy who were absent from their cures and took no care for their flocks. He also began to inveigh against what he called "blind superstitions", such as setting up of candles, running off as pilgrims, and the many follies which obscured the glory of God and the proper works of mercy. "Oh, how vehement was he in rebuking all sins, namely idolatry, false and idle swearing, covetousness, and whoredom! Again, how sweet and pleasant were his words in exhorting unto virtue! He spake nothing but it left as it were certain pricks or stings in the hearts of the hearers, which moved them to consent to his doctrine." So wrote Thomas Becon in *The Jewel of Joy*, and he then went on to add: "I leave off to report his free speech against buying and selling of benefices, . . . against popish pardons, against the reposing our hope in our own works or in other men's merits, against false religion. Neither do I here rehearse how beneficial he was, according to his possibility, to poor scholars and other needy people; so conformable was his life to his doctrine, so watered he with good deeds whatsoever tofore he planted with godly words, so laboured he with all main both in word and deed to win and allure other unto the love of Christ's doctrine and His holy religion. There is a common saying which remaineth unto this day: When Master Stafford read and Master Latimer preached, then was Cambridge blessed."[1] Latimer had found his true vocation, and these three years helped to mould and mature his character and conviction. His call was not that of a monk, seeking peace in cloistered meditation; it was that of a preacher, moving the minds of his hearers with a happy mixture of impassioned eloquence and effective raillery. He was

[1] Thomas Becon, *Catechism with other Pieces*, p. 425.

rising in power and could not be ignored. "I have an ear for other preachers," Sir John Cheke used to say; "but I have a heart for Latimer."[1]

But new troubles were now at hand. In December 1529, Latimer preached two sermons at St. Edward's which are still famous as his Sermons on The Card. It was customary to mark Christmas celebrations with card games of various descriptions, and he proposed to deal Christ's cards to his hearers and to explain how to play them so as to win and not to lose.[2] Thus if some sin should surge up in their hearts, they were to take Christ's card, a card wherein they could perceive Christ's rule; for if they were to lay this card upon their heart, they would have won the game. But these Sermons with their homely illustrations seized the public fancy and filled Cambridge with fresh strife and debate. A Dominican Friar named Buckenham came out with an attack upon Latimer's assumption that all men should have the Scriptures in their own hands ready for use. Latimer's Christmas Cards were now matched with Buckenham's Christmas Dice. His aim was to show his hearers how to cast cinque and quatre; the quatre were four of the Fathers, and the cinque were five quotations from the New Testament which he used to argue against the free circulation of the Scriptures. "So," he said, "when Master Latimer deals out his cards, we cast our cinque-quatre upon them, and lo! we have won the game!"[3] Buckenham, however, was no match for his foe and was routed amid universal laughter. But the controversy spread ever more widely until Cambridge as a whole was involved in hot verbal warfare. It was isolated academic warfare, but it was an outbreak of the struggle which had begun to arm the whole realm in two camps. But the time had not yet come when Cambridge was to fight it out to the end, for a second issue was now to grasp men's minds. The Royal Almoner wrote to the Vice Chancellor in words that took stock of the whole controversy and put down the opposition to the malice of Hugh Latimer's opponents: "which malice peradventure cometh partly for that Mr. Latimer favoureth the King's Cause; and I assure you it is so reported to the King."[4] Thus in January 1530, the Vice Chancellor summoned all the antagonists to the Senate and required them under pain of the

[1] Demaus, p. 55.   [2] *Sermons*, p. 8.   [3] Demaus, p. 68.   [4] Ibid., p. 70.

King's displeasure not to disturb the peace with fresh wrangles. Latimer was ordered "to touch no such things in the pulpit as had been in controversy between him and others", and was warned with threats of excommunication "to be circumspect and discreet in his sermons, and speak no such thing as might be occasion of offence".[1]

Thus the strife caused by the Sermons on The Card was allayed only to make room for the great controversy on the subject of "the King's Cause". In February 1530, the Vice Chancellor was required to submit the whole question to the judgment of the University. It was referred to a committee of which Crome and Latimer were both members. Sir William Butts, the Royal Physician, was in Cambridge when the debate took place, and he at once perceived how valuable an ally the King already had in Latimer. Butts secured an invitation for the Cambridge preacher to wait on the King at Windsor where he had gone for Lent, and he thus preached his first sermon before the Court in March 1530. The Vice Chancellor of Cambridge had arrived at the same time, and just after the sermon found himself summoned into the King's presence. The judgment of Cambridge on the King's Cause was placed by him in the King's hands, and he recalled that "His Highness gave me there great thanks, and talked with me a good while". But Henry then began to converse with certain others, and in a voice that all might hear, "greatly praised Mr. Latimer's sermon".[2] Latimer recognised that this was a momentous occasion, and he never forgot the scene. "I was called to preach before the King, which was my first sermon that I made before His Majesty, and it was done at Windsor: where His Majesty after the sermon was done did most familiarly talk with me in a gallery."[3] In May, he was named as one of the twelve Cambridge divines who were chosen with twelve Oxford divines to confer in London with those whom the King had nominated on the circulation of heretical books. After twelve days, they ended their labours at a solemn meeting in the presence of the King in St. Edward's Chamber at Westminster Palace. Latimer was compelled to add his name to a condemnation of the works of Tyndale which said that his translation of the Scriptures was full of error and heresy. Foxe

[1] Demaus, p. 70. [2] Ibid., p. 77. [3] *Sermons*, p. 335.

says that he spent the summer as the guest of Sir William Butts, and that he was often preaching in the City. Tunstall had just gone to Durham, and the Bishop-elect, Stokesley, was still abroad: for this once there was no one to say him nay in London.[1] Perhaps he returned to Cambridge in the autumn and drew up the noble letter in which he urged the King to grant the free circulation of the Scriptures in the language of the people.[2] Henry was not prepared to take this step as yet, but he was so far from taking offence that Latimer was appointed as one of his Chaplains.

But he had no more love for Court intrigue than for Cambridge quarrels, and, in January 1531, he was instituted to the living of West Kington in the Diocese of Salisbury. It was just a pocket village on the fringe of Wiltshire fourteen miles from Bristol, and he was soon absorbed in a pastoral ministry in a parish which must have made him think of old days in Thurcastone. "Sir," he told Sir Edward Baynton, "I have had more business in my little cure since I spake with you . . . than I would have thought a man should have in a great cure. I wonder how men can go quietly to bed which have great cures and many, and yet peradventure are in none of them all."[3] But his efforts soon branched from West Kington to the country about; "his diligence was so great, his preaching so mighty, the manner of his teaching so zealous, that he could not escape without enemies".[4] In March 1531, Stokesley prepared certain items on which to charge Latimer, Bilney, and Crome with heretical preaching in London. Latimer and Bilney were not within his reach, but Crome was forced into a pitiful recantation. However, Latimer was stirred by this threat to condemn the conduct and outlook of the rulers of the Church in a bold sermon in the village of Marshfield, near Kington. We find him in London itself during the summer of 1531, and he declined more than once the earnest request of those who wished to hear him preach. But at length he agreed to preach at St. Mary Abchurch to those who had a "great hunger and thirst of the Word of God and ghostly doctrine"[5]; though not until he had obtained the full consent of the Curate, and had made it clear that he did not hold Stokesley's

[1] *John Foxe*, Vol. VII, p. 454. [2] *Remains*, pp. 297: 309. [3] Ibid., p. 350.
[4] *John Foxe*, Vol. VII, p. 454. [5] *Remains*, p. 323.

licence. But his letter to Sir Edward Baynton proves that he was not at all sure that there was not some trap,[1] and his sermon pictured St. Paul himself on a charge of heresy. "Oh! it had been a godly sight to have seen St. Paul with a fagot on his back," he said, "even at Paul's Cross, my Lord of London, bishop of the same, sitting under the cross!"[2] Such a sermon could not fail to excite Stokesley's indignation, but he returned to West Kington in peace. He did not know how soon the year would be darkened with news of the burning of Bilney, and Bayfield, and Tewkesbury; but that news would make him feel as though the darkness had now begun to hem him in at West Kington. Bilney's death was a shock to his inmost being; who could tell when his own dark hour might come?

Stokesley soon brought pressure to bear upon Hiley, the Chancellor of Salisbury, to send Latimer up to London as a prisoner to stand on trial for his sermon in St. Mary Abchurch. Latimer was summoned before the Chancellor; but he convinced him that he was too weak and frail to make such a journey in the depth of winter and that it was his own proper duty, acting for the Ordinary, to correct or reform him as far as need might demand.[3] Hiley seemed quite content with this reply, but he went home to West Kington with an oppressed spirit. "The matter is weighty," he told Sir Edward Baynton, "and ought substantially to be looked upon, even as weighty as my life is worth; but how to look substantially upon it, otherwise know not I than to pray my Lord God day and night, that as He hath emboldened me to preach His truth, so He will strengthen me to suffer for it."[4] Latimer drew up a long account of all his trials for Sir Edward Baynton, who showed it to some of his friends. But they hotly opposed it on the ground that God alone knew the truth for certain, and Sir Edward himself was also in favour of great caution. Latimer was far from books and men of learning, and had never been so occupied with parish duties.[5] But he sat down to write a long reply to his critics, and his letter shows how the gap between him and the old school was now slowly widening. "Ye mislike that I say I am sure that I preach the truth; saying in reproof of the same that God knoweth certain truth.

---

[1] *Remains*, p. 324.   [2] Ibid., p. 326.   [3] Ibid., p. 323.
[4] Ibid., p. 333.   [5] Ibid., p. 350.

Indeed, alone God knoweth all certain truth, and alone God knoweth it as of Himself; and none knoweth certain truth but God and those which be taught of God. . . . But as to my presumption and arrogancy: either I am certain or uncertain that it is truth that I preach. If it be truth, why may I not say so? . . . If I be uncertain, why dare I be so bold to preach it? And if your friends in whom ye trust so greatly be preachers themselves, after their sermon I pray you, ask them whether they be certain and sure that they taught you the truth or no; and send me word what they say, that I may learn to speak after them."[1]

But he was still engaged in this animated reply when a summons reached him which he could not refuse. "Sir," he wrote, "I had made an end of this scribbling and was beginning to write it again more truly and more distinctly, and to correct it; but there came a man of my Lord of Farley with a citation to appear before my Lord of London in haste, to be punished for such excesses as I committed at my last being there."[2] Hiley had yielded to Stokesley's demands, and the citation required him to appear before the Bishop of London in the Consistory Court at St. Paul's. "Jesu! mercy!" he exclaimed; "what a world is this that I shall be put to so great labour and pains, besides great costs, above my power, for preaching of a poor simple sermon!"[3] Thus on Monday, January 29th, 1532, his trial opened before Stokesley and a group of Bishops. He knew that the fate which he must expect if he were found heretical would be that of Little Bilney; but he had not as yet diverged from the orthodox tradition of the Church in theology. He was repeatedly cross-examined, but no definite charge of heresy could be fastened on his statements. Three times a week he was grilled and questioned in the presence of five or six Bishops, and he believed that it was God indeed Who gave him wisdom how to reply.[4] The day came when he was taken into the room where these cross-examinations were held, and he noticed that for the first time there was no fire in the grate; and he was placed between the table and chimney which had now been covered with a piece of arras. One old Bishop who had been a good friend to him in the past now sat near the end of the table and asked him a very subtle

---

[1] *Remains*, p. 336.   [2] Ibid., p. 350.
[3] Ibid., p. 351.   [4] *Sermons*, p. 294.

question which he hardly knew how to meet. "Master Latimer," he said, "do you not think on your conscience that you have been suspected of heresy?" To say nothing would be tacit consent that he had been at fault; but to answer it at all would be full of risk. Latimer was silently turning it over in his own mind when the Bishop surprised him with a sharp request that he should speak up since he was hard of hearing. Misgiving suddenly sprang up in his heart, and he gave an ear to the chimney. "And Sir," he recalled, "there I heard a pen walking in the chimney behind the cloth! They had appointed one there to write all mine answers." He had never been in a place where his wit and skill were so sorely needed, but we do not know what answer he coined for the emergency. "God was my good Lord, and gave me answer," he said; "I could never else have escaped."[1]

Stokesley prolonged the trial for no less than six weeks without result and then referred it to Convocation. Latimer was thus called before Convocation on March 11th and was asked to subscribe to a series of fifteen articles.[2] They had been framed with no little cunning on such subjects as purgatory and pilgrimages, and they represented that class of things which had been so greatly abused in the common life of the day. Latimer's emphasis had been on the fact that these things did not matter half so much as the plain duties laid down in the Scriptures; he was even prone to suspect that they had no solid authority in the Scriptures at all. Thus to accept the articles would be to endorse the kind of practice which he had so often denounced, while to reject them would be to imply the kind of teaching which would brand him as a heretic. To his credit, he refused to subscribe; and he refused, not once, nor twice, but a third time as well. Warham of Canterbury then pronounced him contumacious, excommunicated him, and remanded him to lie in custody at Lambeth until Convocation should declare its will. Ten days were to elapse before his next summons before Convocation, and they were spent in the greatest mental distress. In his uncertainty, he drew up a touching appeal to the Archbishop of Canterbury, in which we learn that he could not come to Lambeth on account of sickness. "And that your Lordship may not any longer in vain expect my arrival, lo, I send you this

[1] *Sermons*, pp. 294, 295.   [2] *Remains*, pp. 218, 219.

strange sheet," he wrote, "blotted by my own hand, which will be a satisfactory evidence to you of the truth of my excuse."[1] He was disturbed by his long absence from his flock, and he complained of the harsh and unfair treatment he had received. He had been called up to appear before the Bishop of London, but the process had been transferred to the Convocation; he had been charged with one particular breach of authority, but so many extraneous questions had been brought in that he could see no end to them.[2] If his preaching had been obscure, he was ready to explain it, for he had taught nothing against the Truth or the decrees of the Fathers. "It is lawful I own to make use of images; it is lawful to go on pilgrimage; it is lawful to pray to saints; it is lawful to be mindful of souls abiding in purgatory: but these things which are voluntary are so to be moderated that God's commandments of necessary obligation . . . be not deprived of their just value. . . . But what can be more unseemly than to employ our preaching in that which God would neither command nor counsel, so long at least as those things thereby fall into neglect which are commanded! I therefore hitherto stand fixed on the side of the commandments of God."[3]

Latimer was still determined not to subscribe. "I dare not, Most Reverend Father, subscribe the bare propositions which you require of me; being unwilling as far as I may to be the author of any longer continuance of the superstition of the people."[4] On March 21st, he came before Convocation again, and the Bishops offered to release him from the pains of excommunication if he would subscribe to the two Articles which dealt with Lent and the Crucifix. Latimer agreed to accept this compromise: but he found that he was also required to read out a prepared statement with a promise to make amends for his reckless preaching. He then knelt down to sue Stokesley's pardon, only to find that his case was again deferred for three more weeks. On April 10th, he appeared before Convocation, and is said to have signed the whole series of fifteen Articles; but he was still required to remain in London and to appear again. Meanwhile, whispers reached the Bishops' ears of a new offence. Greenwood, one of his old Cambridge antagonists, had heard of his fall and had been loud

---

[1] *Remains*, p. 351. [2] Ibid., p. 352.
[3] Ibid., pp. 353, 354. [4] Ibid., p. 355.

in triumph. Latimer at once prepared a strong protest, the more indignant perhaps because his own conscience told him that there was some ground for Greenwood's exultation. "As to my preaching," he wrote, "as I was not conscious of having preached any error, I have not made any public acknowledgment of any error; though peradventure more out (outspoken) some time than well advised."[1] But this letter was placed in the hands of Convocation, and the Bishops saw that Latimer's submission would be worthless if he were to preach as before and to boast that he had never confessed to an error. Therefore he was summoned before Convocation on April 15th and again on the 19th to answer for his statements in reply to Greenwood. He could now see no end to these delays, and he made a sudden appeal from the Convocation to the King's Grace. Henry approved of his appeal on the understanding that he should make a full apology to the Bishops and should promise to preach with more care in future. It was Stephen Gardiner who made the King's decision known to Convocation, and on April 22nd, Latimer confessed that he had erred both in doctrine and discretion, and on his knees implored the pardon of Convocation. Then at the King's desire, he was absolved by Stokesley and dismissed with the warning that the old charge would be revived should he relapse.

Thus he was free once more after three months of great anxiety; but the darkest page of his life had been written in the terms of his own vacillation. Before he left London, there was another incident which must have made him feel deeply ashamed at the excess of his caution. His friends Ralph and William Morice induced him to pay a visit to James Bainham who was then in Newgate. He had once been forced to recant and had borne a faggot to the Cross at St. Paul's; but he had braved torture on his second arrest and had now been sentenced to death. But the precise reason for which he was condemned had not been made public, and this visit was to find out the real ground for which he was to suffer. Latimer and the two brothers found him the night before his death, sitting on a straw couch in the darkness, with a book in one hand and a candle in the other, reading and praying. Latimer's opening words were staid and cautious, for he felt that it must be a weighty matter for which a man

[1] *Remains*, p. 357; Demaus, p. 123.

would be willing to die. "The truth is," said Bainham, "I spake against Purgatory, that there was no such thing, but that it picked men's purses; and against satisfactory masses: which (assertions of mine) I defended by the authority of the Scriptures." Latimer comforted him in the face of death, and then heard him say in reply: "And I likewise do exhort you to stand to the defence of the truth; for you that shall be left behind had need of comfort also, the world being so dangerous as it is."[1] The next morning, he went to his death at the stake, firm and constant in the hour of trouble. Latimer for his part returned to West Kington: but the words of Bainham were now added to the death of Bilney, nor could he shake himself free from their hold upon his mind. It was his own conduct which he would find himself forced to pass in judgment; it was his own doctrine which he would now have to judge more firmly by the authority of the Scriptures. He did not stir from his rural retreat at West Kington during the months at hand, and we may well suppose that his leisure was spent in thought and prayer for divine help and guidance. Could it be that Bainham was right when he said that Purgatory was no more than a cruel pick-purse?

In March 1533, Latimer reappeared on the public stage of England just when times were proving favourable to the cause of reform. He had emerged from his meditative retreat in the month of Cranmer's consecration to lift up his voice in Bristol. The whole city soon rang with his sermons. Complaints were addressed to Convocation, but that body had lost its powers with the abolition of the Papal Supremacy. He was asked by the Mayor to preach again during Easter, but the result was a prohibition to preach in any part of the Diocese without the Bishop of Worcester's licence. Having thus been put to silence, he was assailed with a scurrilous fusillade by such nonentities as Powell, Wilson, and Hubbardin, and a controversy raged in Bristol with far more din than in the old days at Cambridge. At length, Cromwell himself was forced to take notice, and, in July, Commissioners were sent down to investigate for the Council. Latimer's opponents had rashly outrun the proper limits of zeal, and had condemned the King's Divorce and the marriage with Anne Boleyn. They found themselves under the iron heel of the

[1] *Remains*, p. 223.

law, and were driven from the field in disgrace. Latimer, however, was to receive a licence from Cranmer which would permit him to preach in all parts of the Southern Province, and he seems to have been allowed to return to Bristol for an exposition of the doctrines which had stirred up so much trouble. The whole storm had helped him to break free from a few more bonds of the traditional theology in which he was so long enmeshed. His sermons have vanished; but his answer to the Articles imputed to him by Powell and his letter on the subject to Ralph Morice have been preserved. His bold statements on the Virgin Mary, and Saints, and Pilgrimages, and Purgatory, show how far his thoughts had travelled during the past twelve months. There was more than a touch of quiet humour in what he thought fit to say of Purgatory. "I had rather be in purgatory than in the Bishop of London's prison: for in this I might die bodily for lack of meat, in that I could not; in this I might die ghostly for fear of pain or lack of good counsel, in that I could not; in this I might be in extreme necessity; in that I could not, if extreme necessity be peril of perishing;"[1] "in this I might be craftily handled, in that I could not; in this I might be brought to bear a fagot, in that I could not; in this I might be discontented with God, in that I could not. . . . Ergo, I had rather to be there than here. For though the fire be called never so hot, yet if the Bishop's two fingers can shake away a piece, a friar's cowl another part, and scala coeli altogether, I will never found Abbey, College nor Chantry for that purpose."[2]

In April 1533, Stokesley promulgated a fresh edict to prevent all preaching in his Diocese unless the preacher held his special licence, and the Bristol controversy led him to inhibit Latimer by name for pestiferous doctrine. But since he held Cranmer's licence for the Southern Province, he could afford to disregard Stokesley's thunder, and, in October, he ventured to preach in the Church of the Augustine Friars in London. Stokesley was so provoked that he issued a most peremptory inhibition, to forbid his clergy under the pains of the law from allowing Latimer to preach until he had appeared to purge his fault. But he was now beyond Stokesley, and he returned to West Kington for the winter without care or trouble. Then in January 1534, Cranmer

---

[1] *Remains*, p. 237.   [2] Ibid., p. 362.

secured him an invitation to preach before the King on the Wednesdays of Lent and wrote some sage advice: "I would ye should so study to comprehend your matters that in any condition you stand no longer in the pulpit than an hour, or an hour and a half at the most!"[1] Thus he would preach before the Court during the six weeks from February 18th until April 1st, but the sermons have not survived. They would no doubt deal with subjects chosen on the advice of Cranmer and Cromwell, and he was a guest at Lambeth Palace for a fortnight at least after Easter. Thus on April 13th, Sir Thomas More was asked to wait in the Palace garden while his case was being discussed by the Commissioners. "And thereupon," he told his daughter, "I tarried in the old burned chamber that looketh into the garden, and would not go down because of the heat. In that time saw I Master Doctor Latimer come into the garden, and there walked he with divers other doctors and chaplains of my Lord of Canterbury. And very merry I saw him."[2] And good cause he now had. It was only two years since all had been hostile, and now he was high in favour. He would return to West Kington with an authority which could not be denied, for he had been placed in control of the issue of a licence for all preachers in the west of England. This was dependent on the injunctions which compelled the preacher to own the King's marriage and to uphold his heirs. It was to be at his "instance and request" that preachers would be licensed; it was to be on his judgment and advice that a licence might be withdrawn.[3]

On August 20th, 1535, Latimer was installed by the Prior as Bishop of Worcester, and, on September 26th, he was consecrated by Cranmer at Winchester. The Diocese of Worcester was the most neglected See in England; nowhere was the blight of foreign rule so harsh or severe. It had been farmed out to Italian prelates for forty years, and not one of them had ever set his foot in the See. It was so large that the modern Sees of Bristol and Gloucester formed part of its jurisdiction, and its landed estates were the source of princely revenue. The main episcopal seat was the stately Castle of Hartlebury, but the Bishop also found himself possessed of certain other country manors and a

[1] Cranmer, *Works*, Vol. II, p. 308. [2] Demaus, p. 157.
[3] Cranmer, *Works*, Vol. II, p. 297.

noble London mansion. There had been an absenteeist régime for
so long that the plain duties of the See would call for the full
expense of the time and strength of the most energetic Diocesan.
There are but few records of the daily round of episcopal cares
and labours which now occupied Latimer, but he gave his whole
mind to the task with unflagging devotion. "The days," says
Foxe, "were so dangerous and variable that he could not in all
things do that he would: yet what he might do, that he performed
to the uttermost of his strength."[1] He was appalled at the state of
ignorance which he discovered, and the moral situation made his
heart burn. It made him long for the revival of true discipline in
Church affairs, and that longing found an echo in his last great
sermon before Edward VI: "And here I will make a suit to your
Highness to restore unto the Church the discipline of Christ in
excommunicating such as be notable offenders; nor never devise
any other way. For no man is able to devise a better way than
God hath done, which is excommunication, to put them from
the congregation till they be confounded. Therefore restore
Christ's discipline for excommunication; and that shall be a means
both to pacify God's wrath and indignation against us; and also
that less abomination shall be used than in times past hath been,
and is at this day. I speak this of a conscience, and I mean and
move it of a goodwill to your Grace and your Realm. Bring into
the Church open discipline of excommunication, that open
sinners may be stricken withal."[2]

"You that be of the Court, and especially ye sworn chaplains,"
said Latimer in a sermon before Edward VI, "beware of a lesson
that a great man taught me at my first coming to the court: he
told me for good-will; he thought it well. He said to me, 'You
must beware, howsoever ye do, that ye contrary not the king;
let him have his sayings; follow him; go with him.' Marry, out
upon this counsel!"[3] He was soon put on his mettle in such
matters himself. He took his seat in the House of Lords in
February 1536, when the business before each House was the
dissolution of the lesser monasteries. Latimer had been vehement
in his condemnation of the conventual orders, but he could not
approve of the way in which the monastic revenues were seized
to line the purse of a greedy nobility. Certain abbeys had been

[1] *John Foxe*, Vol. VII, p. 461.   [2] *Sermons*, p. 258.   [3] Ibid., p. 231.

reserved for the royal stud, and this provoked his bold rebuke. "I was once offended with the king's horses," he recalled, "and therefore took occasion to speak in the presence of the King's Majesty . . . Abbeys were ordained for the comfort of the poor: wherefore I said it was not decent that the king's horses should be kept in them." Afterwards he was admonished by one of the lay lords who asked him what concern of his it was. "I spake my conscience," he replied, "as God's Word directed me."[1] But such outspoken honesty was not without its own difficulties. On one occasion Latimer was in the King's presence when one of the others who were present suddenly knelt down and accused him of sedition. Latimer faced his accuser and said: "Sir, what form of preaching would you appoint me to preach before a king? Would you have me for to preach nothing as concerning a king in the king's sermon?" Then he turned to the King and knelt down with words of dignified submission. "I never thought myself worthy, nor I never sued to be a preacher before Your Grace," he said, "but I was called to it, and would be willing, if you mislike me, to give place to my betters. . . . But if Your Grace allow me for a preacher, I would desire Your Grace to give me leave to discharge my conscience; give me leave to frame my doctrine according to mine audience." Certain of his friends came to him later with tears in their eyes and told him that they looked to have seen him in the Tower the same night. But the King was pleased to accept his own statement, and the subject was dropped once and for all.[2]

In June 1536, Convocation met for the first time since the fall of the Papal Supremacy, and Latimer was invited not merely to attend, but to preach the sermon. It was a most momentous occasion, and the preacher rose to it with magnificent courage. He would preach in Latin, but the sermon was soon in print in the language of the people; and it was read with an astonishing avidity by high and low, for no preacher could have been a better spokesman for the mind of England. He passed over the more subtle points of theology to give his whole strength to the most direct moral issues. It was not the teaching of the Church, but the practice of Churchmen, which he castigated. "The end of your Convocation shall show what ye have done," he said,

[1] *Sermons*, p. 93.　　　　[2] Ibid., pp. 134, 135.

". . . for what have ye done hitherto I pray you, these seven years and more? . . . What one thing that the people of England hath been the better of a hair? . . . I am bold with you; but I speak Latin and not English, to the clergy, not to the laity; I speak to you being present, and not behind your backs. God is my witness, I speak whatsoever is spoken of the goodwill that I bear you; God is my witness, which knoweth my heart, and compelleth me to say that I say!"[1] What had they done, who had met so often? They had gone about to burn him alive! His thoughts were on his own experience before this same body, though he spoke of himself in an oblique manner. "This other," he said, "which truly never hurt any of you, ye would have raked in the coals, because he would not subscribe to certain articles that took away the supremacy of the king."[2] Then he asked: "How chanced this? How came it thus? Because there were no children of light, no children of God amongst you? . . . I think not so. God forbid that all you which were gathered together under the pretence of light should be children of the world! Then why happened this? Why, I pray you? Perchance either because the children of the world were more in number in this your congregation, . . . or at the least of more policy than the children of the light."[3] And he could not refrain from an illustration of the policy of the children of the world in one point: "They begot and brought forth that our old ancient purgatory pick-purse."[4] And there was so much else to say as well. "What think ye of these mass-priests, and of the masses themselves? What say ye? Be all things here so without abuses that nothing ought to be amended?"[5] Then the sermon concludes: "If ye will not be the children of the world, be not stricken with the love of worldly things. . . . Feed ye tenderly with all diligence the flock of Christ. Preach truly the Word of God. Love the light, walk in the light, and so be ye children of light while ye are in this world that ye may shine in the world that is to come bright as the sun."[6]

The Ten Articles which were drawn up as a result of this Convocation were signed by Latimer with his most careful signature; his handwriting was seldom so legible. The Cotton

[1] *Sermons*, pp. 45, 46.   [2] Ibid., p. 46.   [3] Ibid., pp. 46, 47.
[4] Ibid., p. 50.   [5] Ibid., p. 55.   [6] Ibid., p. 57.

Manuscripts have preserved an interesting letter in this connection; it supplies his arguments against Purgatory, together with the King's marginal annotations in its defence. Latimer's arguments were based on the Scriptures, and he claimed the right to differ from the Fathers on their authority. But the Ten Articles did not meet with general acceptance, and he was called back to London to take part in a Royal Commission which was to draw up a still more ample statement. This body of Bishops was in session from May until August, even though the plague had driven Henry and Cromwell and many others out of London. By the end of July, they could go no further without Cromwell's help and authority, and Latimer wrote anxiously to him: "This day Sir which is Saturday (July 21st), we had finished I trow the rest of our book if my Lord of Hereford had not been diseased, to whom surely we owe great thanks for his great diligence in all our proceedings. Upon Monday I think it will be done altogether, and then my Lord of Canterbury will send it unto your Lordship with all speed. . . . As for myself, I can nothing else but pray God that when it is done, it be well and sufficiently done, so that we shall not need to have any more such doings. For verily for my part, I had lever be poor parson of poor Kington again than to continue thus Bishop of Worcester." Then his letter closed with a sad note of the times: "Sir, we be not here without all peril; for beside that two hath died of my keeper's folks, out of my gate-house, three be yet there with raw sores; and even now Master Nevell cometh and telleth me that my under cook is fallen sick, and like to be of the plague."[1] This book was *The Pious and Godly Institution of A Christian Man*, commonly known as The Bishop's Book, and it was no sooner finished than Cranmer and Cromwell obtained Henry's consent for the publication of an English version of the Bible. This was indeed a large answer to the appeal which had been drawn up by Latimer in 1530, and it rejoiced his heart as he returned to his Diocese.

It was at the end of August that he returned home to set on foot a Diocesan Visitation. The Articles or Injunctions seem to have been compiled with the help of Cranmer, and they furnish a most lamentable sketch of Diocesan affairs. There were clergy

[1] *Remains*, pp. 379, 380.

who had neither a Bible nor a Testament; there were communicants who did not know the Lord's Prayer in English. Sermons had been curtailed by bead-telling or long prayers for the dead; sometimes they were entirely omitted for the sake of other dumb dark ceremonies.[1] Latimer's convictions on the supreme duty of the preacher were shocked indeed by the neglect which he everywhere discovered, and his sermons refer more than once to pulpits which were like bells without clappers or to people who were more in love with Robin Hood than with the Word of God.[2] But he carried out the Visitation with a resistless energy which taxed his strength to the utmost. In October, we find him in Hartlebury, thankful for the birth of a prince: "God give us all grace to yield due thanks to our Lord God, God of England!"[3] In November, he was in London to preach in connection with the burial of Jane Seymour; but he was in a state of great fatigue and had to brace himself to stand in the pulpit.[4] Robert Barnes went home with him for Christmas and spent some weeks in the blind ends of the Diocese, preaching with singular power and ability. Latimer's opinion of Barnes stood high, for, in July, he had written: "I pray God continue with him, for then I know no one man shall do more good."[5] Now he declared of his preaching: "Surely he is alone in handling a piece of Scripture, and in setting forth of Christ he hath no fellow."[6] Meanwhile, his own health was never robust, and it was in April this year perhaps (1538) that he informed Cromwell: "I am light-headed for lack of sleep: not that I can sleep, and will not; but that I would sleep, and can not."[7] This may have been partly owing to the fact that much of his time in the new year had been occupied with the exposure of false relics such as the Rood of Ramsbury. Then the famous statue of the Virgin in Worcester Cathedral was stripped and was found to be the statue of a bishop. He could only ask for consent to throw this "great Sibyll" into the flames.[8] Finally, in October, he was appointed to a Commission to visit the monastery of Hales and to investigate what was known as the Blood of Hales. He had told Ralph Morice while he was still at West Kington: "I dwell within half a mile of the Fossway, and

[1] *Remains*, pp. 242:244.   [2] *Sermons*, pp. 207, 208.   [3] *Remains*, p. 385.
[4] Ibid., p. 386.   [5] Ibid., p. 378.   [6] Ibid., p. 389.   [7] Ibid., p. 391.
[8] Ibid., p. 395.

you would wonder to see how they come by flocks out of the west country to . . . the Blood of Hales."[1] Now he exposed the fraud which had so vexed his soul, and it was proved that the Blood of Christ was only melted honey coloured red with saffron.[2]

In spring 1539, Latimer was summoned to London for Parliament and Convocation which met late in April. Neither body had met during the three years since 1536, nor could it be known in advance what the course of events was now to be. On May 5th, Latimer formed one of a committee of nine who were to meet at St. Paul's to devise some bond of general unity. A fortnight of debate failed to produce any such articles of agreement. The King therefore transferred the whole matter to a fresh court, and the Duke of Norfolk was sent to ask the House of Lords for a verdict upon the six items which were most in dispute. There were long and earnest debates until the King himself appeared to join issue with the Reform party. Cranmer carried on the struggle alone when his friends had fallen silent, but all to no avail. In June, an act was passed in both Houses which gave the Six Articles a firm place in the laws of the Kingdom; they were to be enforced by a bill of penalties which was to take effect as from July 12th. Latimer could still accept the first Article on Transubstantiation, but the other five raised problems with which he had long been vexed and troubled. He was absent from the House of Lords for three days after June 28th, the day on which the act was passed; he was perhaps far too oppressed with sorrow and anxiety to appear in public. The Act did not compel him to teach the doctrine laid down by the Articles, but it forbade him to deny or oppose it. He had nothing to fear as a private person, but he was a Bishop who might be called on to preside at the trial of offenders. Would he have to condemn those whose only fault was that they dared to proclaim the truths which he also believed? Such a line of thought would make him wish to retire into private life: had he not declared before this that he would prefer the life of West Kington to that of a Diocesan Bishop? On the other hand, to desert Cranmer, and to withdraw from the conflict at this sudden reverse, would be highly questionable as an act of wisdom or of necessity. And yet three days later, on

[1] *Remains*, p. 364.   [2] Ibid., pp. 407, 408.

July 1st, he resigned from the See of Worcester. Cromwell appears to have made him think that it was the King's wish that he should resign; and so resign he did. Why did Cromwell act so strangely? Was it because he could not get Latimer to follow his policy? Latimer was seized with deep regret when he ascertained the truth. "He was deceived," so he told the Council in May 1546, ". . . when he left his bishopric; being borne in hand by the Lord Cromwell that it was his Majesty's pleasure he should resign it; which his Majesty after denied, and pitied his condition."[1]

"At what time he first put off his rochet in his chamber among his friends, suddenly he gave a skip on the floor for joy, feeling his shoulder so light and being discharged as he said of such a heavy burden."[2] This quaint remark by Foxe bears all the marks of truth and is quite in harmony with his character. Nevertheless, Latimer's retirement at this stage was a grave loss to the cause of the Reformation, for it meant that the voice of the finest preacher in all England was for eight years put to silence. Henry may have pitied him for being deceived, but he ordered him to be placed in ward in the house of Sampson of Chichester. "When I was in trouble," he said, "it was objected and said unto me that I was singular; that no man thought as I thought; that I loved a singularity in all that I did; and that I took a way contrary to the King and the whole Parliament."[3] Sampson's house in London lay on the east side of Chancery Lane with a pleasant outlook over Lincoln's Inn Fields, and the custody in which Latimer now found himself was an honourable form of imprisonment in which he was free to receive his friends.[4] But the King was irritated by the circulation of a letter from Melancthon with reference to the Six Articles in which he commented: "Beside all this I hear of divers good men, excelling both in doctrine and virtue, to be detained in prison, as Latimer, Crome, Shaxton, and others, to whom I wish strength, patience, and consolation in the Lord."[5] But men who were "lanthorns of light" in the eyes of Melancthon were for a time in no little danger. Latimer considered himself as marked out for execution. "I looked that my part should have been therein," he said; "I looked every day to be called to it

[1] Demaus, pp. 323, 324.   [2] *John Foxe*, Vol. VII, p. 463.
[3] *Sermons*, p. 136.   [4] Ibid., p. 164.   [5] *John Foxe*, Vol. V, p. 351.

myself."[1] But then, in the spring of 1540, Sampson himself was
sent to the Tower of London, and, in July, Latimer found himself
at liberty on the understanding that he was to refrain from all
preaching and was not to approach within six miles of the cities
of Oxford, Cambridge, London, or Worcester.[2] It was just at this
time that Barnes was in prison, and on July 20th, he went to his
death at the stake. Latimer seems to have used his new liberty to
speak for Barnes, for in the last letter that Barnes ever wrote he
declared: "Although many persons approve my statements, yet
no one stands forward except Latimer."[3] Barnes had been a
stormy petrel, and his course was far from even; but the Prior
who had received Latimer into his pulpit at Cambridge had now
sealed his testimony like Bilney; like Bainham.

We have nothing but the vaguest information for the six years
after July 1540, for even his correspondence has been lost to
posterity. He was condemned to silence and obscurity, and he
seems to have spent his time in hospitable country homes. Thus,
when Thomas Becon was in trouble, about the year 1545, and had
to go into hiding, he met Latimer at a home in Warwickshire
and was captivated by his conversation. It made him feel as if he
had been "clean delivered from Egypt, and quietly placed in
the new glorious Jerusalem".[4] But those years of silence must
have brought the rest and change which his broken state of health
so greatly needed, as well as the peace and leisure which his
slowly changing state of mind would require. Certain it is that
he emerged from those years with a new richness of experience
and an accuracy of statement which far surpassed all that he
had enjoyed before. At length, in the spring of 1546, he returned
to London to stand by his old friend Crome who was in trouble
for a sermon which had attacked the doctrine of Purgatory.
Crome was forced to recant, and the Council then turned its full
attention upon Latimer. In May, the Council at Greenwich was
thus mentioned in a letter from one of its members: "This day
we look for Latimer, the Vicar of St. Bride's (John Taylor, otherwise Cardmaker), and some others that have specially comforted
Crome in his folly."[5] On May 13th, Latimer was examined, and
he admitted that he had been with Crome on various occasions.

[1] *Sermons*, p. 164. [2] *Original Letters*, Vol. I, p. 215. [3] Ibid., Vol. II, p. 617.
[4] Thomas Becon, *The Catechism with Other Pieces*, p. 426. [5] Demaus, p. 322.

He was then placed on oath and was told to prepare a written answer to certain questions. It was not long before he sent back a message to say that he could not proceed until he had spoken to the Council again. Tunstall and Sir John Gage saw him and brought back the report that he wished to clear his conscience with the Council. He was brought back and said that he "doubted whether it were His Highness's pleasure that he should be thus called and examined; desiring therefore to speak with His Majesty himself before he made further answer."[1] When the Council compelled him to proceed, he proved too shrewd for them. "He hath since answered," the Council reports; "but in such sort as we be for the purpose as wise almost as we were before; saving that by the same he doth so open himself as it should appear that he is as Crome was, which we shall this night know thoroughly. For this afternoon my Lord of Worcester and the rest of the Doctors talk frankly with him in the matter of the Articles to fish out the bottom of his stomach, whereby His Majesty at his coming shall see further in him."[2] But the curtain falls at this point, and we only know that he was sent to the Tower, where he remained in close confinement until the King's death.

On the Coronation of the Boy-King, Edward VI, Latimer was released from his imprisonment; but he did not resume the life of a Diocesan Bishop. On January 8th, 1549, the House of Commons moved an address to the Duke of Somerset, requesting him to restore Latimer to his old See. Again, in February 1550, rumour was active: "They say that a bishopric has been offered to Latimer, the king's preacher."[3] But age and failing health had made Latimer averse to the cares and anxieties of the episcopate, and he declined. He was to do more real service to the cause of Reformation in the reign of Edward by his occasional sermons than he had done by his episcopal labours in the reign of Henry. His great sermon before the Convocation of 1536 had won him a place in the heart of all England which no other preacher could claim, and he was now more than ever revered by the common people because he had refused the lure of wealth and high office held out in the offer of a Diocese. In 1547, he received a licence under seal which restored to him the right to preach where he

[1] Demaus, p. 323.   [2] Ibid., pp. 324, 325.   [3] *Original Letters*, Vol. II, p. 465.

would in any part of the realm. Thus "the golden mouth of this preacher . . . was opened again", and he was to continue preaching for the most part twice each Sunday throughout this reign.[1] He was now the recognised exponent of the moral teaching of the Reformation, and the practical character of his oratory was the surest means to arouse the conscience of England. We must look to Ridley or to Cranmer for the theology of the movement, but his was the voice for righteousness. No one could have been more vigorous in his condemnation of the common faults and superstitions of the priests and people than he was at Paul's Cross; he was just as unsparing in his condemnation of the social greed and rapacity of the peers and prelates when he preached before them at Court. There was nothing crude or vulgar in his sermons; they were plain and opportune, shrewd and vigorous, with a touch of racy humour, and a flair for homely illustration, and a magnificent verve, and a colloquial dash, that gave his words instant penetration. "If," says Ryle, "a combination of sound Gospel doctrine, plain Saxon language, boldness, liveliness, directness, and simplicity can make a preacher, few I suspect have ever equalled old Latimer."[2] The high standard which he set for moral truth and holy living was of supreme value to the Reformation. The State Paper Office and the British Museum contain many proofs of the wide extent of his influence on the opinions of his hearers: they prove in fact beyond all doubt that his preaching left a broad mark on the mind of England which the lapse of time has yet to efface from the national character.[3]

Thus on January 1st, 1548, he resumed his career as a preacher with a sermon at Paul's Cross, where he preached again each week during the month. The fourth sermon in this series is renowned in English Literature as the Sermon of The Plow, and there could be no better illustration of his style and ability, his trenchant wit, his homely traits, his discursive qualities and quaint expressions. It was no dry logic which he had to offer, but truth spoken with a force and fire which could not be hid. "I liken preaching to a plowman's labour, and a prelate to a plowman," he said. ". . . For as the plowman first setteth forth his plow, and then tilleth his land, and breaketh it in furrows,

[1] *John Foxe*, Vol. VII, p. 463.   [2] Ryle, p. 164.   [3] Demaus, p. 232.

and sometimes ridgeth it up again, . . . so the prelate, the preacher, hath many diverse offices to do: . . . now casting them down with the law, . . . now ridging them up again with the Gospel, . . . now weeding them by telling them their faults, . . . now clotting them by breaking their stony hearts."[1] But what if one were to ask how it was that there were so many prelates who did not set forth their plow in preaching? "Ye would have me here to make answer, and to show the cause thereof! Nay, this land is not for me to plow; it is too stony, too thorny. . . . But this much I dare say, that since lording and loitering hath come up, preaching hath come down, contrary to the Apostles' times: for they preached and lorded not, and now they lord and preach not. For they that be lords will ill go to plow; it is not seeming for their estate. . . . For ever since the prelates were made lords and nobles, the plow standeth; there is no work done; the people starve. They hawk; they hunt; they card; they dice . . . so that plowing is set aside."[2] These were bold words; they led up to the most famous passage of all in its indignant eloquence. "And now I would ask a strange question: who is the most diligentest bishop and prelate in all England? I can tell, for I know him, who it is; I know him well. But now I think I see you listening and hearkening that I should name him. There is one that passeth all the other, and is the most diligent prelate and preacher in all England. And will ye know who it is? I will tell you: it is the devil. He is the most diligent preacher of all other; he is never out of his diocese; he is never from his cure; ye shall never find him unoccupied; he is ever in his parish; . . . ye shall never find him idle, I warrant you."[3] And to drive home this mighty metaphor, his voice rang out: "Where the devil is resident and hath his plow going, there away with books and up with candles! Away with Bibles and up with beads! Away with the light of the Gospel, and up with the light of candles, yea, at noon-days!"[4]

Latimer's eloquence was soon to pour itself out in a new environment, for he was called to preach on the Wednesdays of Lent before the King and Court. A large pulpit was built in the garden at Westminster so that he might be heard by three or

---

[1] *Sermons*, p. 61. [2] Ibid., pp. 65, 66.
[3] Ibid., p. 70. [4] Ibid., p. 70.

four times as many as the Chapel Royal could accommodate. His theme before Edward and his Court was Restitution, and he addressed the most forceful appeals to all classes in his auditory. In Lent 1549, he preached before the Court again, and "the famous Friday sermons" were again most carefully adapted to his hearers.[1] Once more he dealt with the values of preaching and the dangers of neglect. "I had rather ye should go a napping to the sermons than not to go at all," he said; "for with what mind so ever ye come . . . ye may chance to be caught or ye go."[2] "If a priest should have left mass undone on a Sunday within these ten years, all England should have wondered at it; but they might have left off the sermon twenty Sundays, and never have been blamed."[3] In Lent 1550, he preached once more before the Court; it was on March 10th, and the sermon was in two parts, before noon and after. His health had failed so much that he knew that it would be his last sermon before the King. "I come now to take my leave and to take my ultimum vale, at least-wise in this place," he said; "for I have not long to live, so that I think I shall never come here into this place again."[4] It was a most powerful homily which caught up the theme of Hooper's Wednesday lectures on the Book of Jonah. "Take heed and beware of covetousness," so it began; "take heed and beware of covetousness; take heed and beware of covetousness! And what if I should say nothing else these three or four hours but these words? It would be thought a strange sermon before a king, to say nothing else but Beware of covetousness. And yet, as strange as it is, it would be like the sermon of Jonas that he preached to the Ninivites."[5] "And I say Ninive shall arise against England, thou England; Ninive shall arise against England, because it will not believe God, nor hear His preachers that cry daily unto them."[6] It was indeed a great loss when that voice was heard no more by King and Court: no more fitting tribute could have been paid to his name than in the words of Thomas Becon. Latimer lived in Becon's mind and memory as "a man worthy to be loved and reverenced of all true-hearted Christian men, not only for the pureness of his life which hath always before the world been innocent and blameless, but also for the sincerity and godliness of

[1] *Sermons*, p. 82.   [2] Ibid., p. 201.   [3] Ibid., p. 203.
[4] Ibid., p. 243.   [5] Ibid., p. 239.   [6] Ibid., p. 242.

his evangelic doctrine, which since the beginning of his preaching hath in all points been so conformable to the teaching of Christ and of his apostles".[1]

Latimer had been one of Cranmer's guests at Lambeth since his release, and his mind was cleared and strengthened in conference and fellowship with the Divines whom he met there. In Lent 1548, he tells us how crowds of those who were hapless victims of law's delays came to Lambeth and sought his help. He could hardly go to his book for the numbers who came; he could not walk in the garden without some call on his goodwill. "I am no sooner in the garden and have read awhile, but by and by cometh there someone or other knocking at the gate. Anon cometh my man and saith, Sir, there is one at the gate would speak with you."[2] The fact was that he had become known as the poor man's friend, and he did not mince words before the King: "They in Christ are equal with you. Peers of the realm must needs be. (But) the poorest plowman is in Christ equal with the greatest prince that is."[3] In Lent 1549, he told how he used to cross the Thames in a wherry on his way to the New Palace at Westminster, and how the watermen used to crowd round the steps at Lambeth for his custom.[4] And we hear him refer to the hours which he spent among Cranmer's wonderful collection of books: "I chanced to meet with his book," he said, "in my Lord of Canterbury's library."[5] On August 1st, 1548, Bartholomew Traheron told Henry Bullinger how earnestly Latimer used to listen to the conversation of the foreign divines then at Lambeth when Eucharistic doctrine was being discussed: "as one who is beyond measure desirous that the whole truth may be laid open to him, and even that he may be thoroughly convinced."[6] On September 28th, he wrote again: "That you may add yet more to the praises of God, you must know that Latimer has come over to our opinion respecting the true doctrine of the Eucharist, together with the Archbishop of Canterbury."[7] But after Lent 1550, he ceased to be "the king's preacher", and his failing health seems to have driven him into the country.[8] The Duchess of Suffolk was his hostess for the greater part of the time, and he

---

[1] Thomas Becon, *The Catechism with Other Pieces*, p. 424. [2] *Sermons*, p. 127.
[3] Ibid., p. 249.   [4] Ibid., p. 205.   [5] Ibid., p. 209.
[6] *Original Letters*, Vol. I, p. 320.   [7] Ibid., p. 322.   [8] Ibid., Vol. II, p. 465.

preached a noble course of sermons in the Hall at Grimsthorpe
Castle and in neighbouring parts of Lincolnshire during 1552.
He was also a not-infrequent visitor to John Glover of Baxterley
Hall in Warwickshire, and his voice was heard there also. These
last sermons are marked by a ripeness of experience and a richness
of exposition which add greatly to their value: they have less of
declamation and more of the pure Word of God than the older
sermons. John Foxe has left us a delightful photograph of his life
and habits at that time, though they seem so strange to our
modern ideas. He not only carried on his calling as a preacher for
the most part twice each Sunday, but "in his own private studies,
notwithstanding both his years and other pains in preaching,
every morning orderly, winter and summer, about two of the
clock in the morning, was at his book most diligently".[1]

Mary Tudor came to the Throne amid universal acclamation
in mid-July 1553. Latimer seems to have been buried in the
country with John Glover and had no share in the attempt to
crown Lady Jane Grey as Queen. But his reputation with the
common people was too high for him to escape notice, and, on
September 4th, Gardiner moved the Council to send him a
summons by hand. He was warned by a friend named John
Careless of Coventry that the summons for his arrest was on the
way: "yet so far off was it that he thought to escape that he
prepared himself towards his journey before the said pursuivant
came to his house."[2] The messenger was most surprised to find
him thus prepared; he was still more surprised to hear him say:
"My friend, you be a welcome messenger to me: and be it
known unto you and to all the world that I go as willingly to
London at this present, being called by my prince to render a
reckoning of my doctrine, as ever I was at any place in the world."[3]
But the messenger departed and left him to follow at will: for
the Council "would not have him appear, but rather to have
fled out of the realm".[4] Latimer had no mind to play the fugitive
and set out at once for London; and he could not resist a brief
quip that "Smithfield had long groaned for him".[5] On September 18th, he came before the Council: "and for his seditious
demeanour was committed to the Tower, there to remain a close

[1] *John Foxe*, Vol. VII, p. 463.　　　　　　[2] Ibid., p. 464.
[3] Ibid., p. 464.　　　[4] Ibid., p. 464.　　　[5] Ibid., p. 464.

prisoner," though still allowed to retain his servant Bernher.[1] "I had nothing but scornful taunts," he told Ridley, "with commandment to the Tower."[2] Ridley had been there for some time, and the next day Cranmer arrived. As close prisoners, they were confined to their cells, which were cold and damp and unwholesome. But this told on their health so much that a Council order allowed them "to have the liberty of the walk within the garden of the Tower".[3] Latimer was without a fire during winter and felt half dead with cold; but he sent a teasing message to the Lieutenant of the Tower to say that if he did not look to him better, he would perchance find himself deceived. This brought the Lieutenant to his door, anxious to find out if he had planned an escape. "Yea, Master Lieutenant," quoth he; "for you look I think that I should burn; but except you let me have some fire, I am like to deceive your expectation, for I am like here to starve for cold."[4]

But the winter lost its sense of tedium as a result of the discussion which he carried on with Ridley by the exchange of hand-written papers. Ridley set out to arm himself for the coming conflict on the Doctrines of the Mass and the Lord's Supper, and was anxious to prepare the veteran Latimer as well. Latimer saw at once that Ridley in this humble-minded approach was now playing the same role as Bilney had done at the time of his conversion. "Better a few things well pondered than to trouble the memory with too much," he wrote; ". . . I intend not to contend much with them in words, after a reasonable account of my faith given; for it shall be but in vain."[5] He had lost his freshness in memory and could not trust his skill in argument. It was long since those first days of strife in Cambridge; but he was in no doubt as to the Mass. "The very marrow-bones of the Mass are altogether detestable, and therefore by no means to be borne withal," he wrote; "so that of necessity the mending of it is to abolish it for ever. For if you take away oblation and adoration which do hang upon consecration and transubstantiation, the most papists of them all will not set a button by the mass."[6] Latimer, however, wrote much less than Ridley, con-

[1] Demaus, p. 409.　　　　　　[2] *John Foxe*, Vol. VII, p. 411.
[3] Demaus, p. 411.　　　　　　[4] *John Foxe*, Vol. VII, pp. 464, 465.
[5] Ibid., p. 411.　　　　　　　[6] Ibid., p. 412.

scious that he had more to learn than to impart. "Who am I, that I should add anything to this which you have so well spoken? Nay, I rather thank you that have vouchsafed to minister so plentiful armour to me, being otherwise altogether unarmed, saving that he can not be left destitute of help which rightly trusteth in the help of God. I only learn to die in the reading of the New Testament, and am ever now and then praying unto my God that He will be a helper unto me in time of need."[1] Latimer brought the Conference to an end with a last decisive paragraph. "Sir, I have caused my man not only to read your armour unto me, but also to write it out. For it is not only no bare armour, but also well buckled armour. I see not how it could be better. I thank you even from the bottom of my heart for it, and my prayer shall you not lack, trusting that you do the like for me."[2] Many things wrought confusion in his memory, but he knew the ground on which he would take his stand; there he would stand, let them say or do what they list. To use many words in reply would be in vain, but he meant to give a reasonable account of his faith if they would only listen. "Lo Sir, here have I blotted your paper vainly and played the fool egregiously; but so I thought better than not to do your request at this time. Pardon me, and pray for me; pray for me, I say; for I am sometimes so fearful that I would creep into a mouse-hole. . . . Fare you well once again, and be you steadfast and unmovable in the Lord."[3]

In Lent 1554, the Tower was so crowded that Cranmer and Ridley, Bradford and Latimer were placed in a common prison. "We four," said Latimer, "were thrust into one chamber, as men not to be accounted of, but God be thanked, to our great joy and comfort! There did we together read over the New Testament with great deliberation and painful study."[4] This was to see if they could find any statement which might favour the Mass, but it left them more than ever convinced that God required nothing apart from the death of Christ on the Cross. Then in April, Cranmer, Ridley, and Latimer were sent down to Oxford for a Disputation as to the presence, substance, and sacrifice of the Sacrament, with a group of divines from the two Universities. But they were no longer to share the same prison, and

[1] *John Foxe*, Vol. VII, p. 419.   [2] Ibid., p. 422.
[3] Ibid., p. 423.   [4] *Remains*, p. 259.

Latimer was now lodged in the house of one of the city bailiffs. On Saturday, April 14th, 1554, the proceedings were opened with a Mass of the Holy Ghost, sung by the choir of Christ Church. Then an imposing procession took place: the cross in front, followed by choristers, regents, doctors of law, doctors of divinity; with beadles to precede the chief dignitaries in the centre, and with students to bring up the rear. They met in St. Mary's Church, where the thirty-three Commissioners had seats of state in front of the altar and where crowds of interested people found a place in the nave. Cranmer was the first to appear, and then Ridley. "Last of all came in Master Latimer in like sort, with a kerchief and two or three caps on his head, his spectacles hanging by a string at his breast, and a staff in his hand, and was set in a chair; for so was he suffered by the Prolocutor."[1] He refused to subscribe to the Articles which had been compiled for the Disputation, and was ordered to prepare to defend himself on the coming Wednesday. "He alleged age, sickness, disuse, and lack of books, saying that he was almost as meet to dispute as to be a captain of Calais; but he would declare his mind either by writing or word, and would stand to all they could lay upon his back: complaining moreover that he was permitted to have neither pen, nor ink, nor yet any book but only the New Testament there in his hand, which he said he had read over seven times deliberately, and yet could not find the Mass in it, neither the marrow bones nor sinews of the same."[2] Weston said that he would compel him to retract those words, but he replied: "That you will never do, Master Doctor."[3] He was at once put to silence and sent back to the bailiff.

On the Wednesday morning at eight o'clock, Latimer reappeared to make reply to the Articles. "I pray you, good Master Prolocutor," he began, "do not exact that of me which is not in me. I have not these twenty years much used the Latin tongue."[4] Weston agreed; and he then asked leave to confess his faith as one who could no longer dispute. He had with great labour written out his answers in the hope that he would be spared from the trial and fatigue of an oral Disputation, and this written statement was now placed in the hands of the Prolocutor.

[1] *John Foxe*, Vol. VI, p. 443.
[3] Ibid., p. 443.
[2] Ibid., p. 443.
[4] Ibid. p. 501.

"Thus lo," so it ran, "I have written an answer to your conclusions, even as I will answer before the Majesty of our Lord
and Saviour Jesus Christ; by Whose only sacrifice I hope to
possess heaven. Therefore I beseech your good Masterships to
take it in good part, as I have done it with great pains, having no
man to help me, as I never was before denied to have. O Sir, you
may chance to come to this age and weakness that I am of; and
then you would be loth to be used as I am at your hands; that no
man may come to me to help me for any need; no, not so much
as to mend my hose or my coat. . . . I have spoken in my time
before two kings, more than one, two, or three hours together
without interruption; but now, when I should have spoken the
truth out of God's Book, for that I ever took for my warrant,
I could not be suffered to declare my faith before you, (for the
which, God willing, I intend to give my life), not by the space of
a quarter of an hour, without snatches, rages, revilings, checks,
rebukes, and taunts, such as I never heard the like, in such an
audience, all my life long. Sure it can not be but I have made some
heinous offence. Forsooth I think it be this; I have spoken against
the Mass, and did ask if their god of the altar had any marrow
bones."[1] In the Harleian Manuscripts there is a most important
addition to this statement. "Forsooth I had spoken of the four
marrow bones of the Mass. I could not be allowed to tell what I
meant by the metaphor: but now Sir, by your favour, I will tell
your Mastership what I meant. The first is the popish consecration, which hath been called God's body-making. The second
is transubstantiation. The third is the missal oblation. The fourth
the adoration."[2] Latimer was not unmindful of the issue of his
trial in 1532, and he did not intend to risk conscience again for
the sake of safety. The end of his statement ran as follows:
"Thus have I answered your conclusions, as I will stand unto,
with God's help, to the fire. And after this I am able to declare to
the Majesty of God by His invaluable Word that I die for the
truth: for I assure you, if I could grant to the Queen's proceedings
and endure by the Word of God, I would rather live than die;
but seeing they be directly against God's Word, I will obey God
more than man, and so embrace the stake."[3]

But this statement was not even perused by the Commissioners,

[1] *Remains*, pp. 256: 258.   [2] Ibid., p. 481.   [3] Ibid., p. 262.

and the Disputation went on until almost eleven o'clock. It all began when the Prolocutor brushed aside his written statement and pounced on his remark of the Saturday with regard to the marrow bones of the Mass. "We will find a Mass in that Book," declared Weston. "No good Master Doctor, ye can not." "What find you then there?" "Forsooth," said Latimer, "a communion I find there."[1] And so whether he would or not, he found himself caught in the toils of a Disputation. He was very faint and afraid even to drink lest he should begin to vomit. He was assailed with taunts and jibes, and his defence was much interrupted with hissing and laughter. But he made a further effort to shake off the burden. "I trust I have obtained of Master Prolocutor," he said, "that no man shall exact that thing of me which is not in me. . . . Disputation requireth a good memory. My memory is gone clean, and marvellously weakened, and never the better, I wis, for the prison."[2] He was driven by the failure of his memory to pass by the Fathers and to prove his statements by a simple appeal to the Scriptures. Weston asked him how long he had held his present doctrine, for all men knew that the time was when he would have said his Mass "full devoutly". "I have long sought for the truth in this matter of the Sacrament," Latimer replied, "and have not been of this mind past seven years: and my Lord of Canterbury's book hath especially confirmed my judgment herein."[3] Tresham declared that he had once heard him preaching before King and Court at Greenwich, when he had affirmed that no Christian man ought to doubt of the true and real presence of Christ's body in the Sacrament: why then did he deny at this present that which he had once held that it was not lawful to doubt?[4] Latimer insisted again that he could not speak in Latin "so long and so largely" as in English,[5] and his reply was based on the treatment of the Fathers which he had been taught by Cranmer. "The Romish Church begat the error of transubstantiation," he said: "my Lord of Canterbury's book handleth that very well."[6] Latimer reverted so often to Cranmer that Weston was irritated: "Your learning is let out to farm, and shut up in my Lord of Canterbury's book."[7] But he was not deterred and, when challenged as to the faith of the Fathers,

---

[1] *John Foxe*, Vol. VI, p. 503.   [2] Ibid. p. 505.   [3] Ibid., p. 505.
[4] Ibid., p. 506.   [5] Ibid., p. 507.   [6] Ibid., p. 508.   [7] Ibid., p. 509.

replied once more: "I am of their faith when they say well; I refer myself to my Lord of Canterbury's book wholly herein."[1] Weston summed up at last with an appeal to fear: "Your stubbornness . . . will do you no good when a fagot is in your beard. And we see all how little cause you have to be stubborn, for your learning is in feoffer's hold. The Queen's Grace is merciful, if ye will turn." But he knew what anguish of mind men like Bilney, and Bainham, and Barnes, had once endured, and he would now rather have that fagot in his beard than fail in this time of trial. "You shall have no hope in me to turn," he said; "I pray for the Queen daily . . . that she may turn." Weston at once closed the Disputation with the verdict: "He denieth all Truth, and all the old Fathers."[2]

On the Friday, the three men were brought back to St. Mary's to hear words of formal condemnation pronounced by the Prolocutor: they were declared to be no members of the Church and were condemned as heretics. Latimer's comment was brief: "I thank God most heartily that He hath prolonged my life to this end that I may in this case glorify God by that kind of death."[3] The whole Disputation came to an end the next morning with a Mass and general procession. Latimer was brought out to look on, and "thought that he should have gone to burning"[4]; but when he reached Carfax and saw what it all was, he turned aside and refused to look. There are but few details of his imprisonment with the city bailiff in the eighteen months which were now to drag slowly away; but of all the martyrs in the years now at hand, he was said to have had "the plainest and simplest heart".[5] John Foxe helps to enlarge our thoughts with a noble picture: "Albeit Master Latimer by reason of the feebleness of his age wrote least of them all in this latter time of his imprisonment, yet in prayer he was fervently occupied, wherein oftentimes so long he continued kneeling that he was not able to rise without help; and amongst other things, these were three principal matters he prayed for. First, that as God had appointed him to be a preacher of His Word, so also He would give him grace to stand to his doctrine until his death. . . . Secondly that God of His mercy would restore His Gospel to England once again; and these

---

[1] *John Foxe*, Vol. VI, p. 510.   [2] Ibid., pp. 510, 511.
[3] Ibid., p. 534.   [4] Ibid., p. 534.   [5] Ryle, p. 164.

words, 'once again, once again,' he did so inculcate and beat into the ears of the Lord God, as though he had seen God before him and spoken to Him face to face. The third matter was to pray for the preservation of the Queen's Majesty that now is (Elizabeth), whom in his prayer he was wont accustomably to name, and even with tears desired God to make her a comfort to His comfortless realm of England."[1] We can also quote one lovely fragment from his letter to All Unfeigned Lovers of God's Truth, written from the Bocardo on May 10th, 1555. "Die once we must," he wrote; "how and where we know not. Happy are they whom God giveth to pay nature's debt (I mean, to die,) for His sake. Here is not our home: let us therefore accordingly consider things, having always before our eyes that heavenly Jerusalem and the way thereto in persecution. And let us consider all the dear friends of God, how they have gone after the example of our Saviour Jesus Christ; Whose footsteps let us also follow, even to the gallows if God's will be so, not doubting but as He rose again the third day, even so shall we do at the time appointed of God, that is, when the trump shall blow, and the angel shall shout, and the Son of Man shall appear."[2]

A letter from Ridley to John Bradford notes that Latimer's health was utterly shattered during this long imprisonment.[3] "Old Father Latimer," so he described him to Mrs. Glover, "whom I do think the Lord hath placed to be His standard-bearer in our age and country against His mortal foe anti-Christ."[4] At length, late in September 1555, Cardinal Pole sent three Episcopal Commissioners down to Oxford with full authority to try and then pronounce judgment upon Ridley and Latimer. On September 30th, their work began at eight o'clock in the Divinity School when Ridley was placed on trial. The bailiffs brought Latimer to the Divinity School long before he was required to appear, and he was forced to wait outside until Ridley's trial was over. Thus his first words were to protest at his treatment. "My Lords," he said, "if I appear again, I pray you not to send for me until you be ready: for I am an old man, and it is great hurt to mine old age to tarry so long gazing upon the cold walls."[5] The Bishop of Lincoln promised more care in the

[1] *John Foxe*, Vol. VII, p. 465. [2] *Remains*, p. 444.
[3] Ridley, *Works*, p. 366. [4] Ibid., p. 384. [5] *John Foxe*, Vol. VII, p. 529.

future. "Then Master Latimer bowed his knee down to the ground, holding his hat in his hand, having a kerchief on his head, and upon it a nightcap or two, and a great cap such as townsmen use, with two broad flaps to button under the chin, wearing an old thread-bare Bristol frieze gown girded to his body with a penny leather girdle, at the which hanged by a long string of leather his Testament, and his spectacles without case depending about his neck upon his breast."[1] The Bishop of Lincoln then urged him to return to the fold of the Church from which like a strayed sheep he had gone out. "Therefore Master Latimer, for God's love consider your estate; remember you are a learned man; you have taken degrees in the school, borne the office of a bishop; remember you are an old man; spare your body, accelerate not your death; and especially remember your soul's health."[2] Latimer listened, his head on his elbow, and then obtained consent to be seated for the ensuing dialogue. "Lo," he said, "you look for learning at my hands, which have gone so long to the school of Oblivion, making the bare walls my library; keeping me so long in prison, without book, or pen and ink."[3] After this informal discussion was over, he agreed to answer the Articles of Inquiry on the understanding that he did so as a subject of the Queen and not in acknowledgment of the authority of Rome. He then denied that the Body and Blood of Christ were in the Sacrament in the sense which the Article demanded. "The bread is still bread, and the wine still wine," he said; "for the change is not in the nature, but in the dignity."[4] "Christ," he went on to say, "made one perfect sacrifice for all the whole world; neither can any man offer Him again . . . neither is there any propitiation for our sins saving His Cross only."[5]

The Bishop of Lincoln then told him that he would have the night in which to reflect on his answers, and that he could alter them if he wished on the morrow. Latimer entreated the three Commissioners to deal with him at once, and not to put him to further trouble in the morning. "Truly, my Lord," he said, "as for my part, I require no respite, for I am at a point. You shall give me respite in vain: therefore I pray you, let me not trouble you to-morrow."[6] But there was no escape. At one o'clock, the

[1] *John Foxe*, Vol. VII, p. 529. [2] Ibid., p. 530. [3] Ibid., p. 532.
[4] Ibid., p. 533. [5] Ibid., p. 533. [6] Ibid., p. 534.

130

court broke up, and he returned with the bailiff. There was a vast concourse at eight o'clock the next morning, for "the whole body, as well of the University as of the town, came thither to see the end of these two persons".[1] Ridley appeared first, and heard the verdict which could only spell his execution. The cloth which lay on the table and the carpet on which Ridley had stood were then removed, for it was said that "Master Latimer had never the degree of a Doctor as Master Ridley had".[2] The Bishop of Lincoln began with an address to Latimer in which he urged him once more to recant. But Latimer interrupted him to deny that the Church of Rome was identical with the Catholic Church. A brief exchange of views followed, and then the Articles of Inquiry were read over to him again. But he had not changed his mind, and he now answered as firmly as before. "Christ made one oblation and sacrifice for the sins of the whole world," he said, "and that a perfect sacrifice; neither needeth there to be any other, neither can there be any other propitiatory sacrifice."[3] The Bishop of Lincoln then read out his formal condemnation, and went on to assert that he could now neither hear him nor talk with him. He was handed over to the Mayor of Oxford with the ominous assertion: "Now he is your prisoner, Master Mayor."[4] There was still a fortnight before the end, but a pall of silence lies on those last two weeks. The one interruption would be on the eve of his death when like Ridley he would be stripped from his robes of office with the traditional forms of degradation. There had always been an honest warmth and plainness about the man which would make him care the less for such things. His practical mind, his eloquent speech, his diligent life, his generous hand, had had but a single keynote, and that was his simplicity. And it was in simplicity that old Father Latimer with that Testament which hung from his girdle in his hands would prepare himself to die.

On the morning of October 16th, 1555, a strong stake was driven into the ground close to Balliol, and Lord Williams of Thame was by the Queen's command early at the site to preserve order. "And when everything was in a readiness, the prisoners were brought forth by the Mayor and the bailiffs."[5] Ridley was

---

[1] *John Foxe*, Vol. VII, p. 534.   [2] Ibid., p. 540.
[3] Ibid., p. 541.   [4] Ibid., p. 542.   [5] Ibid., p. 547.

the first to appear, between the Mayor and an alderman, having put on such clothes "as he was wont to wear, being bishop".[1] "After him came Master Latimer in a poor Bristol frieze frock, all worn, with his buttoned cap, and a kerchief on his head, all ready to the fire, a new long shroud hanging over his hose down to the feet."[2] Ridley soon caught sight of him and called out: "Oh, be ye there?" "Yea," said Master Latimer, "have after as fast as I can follow."[3] Ridley arrived first at the stake, but with "a wonderous cheerful look" ran to meet Latimer with the embrace and kiss of a fellow-martyr. They knelt down on either side of the stake and poured out their hearts in a short season of prayer. Then they stood and talked for a while, but what they said Foxe could learn of no man. Then followed the sermon, only fifteen minutes in length, while they lifted up both hands and eyes to heaven, as if calling God to witness when they thought that he spoke amiss. They were not allowed to speak in reply, but were ordered to make themselves ready. "Master Latimer . . . quietly suffered his keeper to pull off his hose and his other array which to look upon was very simple; and being stripped into his shroud, he seemed as comely a person . . . as one should lightly see."[4] Then the smith took a chain of iron, and girt it round their waists so that they stood back to back at the stake. A bag of gunpowder was hung about their necks, and the fire was kindled from a faggot at Ridley's feet. Then Latimer gave utterance to the noblest sermon he had ever composed: "Be of good comfort Master Ridley, and play the man. We shall this day light such a candle by God's grace in England as I trust shall never be put out!"[5] The fire leapt up towards him and he cried aloud: "O Father of Heaven, receive my soul!"[6] He stroked his face with his hands and then bathed them in the fire; then with little or no pain, as it seemed, very soon after the fire had been kindled, he succumbed. Latimer, the outspoken and eloquent, "the Apostle of England",[7] frail with age and weakness, had, in dying, lit the candle whose flame was to make his death his glory. That light is now in our keeping: God grant that we may never allow its flame to go out!

[1] *John Foxe*, Vol. VII, p. 547.　　[2] Ibid., pp. 547, 548.　　[3] Ibid., p. 548.
[4] Ibid., p. 549.　　[5] Ibid., p. 550.　　[6] Ibid., p. 550.　　[7] Ridley, *Works*, p. 99.

BIBLIOGRAPHY

STEPHEN CATTLEY, *The Acts and Monuments of John Foxe* (8 Vols.), 1841

HUGH LATIMER, *Sermons* (Parker Society Edition), 1844

HUGH LATIMER, *Sermons and Remains* (Parker Society Edition), 1845

THOMAS BECON, *The Jewel of Joy* (*The Catechism with other Pieces*) (Parker Society Edition), 1844

HASTINGS ROBINSON, *Original Letters Relative to the English Reformation* (Parker Society Edition), 2 Vols., 1846

ROBERT DEMAUS, *Hugh Latimer: A Biography*, 1881

JOHN CHARLES RYLE, *Hugh Latimer: Bishop and Martyr* (Chapter VII in *Light From Old Times*), 1898

HAROLD S. DARBY, *Hugh Latimer* (Epworth Press), 1953

NICHOLAS RIDLEY

*Master of Pembroke Hall,
Cambridge*

c. 1500–1555

"Few Englishmen, if any, have ever surpassed Ridley in quiet courage and large-hearted wisdom. Few Divines have ever more perfectly combined reverence with candour, and learning and reason with the life of the Spirit. Few Churchmen have ever more unreservedly loved and served the Church of England. And few Christians have ever more uniformly shone for their Lord, alike in high places, and in prison and death. SIT ANIMA MEA CUM RIDLEIO, by the grace of Ridley's heavenly Master!"

H. C. G. MOULE, *Annual Letter*, November 1st, 1895. (See BULLOCK, *The History of Ridley Hall*, pp. 281, 282.)

Nicholas Ridley was born about
the year 1500 in a Northumbrian home at Willimoteswick, not
far from the Scottish border. This mote was a fortified residence
which stood on rising ground near the junction of the Allon with
the South Tyne. Its old-fashioned turrets were unique in England;
they had been built partly as watch-towers, and partly for beacon
fires in the days when raids were common events. The Ridleys
or Riddles were an ancient house of knights who figured largely
in the border forays of the Middle Ages. They were men of
courage and daring, who shared to the full the life of excitement
and adventure to which they were born in Northumberland. A
rough and racy ballad called "The Death of Featherstonhaugh"
was penned by Sir Walter himself, and the heroes of whose
exploits it tells were all members of the Clan of Ridley. Thus
their family names and ancestral seats are mentioned in lines
which would be sung in the cottage homes of Northumberland
by peasant and plowman until the rafters rang again:

> "Hoot awa', lads, hoot awa',
> Ha' ye heard how the Ridleys, and Thirlwalls, and a',
> Ha' set upon Albany Featherstonhaugh,
> And taken his life at the Deadmanshaugh?
> There was Willimoteswick,
> And Hardriding Dick,
> And Hughie of Hawdon, and Will of the Wa'."[1]

This was, in a slightly altered form, "the rhyme of deadly feud"
to which Lord Marmion had to listen as the guest of Sir Hugh
the Heron, and the Border life of Ridley's boyhood has been
immortalised in *The Lay of The Last Minstrel*.

Ridley was heir to the virtues of this vigorous ancestry, and
his own life was to add new lustre to the name and stock which
were his by birth. Foxe tells us that he was sent to school at

[1] Sir Walter Scott, *The Minstrelsy of The Scottish Border* (One Vol. Edition of
   Poems, 1838).

Newcastle in spite of border clashes, for the Ridleys were no rude and untutored family who knew nothing of letters and learning. Both in 1510 and 1532, the Rector of Simonburn in the North Tyne Valley was a Ridley, so that there was reason why he should take to his grammar "with great dexterity".[1] But while he was only a lad of ten or twelve years old, the Blue Bonnets from the Lowlands fought and lost the day on Flodden Field some forty miles north of his home at Willimoteswick. In 1554, when he was a prisoner in the Tower of London, he recalled how his boyhood had been filled with the sound of such Border warfare. "In Tynedale where I was born," he wrote, "not far from the Scottish borders, I have known my countrymen watch night and day in their harness, such as they had, that is, in their jacks, and their spears in their hands (you call them northern gads), especially when they had any privy warning of the coming of the Scots. And so doing, although at every such bickering some of them spent their lives, yet by such means, like pretty men, they defended their country. And those that so died, I think that before God they died in a good quarrel, and their offspring and progeny all the country loved them the better for their fathers' sakes."[2] In his Farewell Letter from Oxford in 1555, another memory from those years filled his mind: "Ye know, that be my countrymen dwelling upon the borders, where alas! the true man suffereth oftentimes much wrong at the thief's hand, if it chance a man to be slain of a thief (as it oft chanceth there) which went out with his neighbour to help him, . . . that the more cruelly he be slain and the more stedfastly he stuck by his neighbour, . . . the more favour and friendship shall all his posterity have for the slain man's sake of all them that be true, as long as the memory of his deed, and his posterity doth endure."[3]

One of Ridley's uncles was Robert Ridley, then a Fellow of Queens' College, Cambridge, and a Doctor of Divinity of Paris. He had won a Continental reputation through the writings of Polydore Vergil, and he now took a strong personal interest in his nephew. It was at his expense that, in 1518, the lad from the Tyneside came to Pembroke Hall in Cambridge. There had been a wave of activity for some years in Cambridge, largely as a result of the powerful impetus which had come from Erasmus

[1] *John Foxe*, Vol. VII, p. 407.   [2] Ridley, p. 145.   [3] Ibid., p. 398.

and his residence at Queens' from 1511 to 1514. The New Learning brought in its train a thirst for the teaching of the Reformation based on the text of the Greek New Testament, and, as early as in 1521, the White Horse Inn was used as a regular rendezvous by men who were watching Luther with friendly eyes. Men like Barnes and Bilney were among the first to move into the light; men like Frith and Tyndale could not remain impervious to the sunrise. Pembroke itself was to furnish no less than three martyrs for the Reformation: Rogers, Ridley, and John Bradford. Rogers and Ridley were fellow-students in the Fifteen Twenties, and they were to become famous in the battle for Truth. But they only emerged by slow degrees into that bright new day, and their early reading had no affinities with the cause of Luther. Robert Ridley had been chosen as one of the Commissioners whose task was to inspect Luther's writings, and, in 1520, he joined in their condemnation as works of heresy. We may feel sure that he would not let the nephew for whose education he was responsible play with such fire, and there is no sign that his young kinsman even knew of Bilney's friends at the White Horse Inn during his first years at Pembroke. He was content to spend time and talent on the mediaeval studies which were necessary for his degree, and he began to build up a highly honourable reputation as a scholar of undoubted diligence and ability.

His first degree came in 1522 when he graduated as a Bachelor of Arts, and his name stood fourth on the list of forty-one Wranglers. This led to the offer of a Fellowship at University College in Oxford, but he preferred to remain in Cambridge. Then in 1524, he became a Fellow of Pembroke Hall, and was chosen as Magister Glomeriae for Cambridge. This meant that he was head of the "schools of grammar", and that his main duties were to instruct new students in Latin. Then in 1525, he obtained his Master's degree, and, in 1526, he became the College agent for the livings of Tylney, Soham, and Saxthorpe. Meanwhile, the rapid spread of the Reformed doctrines was causing some alarm in high circles, and when Sir Thomas More became High Steward of Cambridge in 1525, strong measures were taken to check such vagaries. But in 1527, Robert Ridley sent his nephew abroad to read divinity both at Paris and at Louvain, and he applied himself for some three years to the mediaeval style of disputation which still prevailed at the Sorbonne. This was perhaps the most famous school of theology in all Europe, but it was past its prime and he was not greatly impressed. Thus in 1554, when the storm burst round his head at Oxford, it made him think of the "Sorbonical clamours" in Paris.[1] Moule points out that he spoke of the Sorbonne and its tumults as if the dead hand of Rome were the cause of the uproar, and he regards this as a hint that those angry altercations were not merely academic in character or interest. They were just the kind of stormy meetings which sprang direct from the Reformation controversy, and he may have even seen one of the Reformation leaders on trial. It was April 1529, when the gifted de Berquin, friend of Erasmus and Margaret of Navarre, was burnt to death by the Doctors of the Sorbonne in the Place de Grève in Paris.[2] Ridley never referred to this, and there is no further mention of the Sorbonne in his papers. But we may ask ourselves whether he did not owe something to that dying witness as did Saul to Stephen.

Late in 1529 or in 1530, Ridley returned to England and resumed his studies in Cambridge. In 1530, he was Junior Treasurer of Pembroke Hall, and, in 1533, Senior Proctor in the University. In 1534, he took his degree as a Bachelor of Divinity, and was appointed as Public Orator and Chaplain to the University. It was during these years that he built up his great reputation as a student of the Classics of Greece and Rome, while at the same time he was known as a master of the forms of logic cherished by the Schoolmen. William Turner was one of his pupils who could recall his fame as a teacher in the 'Thirties.[3] Cambridge men in those years spoke with one voice in praise of his wide and thorough reading, as well as of his strength and skill in the field of recognised argument. He was himself to pay a fine tribute to his Alma Mater in the Farewell which he composed within a few days of his death; for it was in Cambridge that he had found more true friendship and more of lasting virtue than he ever met with even in the Border country where he was born. "Farewell therefore Cambridge, my loving mother and tender nurse!" he wrote. "If I should not acknowledge thy manifold

[1] Ridley, p. 303.   [2] Moule, pp. 5, 6.   [3] Ridley, pp. 492, 493.

benefits, yea, if I should not for thy benefits at the least love thee again, truly I were to be accounted ungrate and unkind. What benefits hadst thou ever, that thou usest to give and bestow upon thy best beloved children, that thou thoughtest too good for me? Thou didst bestow on me all thy school degrees: of thy common offices, the Chaplainship of the University, the office of the proctorship, and of a common reader; and of thy private commodities, and emoluments in Colleges, what was it that thou madest me not partner of? First to be Scholar, then Fellow, and after my departure from thee thou calledst me again to a Mastership of a right worshipful College. I thank thee, my loving mother, for all this thy kindness; and I pray God that His laws, and the sincere Gospel of Christ, may ever be truly taught and faithfully learned in thee."[1]

The real origins of his decided Protestant convictions are now veiled in obscurity, but like Cranmer, he seems to have felt his way by degrees towards the truth. They were stirring years in Cambridge and in England, but we only know in part what he thought about public affairs. What did he think on the one hand of the death of Bilney and Bayfield in 1531, or on the other hand of the death of More and Fisher in 1535? What did he think of the Coronation of Anne Boleyn in 1533, or the Visitation of the Monasteries in 1536? We know that he had to sign the decree against Papal Supremacy as a Proctor of Cambridge in 1534, and that he was nominated as a Chaplain to Cranmer in 1537. He must have been aware of the struggle for an English version of the Scriptures in the early 'Thirties, and he must have been in accord with the issue of Cranmer's Bible in 1539. It would seem that he had already determined to apply his knowledge to the study of the Greek text in the quiet of his own College environment. The Walk may still be seen where he paced up and down in the Pembroke garden, patiently committing whole chapters of Scripture to the strong grasp of a tenacious memory. He still had those days in mind when he wrote his great Farewell: "Farewell Pembroke Hall, of late mine own College, my cure and my charge! What case thou art in now, God knoweth, I know not well. Thou wast ever named sithens I knew thee, which is now a thirty years ago, to be studious, well learned, and a great setter

[1] Ridley, p. 406.

forth of Christ's Gospel and of God's true word: so I found thee, and blessed be God, so I left thee indeed! . . . In thy orchard (the walls, butts, and trees, if they could speak, would bear me witness), I learned without book almost all Paul's Epistles, yea, and I ween all the Canonical Epistles save only the Apocalypse. Of which study, although in time a great part did depart from me, yet the sweet smell thereof, I trust, I shall carry with me into heaven: for the profit thereof I think I have felt in all my life-time ever after."[1]

Ridley must have become known to Cranmer as a friend to Reform, and, in 1538, he was instituted to the living of Herne in Kent. The times were not easy for the Reform party, for the King's last years were marked by growing persecution. The Six Articles in 1539 and the fall of Cromwell in 1540 showed that the tides were out. Cranmer fell under a shadow, with foes at Court, among the Squires of Kent, within the precincts of his own Cathedral, even within the walls of his own house. But the Vicar of Herne was still in the King's eye, and honours still accrued to him. Thus in 1540, he was named as one of the King's Chaplains, and new laurels were heaped upon him at Cambridge; he was awarded a Doctorate in Divinity and was appointed to the Mastership of Pembroke Hall. Thus his Cambridge career had not come to an end, even though he chose to reside mainly at Herne; it was interrupted, but not terminated, when he went to live and work near Cranmer. His long apprenticeship as a scholar was to govern his work as a Churchman, and his ties with the King could not prevent him from taking his stand more and more on the side of the Reformation. In 1541, he was made a Prebend of Canterbury; in 1545, he was made a Prebend of Westminster. There is still ample proof of his ability as a preacher, and we know well that he never lacked for courage. He was not too timid to preach against auricular confession or to have the Te Deum regularly sung in English at Herne.[2] "Thou hast heard of my mouth oftentimes the Word of God," he wrote of Herne, "preached not after the popish trade, but after the Christ's Gospel."[3] He longed to feel that the fruit had been as the seed, and he rejoiced in one noble convert in the person of the Lady Fiennes. But Herne was for ever memorable to him as the centre

[1] Ridley, pp. 406, 407.   [2] Strype, *Cranmer*, Vol. I, p. 240.   [3] Ridley, p. 407.

of his spiritual enlightenment on the true doctrine of the Lord's Supper. "And yet," he wrote, "I must acknowledge me to be thy debtor for the doctrine of the Lord's Supper; which at that time, I acknowledge, God had not revealed unto me."[1]

It was in this quiet and pleasant country parish that he read the famous Treatise of Bertram, or *Ratramn, De Corpore et Sanguini Domini*. Ratramn had been a monk in the House of Corbie; then he became abbot in the House of Orbais in the ninth century. He stood in high regard as a theologian, and his advice was sought by Charles the Bald in more than one controversy. His last book was written at the request of the Pope in reply to the attacks of the Greek Church, about the year 869. This proves that no taint of heresy could have adhered to him in his own age. About 831, Paschasius Radbertus, who was also in the House of Corbie, wrote a Treatise which taught that the change wrought in the Elements of the Eucharist by the words of Consecration ought to be understood in the most literal sense that faith can conceive. This book was placed in the hands of Charles, who found its teaching so strange that it seemed to require absolute submission or else absolute rejection. He turned to John Scotus Erigena and to Ratramn for help, and this Treatise was the outcome. It was composed as a direct refutation of the thesis put forward by Paschasius, and its great aim was to prove that the Lord's words of Consecration are to be understood as a "figura", not as "veritas". This book almost vanished from sight in the Middle Ages, although Ridley knew that it had received mention by Trithemius in 1494. It was Oecolampadius who secured a reprint of the book in 1531, and the Reformation Divines at once hailed the name of Ratramn as that of an ancient doctor who had taught that the Bread and Wine are the Body and Blood of Christ, "sed in figura, non in veritate". Moule says that Ratramn was the first theologian to treat the doctrine from this standpoint.[2] Ratramn's address to Charles the Bald makes that standpoint quite clear: "Your Majesty's wisdom may thus see from Scripture and the Fathers that the Bread called the Body of Christ is a figure, because it is a mystery. The Body Proper is no figure; it is the manifestation of the Thing itself. For the vision of It, believers long; then shall we be satisfied."[3]

[1] Ridley, p. 407.   [2] Moule, p. 208, n.   [3] Ibid., p. 247.

We do not know just how Bertram's Treatise came into Ridley's hands, but it was to prove a landmark in his career. The grave controversy over the Lord's Supper in which Luther had so strongly opposed the Swiss had come to a head in 1545 when the men of Zurich brought out an Apologia in their own defence. This was read with avidity by men of all parties, and it was bound to win the notice of a man like Ridley. He made up his mind to spend the summer at Herne in a patient study of the points at issue, and he found that the book to which men were turning was *Ratramnus De Corpore et Sanguini Domini*. Ridley was too candid not to peruse such a book for himself, and the result was momentous. He thought that the Bread and Wine of the Sacrament were in literal fact the Body and Blood of Christ, and that this had been the unanimous teaching of the Apostolic Fathers. But here was an honoured theologian to whom both King and Pope had turned as an authority, and he had shown that the work of Paschasius was full of quite unscriptural innovation. Ratramn may have held that the Bread and Wine were the Body and Blood of Christ; but this was in figure, and not in fact. And this was in complete contrast with the mediaeval development which had produced the Doctrine of Transubstantiation. This drove Ridley to the Scriptures and the Fathers with the deliberate resolution to find out what was taught about the Mass in the early Christian centuries. It would appear that he copied out long extracts as he read and studied the works of the Fathers, just as Cranmer did when he was engaged in his work on the Lord's Supper. Thus in 1553 while in the Tower, he wrote: "My memory was never good; for help whereof I have used for the most part to gather out notes of my reading, and so to place them that thereby I might have had the use of them when the time required."[1] But those summer studies left him convinced that the Roman doctrine of the Mass was neither Scriptural nor primitive, but was blasphemous and dangerous.

Ridley had now embraced the truth with a firmness from which he was never to swerve. He had been brought up in mediaeval doctrine and had read more widely than most men in England. But he had now hammered out his own clear convictions and was armed for discussion by a special study of the

[1] *John Foxe*, Vol. VII, p. 414.

Fathers. He saw that the Bread and Wine in the New Testament Sacrament are not identical with the Body and Blood of the Passion, but are emblems which so disclose them to the eye of faith that they may with safety borrow their sacred names. "Of Christ's true Body we say, He is true God, Son of the Father before the worlds; true Man, Son of His mother in the end of the world. But this can not be said of the Body which in mystery we celebrate!"[1] Ridley could not confine the truth to his own mind or his private teaching; he went with it straight to Cranmer, who had so far clung to the old doctrine with an almost jealous sense of alarm at the prospect of change. But in the year 1546, he was moved to review the whole problem, and, to his own surprise, was won over by the weight of Ridley's thought and learning.[2] Nor did this great discovery of truth end at this point, for in 1547, Cranmer in his turn drew Latimer into entire harmony with his brethren.[3] When, in 1551, Cranmer gave the world his masterly discussion of the subject, it was so much in the strain of Ridley's thought that Ridley himself was at least once alleged to have been the author of the volume.[4] These facts explain the taunt which Brooks flung at Ridley in the final Trial at Oxford: "What a weak and feeble stay in religion is this, I pray you? Latimer leaneth to Cranmer, Cranmer to Ridley, and Ridley to the singularity of his own wit; so that if you overthrew the singularity of Ridley's wit, then must needs the religion of Cranmer and Latimer fall also."[5] Truth lay behind the taunt; Ridley was indeed the leader of the English Divines in their movement away from the mediaeval teaching. He had thought out his own faith with calm and sober consistency, and with courage, so as to stand true by the grace of God in the supreme ordeal by fire.

Perhaps there are few books which have endured such long years of obscurity and have risen at last from the grave of neglect with such power and vitality. Ridley referred to it many times in terms of personal gratitude as an authority which should command recognition from all. In December 1548, he mentioned it in the Debate which took place in the House of Lords.[6] In June 1549, he quoted it in the Determination which he delivered at

[1] Moule, p. 243.   [2] Strype, Vol. I, p. 151.   [3] *John Foxe*, Vol. VI, p. 505.
[4] Ibid., p. 436.   [5] Ibid., Vol. VII, p. 538.   [6] Moule, p. 197.

Cambridge.[1] In 1553, in the conversation at the Lieutenant's table in the Tower of London, there was much talk of this book, and Ridley recalled the reference in Trithemius.[2] In 1554, in the Disputation at Oxford, he named Ratramn in a paragraph of great importance because of its bearing on his experience. "I have also for the proof of that I have spoken," he said, "whatsoever Bertram, a man learned, of sound and upright judgment, and ever counted a Catholic for these seven hundred years until this our age, hath written. . . . This Bertram was the first that pulled me by the ear, and that first brought me from the common error of the Romish Church, and caused me to search more diligently and exactly both the Scriptures and the writings of the old Ecclesiastical Fathers in this matter. And this I protest before the Face of God, Who knoweth I lie not in the things I now speak."[3] On the morning before the day of his execution, he asked Brooks of Gloucester, who had come to degrade him from office, to give Bertram a fair hearing. "They would have been gone," so John Foxe tells us; "but Master Ridley said, My Lord, I would wish that your Lordship would vouchsafe to read over and peruse a little book of Bertram's doings, concerning the Sacrament. I promise you, you shall find much good learning therein, if you will read the same with an indifferent judgment."[4] Brooks was not in the mood to seek learning in Bertram, still less to take advice from Ridley; he ignored the appeal and refused to reply. But the Monk of Corbie had set up a signpost in his book whose finger pointed to Truth; and Ridley had followed the way, and found the truth, and held by his guide to the end.

In January 1547, Henry VIII died, and Edward VI came to the Throne. In May, Ridley was inducted to the benefice of Soham for which he had been the College agent in 1526, and he continued to hold it in plurality until 1552.[5] Then on September 5th, he was consecrated with the mediaeval rite of chrism as well as the imposition of hands as the Bishop of Rochester.[6] Ridley had now arrived at that moment when all his gifts would be required, for it was a crucial hour for England and the Reformation. His mind had cleared, and his views on the Lord's Supper were fixed. There was no space in the compass of his mental outlook

[1] *John Foxe*, Vol. p. VI, 334. [2] Ibid., p. 436. [3] Ibid., p. 477.
[4] Ibid., Vol. VII, p. 544. [5] Ridley, p. 536, n. [6] Strype, Vol. II, p. 88.

for the kind of vacillation which had so long troubled Cranmer, and he had now drawn the Primate into the wake of his own calm, firm, and measured progress. The weight of his learning, the force of his judgment, his resolute spirit, his moderate conduct, all served to mark him out as a leading figure. His studies at Cambridge and his preaching at Herne had been the true preparation for the mental address and the invincible courage with which he was to meet the great challenge in the reign of Edward and the supreme ordeal in the days of Mary. His promotion to Rochester placed him beside Cranmer at the helm of the Church, and he was soon wholly absorbed in the task of working out its reform in doctrine and worship. He was Cranmer's right hand as the statesman and pilot of the Reformation, as architect and pioneer for the Articles and the Liturgy. Perhaps there was no one who had so great a hold in all that was spiritual on the mind of Edward VI, "that godly-hearted and peerless young prince."[1] Undoubtedly, next to Cranmer, there was no one who did so much to make the Church pure and reformed for the comfort of the English people. Bishop Moule once declared that he had come from a critical scrutiny of the Works of Ridley with the feeling that he had been in true home-company. "I have learnt to feel with a deeper conviction than ever," he wrote, "that what we understand by Evangelical Church principles are, taken together, the principles of the Reformation as they were embodied in Ridley."[2]

It was Ridley's task in his new See to translate into terms of diocesan and parochial life the measures of reform which soon crowded upon the Church. He had at once enjoined the full distribution of bread and wine in the Eucharistic Service, while he forbade solitary Masses as quite foreign to the purpose of Christ. On the other hand, he preached a sermon at Paul's Cross, in London, so strong in its statement of the divine greatness of this Service that the day came when it was used against him on the ground that he had taught the full Roman dogma. He stood behind Cranmer in the propositions which led to the publication of an Order of Communion to take the place of the Mass at Easter 1548,[3] and he was a member of the Commission which was entrusted with the compilation of the first Book of Common

[1] Ridley, p. 58.   [2] Bullock, p. 282,   [3] Pollard, p. 206.

Prayer during that year. We do not know what part he had in the work, but we may surmise that he would give strong and vigorous oversight to the doctrine of the new Book. Certainly in the December of that same year, he took part in the great debate in the House of Lords on the real nature of the Eucharistic Presence.[1] For three days the Bishops of the old and new schools of thought argued this point with each other, in the presence of the Commons as well as of the Lords. Ridley was a leading speaker on the side of Reform, and it fell to him to close the Debate. Bartholomew Traheron declared that he "handled the subject with so much eloquence, perspicuity, erudition, and power," that "the truth never obtained a more brilliant victory among us".[2] But when the Prayer Book came out in 1549, Ridley was one who felt that its Eucharistic Doctrine was not clearly enough defined. Revision was in the air at once. Peter Martyr discussed the doctrine at Oxford and denied both Transubstantiation and Consubstantiation as well as the view that the bread and wine were but bare signs. In June, Ridley was in Cambridge for a scholastic discussion of the subject, and he wound up the three days' debate in a way that "made all things so clear" that his friends were full of praise.[3] His main judgment was that "Transubstantiation is clean against the words of the Scripture, and consent of the ancient Catholic Fathers".[4]

But he had been sent to Cambridge as a Commissioner to inquire into certain questions of academic legislation, and he arrived just in time to join in energetic opposition to a plan to merge Clare Hall with Trinity Hall. Clare was full of men from the North Country who were loath to submit, and they found a staunch ally in the Master of Pembroke. Ridley knew that its wealth would fall to the spoilers of the Church and the Schools, and that it would divert men who came up to Clare for the study of God's Word to a Hall founded for the study of Law. He said that "the church was already so robbed and stripped that it seemed there was a design laid down by some to drive out all civility, learning and religion, out of the nation".[5] He refused to concur, and composed a noble letter of protest to the Duke of Somerset.

---

[1] Moule, p. 14; cf. pp. 273:278.   [2] *Original Letters,* Vol. I, p. 323.
[3] Strype, *Eccles. Memorials,* Vol. II, p. 329.   [4] *John Foxe,* Vol. VI, p. 332.
[5] Burnet, Vol. II, pp. 191, 192.

In a letter found in the State Paper Office and first published by Robert Demaus, Ridley argued that the Duke ought to spare the Hall which had produced such a man as Latimer. "I consider," he wrote, "not only what learned men may be brought up there in time to come, but also how many hath been already, some such as I think it is hard for the whole University to match them with the like. I will speak now but of one, I mean Master Latimer, which is as I do think, a man appointed of God and endued with excellent gifts of grace to set forth God's Word, to whom in my judgment not only the King's Majesty and his honourable Council, but also the whole realm is much bound."[1] His fellow Visitors complained that they could not complete the King's business, and the Duke wrote him a sharp and chiding letter. But in spite of Somerset's arguments, his firm protest carried the day and saved Clare Hall.[2] But to Ridley, this was just a symptom of the iniquitous greed which marked so many who were in high places and which grew so much worse with the Duke of Northumberland. He looked on with sorrow of heart as he saw the fair name of the Reformation dragged in the mire by its nominal adherents.[3] It was still in his mind when he wrote his Lamentation in the reign of Mary: "Alas England, alas! that this heavy plague of God should fall upon thee! Alas, my dear beloved country, what thing is it now that may do thee good? Undoubtedly thy plague is so great that it is utterly uncurable, but by the bottomless mercy and infinite power of Almighty God."[4] But he was not the man to look on in helpless silence. "I have heard," he wrote in anonymous vein, "that Cranmer and another (that is, himself) were both in high displeasure . . . but specially Cranmer, for repugning as they might against the late spoil of the Church goods."[5]

In September 1549, Edmund Bonner, the Bishop of London, had to appear before Cranmer, Ridley, the Dean of St. Paul's, and the two Secretaries of State, since he refused either to use or to approve the new Prayer Book. "He spake slightingly to them of the whole matter, and turned the discourse off to the Mass, which he wished were had in more reverence."[6] Burnet says that he was

[1] Demaus, p. 376.
[2] Ridley, pp. 327: 330.
[3] Strype, Vol. III, pp. 408, 409.
[4] Ridley, p. 58.
[5] Ibid., p. 59.
[6] Burnet, Vol. II, p. 195.

coarse and brutal, loved by few in England, and that there was little regret either at home or abroad when he was deprived of his See by the King's Commissioners.[1] Ridley was marked out to succeed him as himself the most learned and most widely honoured of the Reformation leaders, and on April 12th, 1550, he was enthroned in St. Paul's with the Te Deum sung in English by a full choir to the strains of the great organ.[2] Ridley made his home in Fulham Palace, but he was careful to give Bonner's mother a warm and daily welcome at his own table. He was wonderfully considerate in his treatment of those who were opposed to him, seeking by gentleness to win them for the truth. Thus when Heath of Worcester was more or less confined in his house for eighteen months from July 1552, Ridley behaved to him with such unfailing courtesy that he lived there as if he were at home.[3] Ridley's love for his own kinsfolk was deep and true, but he would not grant them favours which they did not deserve. He preached regularly in all parts of his See, and the people swarmed to hear him, like bees to the honey-suckle. "Never good child," says Foxe, "was more singularly loved of his dear parents than he of his flock and diocese."[4] He took pains to gather round him the most able men he could find, for he knew that he had daily need of help and counsel from men of true learning. Thus he bestowed Prebends on Grindal, Bradford, and Rogers; he was later to say that they were "men known to be so necessary to be abroad in the Commonwealth" that he could scarce keep them in his own house.[5] Ridley's troubles with the spoilers of Church wealth were clearly illustrated when the Council tried to seize the income from the vacant prebend for which he had proposed Grindal. "Alas, Master Cheke," he wrote, "this seemeth unto me to be a right heavy hearing. Is this the fruit of the Gospel? Speak, Master Cheke, speak for God's sake, in God's cause, unto whomsoever you think may do any good withal. And if you will not speak, then I beseech you, let these my letters speak."[6]

Foxe has drawn a noble picture of his daily routine when at home in Fulham Palace. He gave himself much to prayer and

[1] Burnet, Vol. III, p. 286.
[2] Ibid., Vol. II, pp. 238, 239.
[3] Ibid., p. 497.
[4] *John Foxe*, Vol. VII, p. 407.
[5] Ridley, p. 336.
[6] Ibid., pp. 332, 333.

contemplation, for he was no sterile Churchman in that era of change. "Duly every morning, so soon as his apparel was done upon him, he went forthwith to his bedchamber, and there upon his knees prayed the space of half an hour; which being done, immediately he went to his study (if there came no other business to interrupt him) where he continued till ten of the clock, and then came to the common prayer, daily used in his house. The prayers being done, he went to dinner where he used little talk, except otherwise occasion by some had been ministered, and then was it sober, discreet and wise, and sometimes merry, as cause required."[1] But there was no monastic severity in his outlook on life. William Turner recalled how at Pembroke Hall he would join Ridley for exercise in archery, or for a game of fives.[2] After dinner in his London household, he would spend an hour in conversation or at a game of chess. Then he returned to his study, unless compelled to go abroad, until "five of the clock", when he emerged for prayers as was his wont in the morning. Supper followed, and an hour's chess, and then the rest of the evening was spent in his study. There he remained until eleven o'clock which was his hour for bed, "then saying his prayers upon his knees as in the morning when he rose".[3] William Turner's account makes it clear that Ridley's manner of life was not something which he had just assumed with his Bishop's attire. "Of his beneficence towards the poor, if there were no other witness, I desire to bear my public testimony that before he had arrived at any ecclesiastical dignity, he would take me with him to the nearest hospital, and when I had not where-withal to give to the poor, he in addition to what he largely for his means distributed, would often supply me with somewhat to bestow upon them."[4] Foxe sums up his fatherly character in memorable words: "To be short, as he was godly and virtuous himself, so nothing but virtue and godliness reigned in his house."[5]

In May 1547, Ridley had been named as one of the six preachers for the Visitation under Edward VI, and was sent to Carlisle "to preach to the people . . . and to learn them to worship God truly in heart and mind."[6] In May 1550, as Bishop of London, he was

---

[1] *John Foxe*, Vol. VII, p. 408.
[2] Ridley, p. 493.
[3] *John Foxe*, Vol. VII, p. 408.
[4] Ridley, p. 493.
[5] *John Foxe*, Vol. VII, p. 408.
[6] Strype, Vol. II, pp. 13, 14.

engaged in a stringent Visitation of his new See, and it is clear that this was to mark a fresh stage in the revolution that was going on in England. "The new Bishop of London is now employed in his Visitation," wrote Christopher Hales, "and threatens to eject those who shall not have come to their senses before his next Visitation; and if I know the man, he will be as good as his word."[1] The Articles of Visitation dealt with purity of life and conversation, the repair of house and chancel, and the regular maintenance of Church Services. They asked whether licensed preachers had been secured, whether the new Prayer Book was in use, and whether Masses were still being said in private homes. But the Injunctions which were issued with the Articles had been compiled with a view to sweeping changes which meant that no ceremonies could be used in the Lord's Supper apart from those laid down in the Prayer Book: "That no minister do counterfeit the popish mass in kissing the Lord's Board; washing his hands or fingers after the Gospel or the receipt of the Holy Communion; shifting the book from one place to another; laying down and licking the Chalice after the Communion; blessing his eyes with the sudarie thereof, or paten, or crossing his head with the same, holding his fore-fingers and thumbs joined together toward the temples of his head after the receiving of the Sacrament; breathing on the bread or chalice; saying the Agnus before the Communion; showing the Sacrament openly before the distribution, or making any elevation thereof; ringing of the sacrying bell or setting any light upon the Lord's Board."[2] Further, because some were using the Lord's Board after the form of a Table, and some as an altar, "we exhort the curates, church-wardens and questmen . . . to erect and set up the Lord's Board after the form of an honest table, decently covered, in such place of the quire or chancel as shall be thought most meet, . . . and to take down and abolish all other by-altars or tables".[3]

Thus began "the altar war", the substitution of Communion Tables for sacrificial altars. Ridley was the first to act in this great matter, and his prompt and energetic measures were to set the tone for future legislation. He had made up his mind to bring

---

[1] *Original Letters*, Vol. I, pp. 187, 188.
[7] Ridley, p. 319.   [3] Ibid., p. 320

in one standard and one practice in the way which he thought would best accord with the Gospel, and he broke down the High Altar in St. Paul's Cathedral as an example for the whole Diocese. He was compelled to defend this action, and his defence took the form of "certain reasons" of which the first read thus: "The form of a table shall more move the simple from the superstitious opinions of the popish mass unto the right use of the Lord's Supper. For the use of an altar is to make sacrifice upon it; the use of a table is to serve for man to eat upon. Now, when we come unto the Lord's Board, what do we come for? To sacrifice Christ again, and to crucify Him again, or to feed upon Him that was once only crucified and offered up for us? If we come to feed upon Him, spiritually to eat His body and spiritually to drink His blood, (which is the true use of the Lord's Supper), then no man can deny but the form of a table is more meet for the Lord's Board than the form of an altar."[1] Ridley knew that he had the King's warm but private support, and his action was backed up by letters from the Council which the Sheriff of Essex was sent down to enforce in July.[2] At length, an Order in Council was drawn up in November, and all Bishops were required in the King's name to have altars replaced with tables. The word "altar" itself was left out of the next issue of the Prayer Book, and has never since been restored. The whole struggle proves how fully aware he was of the fundamental "contrast between an altar-sacrifice offered God-ward, and a Sacrament delivered from God man-ward".[3] It was not the former, which is represented by an altar, but the latter, which is represented by a table, which he found in the Scriptural account of the Lord's Supper. That was his great reason why the altar had to make way for the Lord's Board, for the Table where the Feast of Love is spread.

In 1550, Cranmer and his colleagues brought out the first English Ordinal, and it was used for the first time on June 24th when Ridley ordained John Foxe to the Diaconate in St. Paul's Cathedral. But John Hooper declined to be consecrated as Bishop of Gloucester because of the Oath of Office and the Vestments which this new Ordinal required. Both Cranmer and Ridley felt

[1] Ridley, p. 322.   [2] Burnet, Vol. II, pp. 251, 252.
[3] Moule, p. 293.

153

that they must insist on the lawful order of the Church as against private scruples in the case of rites and ceremonies which were free from unwholesome traditions.[1] Ridley and Hooper had several discussions, "not without heat".[2] They cleared up the problem of the Oath of Office, and the only scruple which still remained was as to the Vestments. Cranmer and the Council were inclined to dispense with these, but not Ridley; he could wish that Vestments were laid aside by law, but he would not consent to break the law in things indifferent.[3] At length, in March 1551, Hooper yielded the point and was consecrated in a surplice with full lawn sleeves. Less than four years later, Hooper was to precede both Ridley and Cranmer through the gate of fire to glory, and from Oxford, Ridley wrote a farewell letter which touched briefly on the bygone conflict. "Howsoever in time past in smaller matters and circumstances of religion," he wrote, "your wisdom and my simplicity (I confess) have in some points varied: now I say, be you assured, that even with my whole heart (God is my witness) in the bowels of Christ, I love you."[4] Meanwhile, a brief letter from Ridley to Matthew Parker, in July 1551, shows his constant desire to get the best men to help, as well as his eye for the best men: "Sir, I pray you, refuse not to take a day at the Cross. I may have, if I would call without any choice, enow; but in some alas, I desire more learning, in some a better judgment, in some more virtue and godly conversation, and in some more soberness and discretion; and he in whom all these do meet shall not do well in my judgment to refuse to serve God in that place."[5] Then in April 1552, a new Act of Uniformity enforced the use of the Second Book of Common Prayer, and on All Saints' Day, Ridley employed it for the first time, in St. Paul's, wearing neither cope nor vestment, but his rochet only, preaching in the forenoon in the Choir, and in the afternoon at the Cross until almost five o'clock so that the Mayor and others had to go home by torchlight.[6]

It was Ridley's energetic action which had saved Clare Hall at Cambridge from the threat of spoliation, and he maintained a firm protest against the sacrilegious spirit of grasping politicians.

1 Burnet, Vol. II, p. 243.
2 Ibid., Vol. III, p. 304.
3 Ibid., pp. 304, 305.
4 Ridley, p. 355.
5 Ibid., p. 335.
6 Strype, Vol. II, pp. 406, 407.

It was on his advice that the Boy-King founded his sixteen Grammar Schools for boys and planned to found no less than twelve Halls for students. The most interesting result from these beneficial counsels occurred at the close of Edward's short reign. Ridley had often observed with distress the large crowds of poor and vagrant in the streets of London, and he had them in mind when he heard that an old house of the King's in the City was up for sale. He wrote at once to Sir William Cecil to make the most earnest appeal. "Good Mr. Cecil," he wrote, "I must be a suitor unto you in our good Master Christ's cause; I beseech you, be good to Him. The matter is Sir, alas! He hath lain too long abroad, as you do know, without lodging in the streets of London, both hungry, naked and cold. Now thanks be to Almighty God, the citizens are willing to refresh Him, and to give Him both meat, drink, clothing, and firing. But alas! Sir, they lack lodging for Him. . . . Sir, there is a wide, large, empty house of the King's Majesty called Bridewell, that would wonderfully well serve to lodge Christ in, if He might find such good friends in the Court to procure in His cause. Surely I have such a good opinion of the King's Majesty, that if Christ had such faithful and hearty friends who would heartily speak for Him, He should undoubtedly speed at the King's Majesty's hands. Sir, I have promised my brethren, the citizens, to move you because I do take you for one that feareth God, and would that Christ should lie no more abroad in the streets."[1] But in March 1533, Edward was sinking, and summoned both Houses to Whitehall. Ridley preached on practical charity, and the King was touched to the quick. He thanked Ridley and asked him in private how he could serve all who were in distress. The preacher was silent awhile. Then tears and words broke out together, and he begged for time to take advice. As a result, Edward made grants of lands, houses, and revenues which led to the foundation of Christ's Hospital and St. Bartholomew's Hospital, confirmed and enlarged the grant for St. Thomas's Hospital, and gave the "ancient mansion of many English Kings" at Bridewell for the care or correction of the poor and indolent.[2]

In 1549, the Princess Mary had refused the new Prayer Book, and a special dispensation from the King had then been obtained

---

[1] Ridley, p. 535.   [2] Ibid., p. xiii, n.; cp. Burnet, Vol. II, pp. 351, 352.

so that she might have the Mass for herself and her Chaplains. But in 1550, her two Chaplains were prosecuted for saying Mass in her house, and, in March 1551, she was told that she must relinquish the Mass altogether: the King would not constrain her faith, but it was for her to obey as a subject. But she refused, and the Imperial Ambassador went to Court with a threat of war unless leave were given. The point was then referred to Cranmer, Ridley and Poynet, and they declared that it would be permissible for her to have the Mass in her own house.[1] In September 1552, Ridley was at Hadham in Hertfordshire, and, since Princess Mary was at Hunsdon only two miles away, he rode across to pay her a formal visit. She thanked him for his courtesy, and they conversed pleasantly for some fifteen minutes. She told Ridley that she had known him in Court when he was Chaplain to her father and could still recall one of his sermons before Henry VIII. After dinner, Ridley was again summoned into her presence, when he felt impelled to say: "Madame, I came not only to do my duty, to see Your Grace, but also to offer myself to preach before you on Sunday next, if it will please you to hear me." But the Lady Mary's face grew dark and silent before she thus replied: "My Lord, as for this last matter, I pray you make the answer to it yourself." Ridley affirmed that it was his duty to hold himself ready to preach, and she then said: "If there be no remedy but I must make you answer, this shall be your answer: the door of the parish church adjoining shall be open for you if you come, and ye may preach if you list; but neither I, nor any of mine shall hear you." "Madame," said Ridley, "I trust you will not refuse God's Word." But she replied: "I can not tell what ye call God's Word: that is not God's Word now that was God's Word in my father's days." Ridley answered: "God's Word is all one in all times, but hath been better understood and practised in some ages than in others." Mary rejoined with many bitter words against the Book of Prayer and the Laws of the Realm, and at last sent Ridley away with a final protest: "My Lord, for your gentleness to come and see me, I thank you; but for your offering to preach before me, I thank you never a whit."[2]

But on July 6th, 1553, the King died, and the scene changed at once for Ridley and his colleagues. Rudolph Gualter of Zurich

---

[1] Pollard, p. 260, n.   [2] *John Foxe*, Vol. VI, p. 354.

declared that Edward's "towardliness" to the Reformation was
due above all to Cranmer, Ridley, Hooper, and Latimer,[1] and his
last prayer, before death sealed his lips, had the Reformation at
heart. "O my Lord God," he murmured, "defend this realm from
papistry, and maintain Thy true religion; that I and my people
may praise Thy holy Name, for Thy Son Jesus Christ's sake."[2]
Edward had proposed to translate Ridley to the princely See of
Durham, where he would have lived near his own native Tynedale. His voice like that of Knox who was even further north at
Berwick would have been a mighty force for the Truth in the
Border country; but it was not to be. Both Cranmer and Ridley,
though with pathetic misgiving, agreed to take the side of the
Lady Jane Grey, and in July, Ridley had to preach by command
at St. Paul's Cross against the claims of the Princess Mary. He
seems to have foretold that she would bring in a foreign ruler
to share the Throne, and that she would undo all the good work
of the Reformation. He told how he had toiled to clear up the
errors in her doctrine, and how she had proved so stiff and
intractable that there was no chance of success. But the people
heard with unwonted surliness and with ominous impatience.
Before the month had run its course, Mary had been proclaimed
as Queen. Lady Jane's brief day was to set in blood, for it was all
over with the House of Warwick. Ridley was not blind to the
risks which were crowding round him, and he warned his friends
to fly from England.[3] He rode off at once to salute the Queen at
Framlingham, but there was no welcome for him any more than
for Lord Robert Dudley. The Queen had his sermon at St. Paul's
Cross in mind, and she was glad of the excuse to be the more
severe so as to prepare the way for Bonner's return.[4] Ridley was
deprived of all his dignities and placed under arrest on a charge
of treason. He was then sent back to London on a lame hack and
lodged in the Tower with Cranmer and Latimer. "No man
doubted," he told Bradford, "but Cranmer, Latimer and Ridley
should have been the first to have been called to the stake."[5]

The three friends were detained for nine months in the Tower,
but the severity of their imprisonment varied from time to time.
After the first two months, Ridley was given his freedom within

[1] Strype, Vol. III, p. 383.   [2] *John Foxe*, Vol. VI, p. 352.
[3] Ridley, p. 62.   [4] Burnet, Vol. II, p. 371.   [5] Ridley, p. 370.

the Tower, but he lost it some months later since he would not attend Mass in the Tower Chapel. In Lent 1554, Wyat's rebels so filled the Tower as well as the Fleet and Marshalsea that Cranmer, Ridley, Bradford, and Latimer had to be housed in a single chamber, and they greatly valued the privilege of fellowship which their common quarters forced on them in their last weeks in London. Their great desire from the outset was to strengthen each other in faith; by correspondence while still in separate confinement, by consultation while they were imprisoned together. It is to such correspondence that we owe the record of the notable Conference between Ridley and Latimer. The whole record is just like a written conversation, full of human warmth and personal interest. They went over most of the ground on which they were destined to take their stand. Cranmer's book on the Lord's Supper had been published in 1551 and had provoked a reply from Gardiner of Winchester under the pen-name of Antonius. Ridley's annotations on this book were written out in prison with lead from the windows for want of pen and ink.[1] But he also appealed to both his friends to clear his mind as to Gardiner's arguments, in the belief that he would have to bear the brunt of the attack. "Write again, I beseech you," we hear him say; ". . . Spare not my paper, for I look ere it be long that our common enemy will first assault me; and I wish from the bottom of my heart to be holpen not only by your prayers, but also by your wholesome counsels."[2] Many pages are then taken up with Ridley's statement of the Antonian difficulties, followed by his own replies and then by Latimer's arguments. Ridley who was younger but more learned turned with charming humility to the veteran Latimer; and as "an old soldier",[3] the good Hugh wrote back in reply, his sheets "blotted" with the purest and most nervous English, full of good sense and warm feeling.[4] We who now read what was written in this way can see that the deep sagacity of the younger theologian is as full of human appeal as is the bluff virility of the famous preacher.

Latimer realised that his younger colleague had a double purpose in mind, and his reply to the First Objection of the Antonian was a grateful acknowledgment. "Sir," he wrote, "you

[1] *John Foxe*, Vol. VIII, p. 35.   [2] Ridley, p. 110.
[3] *John Foxe*, Vol. VII, p. 410.   [4] Ibid., p. 423; Moule, p. 28.

make answer yourself so well that I can not better it. Sir, I begin now to smell what you mean by travailing thus with me: you use me as Bilney did once, when he converted me. Pretending as though he would be taught of me, he sought ways and means to teach me; and so do you. I thank you therefore most heartily. For indeed you minister armour unto me, whereas I was un-armed before and unprovided, saving that I give myself to prayer for my refuge."[1] Ridley rehearsed the facts which gave him most offence in the Mass in his Answer to the Second Objection: "the strange tongue, the want of the shewing of the Lord's death, the breaking of the Lord's commandment of having a communion; the Sacrament not communicated to all under both kinds, according to the Word of the Lord; the sign servilely worshipped for the thing signified; Christ's Passion injured for-asmuch as this mass sacrifice is affirmed to remain for the purging of sins."[2] It was the Mass to which he stood opposed, and he stated this most plainly in his Answer to the Eleventh Objection: "I fight in Christ's quarrel against the Mass, which doth utterly take away and overthrow the ordinance of Christ."[3] The whole record of this notable Conference makes it interesting to ask whether Ridley had his books to consult while in prison or whether he had to trust his memory. But there is one pathetic allusion which hints plainly at the loss of his books. "All my notes which I have written and gathered out of such authors as I have read in this matter and such like," he wrote, "are come into the hands of such as will not let me have the least of all my written books. Wherein I am forced to complain of them unto God: for they spoil me of all my labours which I have taken in my study these many years. . . . But who knoweth whether this be God's will that I should be thus ordered and spoiled of the poor learning I had (as methought) in store, to the intent that I, now destitute of that, should from henceforth learn only to know with Paul Christ and Him Crucified?"[4] There were later complaints that his books were being withheld,[5] but it seems that he was at length allowed to have them in his hands again.[6]

While the four friends shared the same room, they pored over

---

[1] *John Foxe*, Vol. VII, p. 410.   [2] Ibid., p. 411.
[3] Ibid., p. 418.   [4] Ibid., p. 414.
[5] Ibid., Vol. VI, p. 438, 471.   [6] Moule, p. 194, n.

the New Testament together, to see if they had missed the way in its teaching on these doctrines. "But," Strype tells us, "they found in that Holy Book that the Sacrifice of Christ upon the Cross was perfect, holy, and good; and that God did require none other, nor that it should be ever done again."[1] Somewhere in the milder moments of this imprisonment, we must plac of conversation on the Eucharistic Presence at the dinner tablee a Sir John à Bruges, Lieutenant of the Tower. Ridley was one in a group of six or seven guests among whom were Sir John Bourn, Secretary to the Queen, and Chomley, late Chief Justice. Ridley's account is not only valuable from the standpoint of his theology, with its rapid statements and its cogent reasons; it is just as interesting as a piece of vivid writing, full of human insight and the sense of humour which marked him to the end.[2] Fecknam maintained that no Divine before Berengarius, Wycliffe, or Huss, had so much as questioned the Doctrine of Transubstantiation. Ridley replied that whole volumes had been written on the subject, such as Bertram's Treatise. Sir John Bourn had never heard of Bertram, and asked many questions. "Sir," quoth Ridley, "I have read his book. He propoundeth the same which is now in controversy, and answereth so directly that no man may doubt but that he affirmeth that the substance of bread remaineth still in the Sacrament." After further talk as to the antiquity of Bertram's work, Sir John Bourn asked: "How can ye than make but a figure or a sign of the Sacrament, as that book which is set forth in my Lord of Canterbury's name? I wis, ye can tell who made it; did not ye make it?" And then Ridley heard a muttered assent round the table, as if they all ascribed that book to him. "Master Secretary," he said, "that book was made of a great learned man, and him which is able to do the like again. As for me, I ensure you, (be not deceived in me), I was never able to do or write any such like thing. He passeth me no less than the learned master his young scholar." There was much more conversation before they broke up in goodwill. "And after I had made my moan for lack of my books, he said they were all once given him: but since I know (said he) who hath them now, write me the names of such as you would have, and I will speak for you the best I can."[3]

[1] Strype, Vol. III, p. 75. [2] Moule, pp. 30, 31. [3] *John Foxe*, Vol. VI, pp. 434: 438.

The first charge of treason was in the end withdrawn, and they were to stand their trial for heresy instead. This trial was to take the form of an academic Disputation in Oxford, and there never was the least doubt that the result would be condemnation and death by fire. In March 1554, Sir John à Bruges had orders to commit the three Bishops to the care of Sir John Williams, soon to be Lord Williams of Thame; as for Bradford, he was kept back to stand his trial before the King's Bench in London. April had come before Cranmer, Ridley, and Latimer set out on the two-day journey, and they spent the night at Windsor on their way to Oxford. They had scarcely a thing with them apart from the clothes which they wore, and the servants who had waited on them in the Tower had now been dismissed. They were separated from each other and were surrounded by strangers. Cranmer was placed in the city gaol called the Bocardo over the north gate, "a filthy and stinking prison" as Foxe called it.[1] Ridley was housed with the Mayor of Oxford, Edmund Irish, who lived close to the Bocardo; and Latimer was lodged with a bailiff. It would appear that Ridley was transferred to the Bocardo for a short time in the spring of 1554 and again in 1555; but he was kept mainly in the Mayor's house.[2] It would be a real though minor burden to have to bear for weeks on end with two people such as were the Mayor and his wife. In a letter to Grindal in May 1555, he sketched his lot in a Latin passage full of patience and quiet humour: "Of all us three at Oxford, I am kept most strait and with least liberty, perhaps because the man in whose house I am imprisoned (although he is Mayor of the City!) is ruled by his wife; a little old lady, peevish and very superstitious, who prides herself on being reported to guard me closely and with the utmost care. Her husband, one Irish, is mild enough indeed to everybody; but to his wife, more than most obsequious. You know I never had a wife; and from my daily intercourse with this pair, I seem to see in some measure how great a calamity and how intolerable a yoke it is to be married to an evil wife!"[3] But his patience told in the end, and she wept on the eve of his death. The civil records of Oxford have an entry four months later in date which tells how Margaret Irish came before the City Council for an offence against Their Majesties. "May not this

[1] Moule, p. 34.   [2] Ibid., p. 53, n.   [3] Ridley, pp. 391, 392; Moule, p. 54.

mean," as Moule suggests, "that the little old lady had spoken out her mind against the persecutors of her martyred inmate?"[1]

It was planned that they should dispute with the Divines of Oxford and Cambridge as to the real Presence, the true Substance, and the nature of the Sacrifice in the Sacrament. Three Articles of Inquiry had been drawn up for this purpose: "First, whether the natural body of Christ our Saviour, conceived of the Virgin Mary and offered for man's redemption upon the Cross, is verily and really in the Sacrament by virtue of God's word spoken by the priest or no? Secondly, whether in the Sacrament after the words of consecration, any other substance do remain than the substance of the body and blood of Christ? Thirdly, whether in the mass be a sacrifice propitiatory for the sins of the quick and the dead?"[2] On April 13th, the Cambridge Doctors arrived in Oxford and were regaled with "a dish of apples and a gallon of wine".[3] The thirty-three Commissioners were a motley body; relatively few were scholars of real merit. On Saturday, April 14th, the first session began with a Mass of the Holy Ghost. Then the Doctors took up their stand before the high altar in St. Mary's, while one by one the three Bishops were brought in to answer certain formal questions. Cranmer was called up for trial on Monday; Ridley had to face the Divines on the Tuesday; Latimer made his appearance on Wednesday; and on Friday, April 20th, all three men were condemned. But the whole thing had been a farce, whether as a trial or as a Disputation; each of the three in turn had been accused, and baited, and goaded with taunts and jibes, with unseemly ridicule and constant interruption. Ridley had been the most direct and forceful in his disavowal of the dogma of Transubstantiation, and he met his judges with words of more resolute quality than the gentle Cranmer had used. He twice composed in Latin an account of that long and stormy day's work, and he told the story as if it were a keen, but not intemperate debate, in which both sides argued with skill and kept to the rules of formal logic. But we know from other information that he framed his report of the debate in this respect as it ought to have been rather than as it was; he summed

---

[1] Moule, p. 55.
[2] Ridley, p. 192; *John Foxe*, Vol. VI, p. 439.
[3] *John Foxe*, Vol. VI, p. 440.

up what was said, but left out, save here and there, the noise and tumult amid which it was said.[1]

But his Preface to the Account does show that it was a loud and disgraceful episode. When he had been brought in on the Saturday and had heard the Articles read out, he at once made answer that their implications were false. He was asked if he would dispute, and he replied: "As long as God gave him life, He should not only have his heart, but also his mouth and pen to defend His truth."[2] Thus the Divines soon found on the Tuesday that his answers were sharp, full of wit, and very learned, and they were at some loss to know how to handle the case. Ridley describes the scene which then ensued: "I never yet in all my life saw or heard anything done or handled more vainly or tumultuously . . . And surely I could never have thought that it had been possible to have found any within this realm, being of any knowledge, learning, and ancient degree of school, so brazen-faced and so shameless as to behave themselves so vainly and so like stage-players as they did in that Disputation. . . . A great part of the time was vainly spent in most contumelious taunts, hissings, clapping of hands, and triumphs, more than intolerable even in stage-plays, and that in the English tongue, to get the people's favour withal. All which things when I with godly grief did suffer and therewithal did openly bewail, . . . I was so far by my such humble complaint from doing good or helping anything at all, that I was forced, what with hissing and shouting, and what with authority, to hear such great reproaches and slanders uttered against me, as no grave man without blushing could abide the hearing of the same spoken by a most vile knave against a most wretched ruffian. At the beginning of the Disputation, when I should have confirmed mine answer to the first proposition in few words, and that after the manner of Disputations, before I could make an end of my probation which was not very long, even the doctors themselves cried out, 'He speaketh blasphemies, blasphemies, blasphemies!' And when I on my knees most humbly and heartily besought them that they would vouchsafe to hear me to the end, whereat the Prolocutor (something moved, as it seemed,) cried out, 'Let him read it, let him read it!' yet when I again began to read it, there was by and by such a cry

[1] Moule, pp. 36, 37.   [2] *John Foxe*, Vol. VI, p. 442.

and noise, 'Blasphemies, blasphemies!' as I to my remembrance never heard or read the like."[1]

It is clear that Ridley's command of logic surprised and dismayed some of those who had come to join in the Disputation. "If there were an Arian which had that subtle wit that you have," Tresham of Christ Church was provoked to say, "he might soon shift off the authority of the Scriptures and Fathers."[2] Weston, who acted as Prolocutor, at length dissolved the court with a Latin cry of triumph: "Here you see the stubborn, the glorious, the crafty, the unconstant mind of this man. Here you see this day that the strength of the truth is without foil. Therefore I beseech you all most earnestly to blow the note (and he began, and they followed,) Verity hath the victory, Verity hath the victory! Vincit veritas, Vincit veritas!"[3] Latimer's appearance on the Wednesday was a fresh farce. "It seemed to me, and a number more," wrote one eyewitness, "that they caused him to be brought forth for nothing else but to laugh at him and mock him; such was their behaviour in the schools that day."[4] On Friday, April 20th, the Doctors and Divines took their seats as before in St. Mary's, and the three friends were then arraigned once more in their presence. Weston asked each in turn whether he would subscribe to the Articles of Inquiry, and he refused to let them make any reply save yea or nay. Cranmer did voice a strong protest because he had not been allowed to speak in accord with the strict rules of Disputation; therefore, he now refused to make answer as they required. Ridley and Latimer refused to revoke their hostility to the Mass and declared that they would still adhere to all that they had said. Then the formal sentence of the court was read out: they were pronounced no true members of the Church, and therefore they were condemned as heretics. Each was asked if he would recant, and each firmly refused. "Although I be not of your company," Ridley dared to say, "yet doubt I not but my name is written in another place whither this sentence will send us sooner than we should by the course of nature have come."[5]

Ridley's prowess as a theologian of the first rank had been

---

[1] Ridley, pp. 303, 304; cp. pp. 199, 200. [2] *John Foxe*, Vol. VI, p. 497.
[3] Ibid., Vol. VI, p. 500. [4] Moule, p. 43.
[5] *John Foxe*, Vol. VI, p. 534.

demonstrated in this Disputation. His own writings were few enough; they form but a single volume in the Parker Society series. They dealt only with those subjects which then seemed most urgent; but these they did handle with "a passionate conviction and an almost wearisome thoroughness".[1] And they prove that he was a great Divine, who well deserved his high reputation among the Exiles in Europe. He was one of the few early English Reformers who had a first-hand knowledge of Continental Theology, and he became the outstanding English Theologian in the reign of Edward VI.[2] His main work was *A Brief Declaration of The Lord's Supper*, and this was a deliberate reassertion, in the leisure of his imprisonment, of the doctrines which had been on trial in Oxford. The book is first mentioned in a letter to John Bradford in the spring of 1554, and this is the only clue we possess as to its date. It was in the hands of Grindal in Frankfort by May 1555, and he knew that it would appear in print once it was known what the Lord had in store for him. The *Brief Declaration* links courage and candour of decision with fairness and restraint of expression in a way that argues a mind of the highest order. It would appear from a comparison of the Scriptural quotations with the English versions known to Ridley that he had to quote from memory, but with recollections of Tyndale and Cranmer as well as of the original text in mind.[3] Ridley closed the book with the words "Vincit Veritas"; a mild echo from the Disputation! But his immense stores of learning allowed him to quote the Fathers with an authority which no one could gainsay, and his testimony was at length to prevail in the Protestant Settlement which took place in the reign of Queen Elizabeth. The redirection of English Theology was in large measure owing to his work, for he it was who did most of all to guide the English Reformation into the Reformed rather than the Lutheran camp. He took up the task just at the point where Luther had left off, and by his learning, and ability, and integrity, he was able to win over to his own standpoint the chief friends of Reform in his own country. He was more forceful, more resolute, and more original in his thinking than Cranmer; he was more wakeful, more sagacious, and more intelligent as a statesman than Hooper. It was indeed Ridley more than any other man

[1] Bromiley, p. 16.   [2] Ibid., p. 5.   [3] Moule, p. 97, n.

who marked out the type of Sacramental Theology which the Church of England was at last to adopt.[1]

"A long silence, as to contact with the outer world," now befell the three Bishops.[2] They were separated from each other, and even their English Prayer Books were taken away. But they were cheered by a series of the finest letters which were somehow conveyed to and from their prison quarters. Ridley thus wrote to John Bradford at a time when the three were in Bocardo together to deny a rumour that they had gone to Mass. "We are in good health," he wrote, "thanks be to God; and yet the manner of our treatment doth change as sour ale doth in summer. . . . We had out of our prison a wall that we might have walked upon, and our servants had liberty to go abroad in the town or fields; but now both they and we are restrained of both. . . . Sir, blessed be God, with all our evil reports, grudgings, and restraints, we are merry in God; and all our care is and shall be by God's grace to please and serve Him!"[3] But early in 1555, Ridley heard that Bradford was soon to die, and he at once wrote a letter which was to be a most tender farewell to one who had proved so worthy of his love and honour. "We do look now every day when we shall be called on, blessed be God!" he went on to say. "I ween I am the weakest many ways of our own company; and yet I thank our Lord God and Heavenly Father by Christ that since I heard of our dear brother Rogers' . . . stout confession of Christ and His Truth even unto the death, my heart (blessed be God!) so rejoiced of it that since that time, I say, I never felt any lumpish heaviness in my heart as I grant I have felt sometimes before. O good brother, blessed be God in thee, and blessed be the time that ever I knew thee. Farewell! Farewell!"[4] One more letter was written, to Grindal, now safe across the sea, to whom Ridley still contrived to smuggle money for the Exiles. They three were in good health, he wrote, though he was the most strictly confined. They looked daily for their execution, and they had in mind those who had gone on before. He gave the names of such men as Rogers, Hooper, Taylor, Ferrar, and then closed his letter with some lines in Latin. "I commend to you my most reverend Fathers and fellow prisoners in the Lord," he wrote,

---

[1] Bromley, pp. 24: 26.   [2] Moule, p. 47.
[3] Ridley, pp. 359, 360.   [4] Ibid., p. 378.

"Thomas Cranmer, now truly right worthy the name of Chief Pastor and Arch-Prelate, and that veteran of our English race, and Christ's true Apostle, Hugh Latimer. Forgive me, brother, my letter's length; for never hereafter dearest brother, so I think, will you be disturbed by letters of mine."[1]

The true quality of his character was brought to light during those long months of imprisonment. He had so far mainly appeared as scholar or churchman, but his prison writings help to portray him as one of the most noble saints and servants of God in our English story. He was master of the New Testament in its spirit as well as its letter, and he won through the long ordeal of tension and suspense in a strength that came from above. Ridley's courage has never been impugned, but he had to face the prospect of death by fire long in advance. There is a moving passage in the *Piteous Lamentation* in which he thought out the alternatives of flight or death, and for himself, he thought it right neither to fly nor to recant, but to die for Truth's sake.[2] He was a man of true learning and breadth of view, calm in counsel, firm in friendship, self-forgetful in his quiet steadfast dignity, self-abasing in his plain downright modesty, one of the most tolerant Reformers of his age in Europe. Had he survived Cranmer and lived in the reign of Elizabeth, he might well have become Primate of All England; and that might have been to impart to the English Reformation more of strength and solidity than it was in fact to possess. Unlike Cranmer, he was never married, but he was a man of deep and generous affections. His love for his sister, at whose name he wept when he was being deprived; his friendship for Bradford, so like that of Tyndale for Frith; and his Farewell Letters before his death all tell of the ties of a warm humanity. He was no cold implacable Churchman, but one who loved England and the Church of England with the love of a true religious patriot. "In fine," said Foxe, "he was such a prelate, and in all points so good, godly and ghostly a man, that England may justly rue the loss of so worthy a treasure."[3] Bishop Moule summed up his judgment after the most careful study of his life and labours in a glowing tribute. "Not many characters in Christian history, so I venture to think," he wrote,

[1] Ridley, pp. 394, 395; Moule, p. 60.
[2] Ibid., pp. 61:65. [3] *John Foxe*, Vol. VII, p. 407.

"bear scrutiny as his does. Sans peur et sans reproche may fairly be written over his whole life. A luminous penetrating mind; a temperate and stedfast will; a heart pure, strong and gentle; a faith laying firm and quiet hold within the veil; all these gifts of God met in Nicholas Ridley."[1] Peter Martyr may be taken as representative of contemporary thought when he told Henry Bullinger in an incidental sentence that Ridley was "a most learned man, and a valiant defender of the Gospel".[2]

Meanwhile, execution of the sentence was put off on account of the then state of the Law in England. It was January 1555 before Pole absolved the Commons from the sin of schism and had the old legislation restored. That cleared a path to the stake for Rogers and Taylor and Hooper in February, and for Ferrar in March. But their burning was so unpopular that the Spanish Consort thought it wise to let things lie for a while. This was why the final ordeal was so delayed in the case of Bradford in the King's Bench and the Bishops who were still in Oxford. Bradford at length suffered at Smithfield in July, and Philip left England in September; but the verdict which had been pronounced against the three Bishops, in April 1554, had become void under the state of law which then prevailed. Thus the Bishops of Lincoln, Gloucester, and Bristol were now named as Commissioners and sent up to Oxford, with full legatine authority to hold a new trial and to pass a new sentence. Cranmer was to appear separately, for his case as Primate required a Bull from Rome. But on September 30th, his two brethren were brought to the Divinity School at eight o'clock in the morning. The Lords Spiritual sat in the seat used for public lectures, and it was "trimmed with cloth of tissue and cushions of velvet."[3] They made up their mind to deal with Ridley before they would examine Latimer, and he was brought into the School to hear the terms of the Commission read out by a Notary. A remarkable scene ensued. Ridley stood bare-headed until the name of Pole as the Papal Legate occurred; then he at once put on his cap. The Bishop of Lincoln then said that the Commissioners did not require cap or knee for themselves, but that formal respect had to be paid at the names of the Pope and his Legate. Ridley removed his cap and bowed his knee each

[1] Moule, p. xiv.   [2] *Original Letters*, Vol. II, p. 486.

[3] *John Foxe*, Vol. VII, p. 518.

time he heard the name of the Queen or of Pole as a member of the Royal House, but he put his cap back on his head when Pole was mentioned as the Papal Legate. Neither threats nor admonition could persuade him, and at length one of the beadles removed it from his head. The Bishop of Lincoln in a long speech then urged him to recant. "Remember Master Ridley," he said, "it is no strange country whither I exhort you to return. You were once one of us; you have taken degrees in the school. You were made a priest, and became a preacher, setting forth the same doctrine which we do now. . . . You see Master Ridley that all Christendom is subject to the Church of Rome. What should stay you therefore to confess the same with St. Augustine and the other Fathers?"[1]

Ridley would have replied at length, but the Bishop broke in to say that they had not come to dispute and must proceed according to their instructions. "Wherefore Master Ridley," he said again, "consider your state; remember your former degrees; spare your body; especially consider your soul!"[2] Ridley answered, in spite of much interruption: "I prefer the antiquity of the Primitive Church before the novelty of the Romish Church."[3] The Bishop of Lincoln then told him that at eight o'clock in the morning he would be required to give his answer to the Articles on which he was to be examined, and that he could have pen, ink, and paper, and such books as might be available, should he need their help in drawing up his reply. The Five Articles were then formally read out, and they charged him with false Sacramental Theology: "We do object to thee, Nicholas Ridley, . . . first, that thou . . . hast affirmed . . . that the true and natural body of Christ after the consecration of the priest, is not really present in the Sacrament of the Altar. . . . Thou hast publicly affirmed and defended that in the Sacrament of the Altar remaineth still the substance of bread and wine. . . . Thou hast openly affirmed and obstinately maintained that in the Mass is no propitiatory sacrifice for the quick and the dead."[4] Then, to Ridley's surprise, the Bishop of Lincoln asked him to make verbal reply at once, saying that the next day he might add to or alter what he said as he would. Ridley remarked that

---

[1] *John Foxe*, Vol. VII, pp. 520, 521.   [2] Ibid., p. 524.
[3] Ibid., p. 525.   [4] Ibid., p. 526.

at the last Disputation, much was promised, but little performed; the Bishop of Lincoln's pretended gentleness was the same that Christ had experienced at the hands of Caiaphas, who would condemn no man to death and yet would not suffer Pilate to release Him! He asked for leave to speak but three words to explain why he disowned the Pope's authority, and was told that the next day he might speak forty. The Articles were ministered to him, and his replies were written down. "Christ," he said, "made one perfect sacrifice for the sins of the whole world, neither can any man reiterate that sacrifice of His; and yet is the Communion an acceptable sacrifice to God of praise and thanksgiving. But to say that thereby sins are taken away (which wholly and perfectly was done by Christ's Passion, of the which the Communion is only a memory), that is a great derogation of the merits of Christ's Passion: for the Sacrament was instituted that we, receiving it, and thereby recognising and remembering His Passion, should be partakers of the merits of the same. For otherwise doth this Sacrament take upon it the office of Christ's Passion, whereby it might follow that Christ died in vain."[1] He was then dismissed until the next day.

At eight o'clock the next morning, the three Episcopal Commissioners repaired to St. Mary's and took their seat on a high throne trimmed with tissue and silk. Ridley stood at a table covered with silk cloth, while the College Heads and certain Gentry sat in framed seats which were arranged in quadrate form round this table. Town and Gown packed the Church to watch the Trial, and one of the beadles roughly snatched the cap off his head. The Trial began with much altercation, but he never lost his sense of humour and smiled quietly at the forlorn attempt of the Commissioners to argue by logic. At length, Ridley drew a sheet of paper from the folds of his cloak and tried to read it out as a prepared statement. But a beadle took it out of his hands, in spite of his protest. "Why, my Lord," he said, "will you require my answer, and not suffer me to publish it? I beseech you, my Lord, let the audience bear witness in this matter."[2] It was secretly examined by John White of Lincoln, who then conferred with the other Bishops, pronounced it full of blasphemies, refused either to let it be read or returned, and paid no regard at

[1] *John Foxe*, Vol. VII, p. 528.   [2] Ibid., p. 537.

all to Ridley's protests. The Five Articles were then read out, and he was asked for a formal reply. But he declared that his answer was in writing and the notaries were compelled to refer to his statement. Brooks of Gloucester at last made an appeal to him, in which the famous words occur: "What a weak and feeble stay in religion is this, I pray you? Latimer leaneth to Cranmer, Cranmer to Ridley, and Ridley to the singularity of his own wit: so that if you overthrew the singularity of Ridley's wit, then must needs the religion of Cranmer and Latimer fall also."[1] Ridley answered that "he was but a young scholar in comparison of Master Cranmer; for at what time he was a young scholar, then was Master Cranmer a doctor; so that he confessed that Master Cranmer might have been his school-master these many years."[2] But Brooks interrupted Ridley's modest self-estimate. "Why, Master Ridley," he said, "it is your own confession; for Master Latimer at the time of his Disputation confessed his learning to lie in Master Cranmer's books, and Master Cranmer also said that it was your doing."[3] The Bishop of Lincoln also pressed him hard to recant, but he only asked for freedom to speak. The Bishop of Lincoln said he might have forty words and began to count them out on his fingers. Ridley was cut short in his first sentence, and his condemnation followed as a matter of course.

Ridley had long foreseen that a fiery chariot would in the end be his way to heaven. Humphrey's *Life* of Jewell tells a story of his travels while Bishop of London which makes this clear. Ridley was caught in a storm at sea, but he cheered his friends with the remark: "Be of good cheer, and bend to your oars: this boat carries a Bishop who is not to be drowned, but burned."[4] There was intelligent foresight in this presentiment, for the precarious health of the King meant that there might be a drastic change of fortune at any time. Ridley had no wish to make his faith an issue of life or death, but that was the issue which the Roman party forced upon him. He was known as the most able theologian of the English Reformation, and the Roman leaders put forth all their strength to induce him to recant. Such a triumph might shake Cranmer himself, and great would be his

[1] *John Foxe*, Vol. VII, p. 538. [2] Ibid., p. 539.
[3] Ibid., p. 539. [4] Ridley, p. xi, n.

fall! Thus Ridley was required to bow without appeal to the ruling of Rome; he was asked to accept, on pain of death, as both true and necessary, doctrines which he believed to be directly opposite to the teaching of the Scriptures. But he held to his faith and did not count the pain of death too great a price to pay when it was forced upon him by others. Thus he was not dismayed when the Bishop of Lincoln at last rose up and read out the sentence of condemnation in its naked severity: "That forasmuch as the said Nicholas Ridley did affirm, maintain, and stubbornly defend certain opinions, assertions, and heresies contrary to the Word of God and the received faith of the Church, as in denying the true and natural body of Christ and His natural blood to be in the Sacrament of the Altar; secondarily in affirming the substance of bread and wine to remain after the words of the consecration; thirdly, in denying the Mass to be a lively sacrifice of the Church for the quick and the dead; and by no means would be induced and brought from these his heresies: they therefore did judge and condemn the said Nicholas Ridley as a heretic, and so adjudged him presently, both by word and also in deed, to be degraded from the degree of a bishop, from priesthood, and all ecclesiastical order; declaring moreover the said Nicholas Ridley to be no member of the Church; and therefore committed him to the secular powers, of them to receive due punishment according to the tenor of the temporal laws: and further excommunicating him by the greater excommunication."[1]

There was yet a fortnight before the end. During those two weeks, Lord Dacre made an offer of ten thousand pounds to the Crown if the Queen would only agree to spare his life; but she refused. Somehow during those two weeks, he wrote his Farewells. They took the form of two Letters which rank with the highest flights of English prose in all our older writings. He had contrived during the year to write his *Piteous Lamentation* in the double strain of pathos and patriotism which shows us all his heart as he looked out from his prison windows upon the fate of the Church in England. "Alas!" he wrote, "what misery is Thy Church brought unto, O Lord, at this day! Where of late the Word of the Lord was truly preached, was read and heard in every town, in every church, in every village; yea, and almost

[1] *John Foxe*, Vol. VII, p. 540.

every honest man's house; alas! now it is exiled and banished out of the whole realm. Of late, who was not glad to be taken for a lover of God's Word, for a reader, for a ready hearer, and for a learner of the same? And now alas! who dare bare any open countenance towards it, but such as are content in Christ's cause and for His Word's sake to stand to the danger and loss of all that they have!"[1] Then the Farewells take up this same lament: "Alas! all that loved God's Word and were true setters forth thereof, are now (as I hear say) some burnt and slain, some exiled and banished, and some holden in hard prisons, and appointed daily to be put to most cruel death, for Christ's Gospel sake."[2] Moule says that these Letters sweep the whole scale of human feeling, "ranging from pathetic tenderness and purest resignation to patriotic and far-seeing appeals and those prophet-like denunciations of the sins of the nation and of the portentous claims of the papal hierarchy with which the first Farewell ends."[3] There were farewells to his Tyneside kinsfolk, to Cambridge and Pembroke, to Herne and Soham, to Rochester and London, and to the fair Realm of England; and at the close of his second Letter, he takes farewell of the true Church on earth in its ideal and its secret reality: "Farewell, thou spiritual House of God, thou holy and royal priesthood, thou chosen generation, thou holy nation, thou won spouse! Farewell, farewell!"[4]

On October 15th, in the morning, Brooks of Gloucester, with the Vice-Chancellor and the College Heads, made his way to the house of Edmund Irish to offer him the Queen's mercy if he would now recant. "My Lord," replied Ridley, "you know my mind fully herein; and as for the doctrine which I have taught, my conscience assureth me that it was sound, and according to God's Word, (to His glory be it spoken); the which doctrine, the Lord God being my helper, I will maintain so long as my tongue shall wag and breath is within my body, and in confirmation thereof, seal the same with my blood."[5] Brooks then told him that they took him for no Bishop, but had come to degrade him from the priesthood. A racy dialogue rapidly developed. Ridley was calm and self-controlled, finding words to match the moment as the

---

[1] Ridley, p. 49.
[2] Ibid., p. 408.
[3] Moule, pp. 62, 63.
[4] Ridley, p. 427.
[5] *John Foxe*, Vol. VII, p. 543.

affair went on. He would not put on the Romish Vestments, or take wafer or cup in his hand of his own accord; but he did not resist the ceremony of Degradation when they were wrapped round his shoulders, or forced into his hand. Brooks began by saying: "Put off your cap, Master Ridley, and put upon you this surplice." Ridley refused: "Not I, truly!" Brooks tried to insist: "But you must!" But he would not flinch: "I will not!" Brooks began to threaten: "You must make no more ado, but put this surplice upon you." But Ridley still affirmed: "Truly, if it come upon me, it shall be against my will."[1] He was then clothed with all the Mass Vestments, although to the indignation of Brooks, he ceased not to inveigh against the Pope. Someone proposed that his mouth should be gagged; but Foxe says that "nevertheless Ridley was ever talking things not pleasant to their ears."[2] When the wretched ceremony came to an end, Brooks was in haste to be away; but not until Ridley had urged him to give a candid reading to the Book of Bertram. "I promise you," he said, "you shall find much good learning therein, if you will read the same with an indifferent judgment."[3] Ridley was then handed over to the bailiffs till his execution, and so the last evening gathered round him. He washed his beard and sat down to supper "as merry as ever he was."[4] When he rose from the table, his brother-in-law offered to spend the night with him. "No, no," he said, "that you shall not. For I mind, God willing, to go to bed and to sleep as quietly to-night as ever I did in my life."[5]

The stake was set up on the morning of October 16th, not far from the city gaol, "in the ditch over against Balliol."[6] Ridley came first, attired with care as a bishop in undress, walking between the Mayor and a bailiff; his black gown furred and faced with foins, his velvet tippet and velvet night-cap in place, and a pair of slippers upon his feet. He looked up to the room which he knew was Cranmer's prison, hoping to see his face at the window and to exchange words of greeting. Cranmer was engaged in debate with a Spanish Friar and could not come to the window in time. But Strype says that as soon as he was free, he looked after his friends with a look of exceeding tenderness, and then

---

[1] *John Foxe*, Vol. VII, p. 543.   [2] Ibid., p. 544.   [3] Ibid., pp. 544, 545.
[4] Ibid., p. 547.   [5] Ibid., p. 547.   [6] Ibid., p. 547.

fell on his knees to pray that the Lord would strengthen them with
faith and patience in their last great ordeal.[1] Bullinger afterwards
told John Calvin that his friends in England had told him how
Ridley and Latimer "were burned in the sight of Cranmer, who
testified that this punishment was more grievous to him than
death itself".[2] Meanwhile, Ridley looked back and caught sight
of Latimer, clad in an old thread-bare Bristol frieze gown, with a
new shroud hanging over his hose down to his feet. Ridley
arrived first at the stake, lifted up his clasped hands and looked
towards heaven as if in prayer; then "with a wonderous cheerful
look", he ran to greet Latimer with the embrace and kiss of a
fellow-martyr.[3] "Be of good heart, brother," he said, "for God
will either assuage the fury of the flame, or else strengthen us to
abide it."[4] They first knelt on either side of the stake in prayer
and then conversed with each other while the bailiffs stood in
the shade. But what was said in those sacred moments, Foxe
could in no wise learn. Then followed that wicked sermon by a
ruthless preacher, based on the text: "If I yield my body to the
fire to be burnt, and have not charity, I shall gain nothing thereby"
(1 Cor. 13:3).[5] Ridley then on bended knee asked Lord Williams
of Thame for leave to speak, and he seemed not unwilling to grant
it. But the bailiffs clapped their hands on his mouth and told
him that he might only speak if he would recant. "Well," quoth
Master Ridley, "so long as the breath is in my body, I will never
deny my Lord Christ and His known truth; God's will be done
in me!" And with that, he rose up and said with a loud voice:
"Well then, I commit our cause to Almighty God which shall
indifferently judge all!"[6]

Then he disrobed and gave away all his outer garments. John
Foxe quaintly observed: "Happy was he that might get any
rag of him!"[7] The smith placed an iron chain about their waists
as they stood back to back, while gunpowder was hung in bags
around their necks. Someone brought a faggot, and the fire was
kindled at Ridley's feet. Their hour had come. But Latimer's
voice broke through the tension of that moment with his im-
mortal utterance: "Be of good comfort, Master Ridley, and play

[1] Strype, Vol. III, p. 200. [2] *Original Letters*, Vol. II, p. 751.
[3] *John Foxe*, Vol. VII, p. 548. [4] Ibid., p. 548.
[5] Ibid., p. 548. [6] Ibid., p. 549. [7] Ibid., p. 549.

the man. We shall this day light such a candle by God's grace in England as I trust shall never be put out!"[1] Ridley saw the flames leap up and cried with a loud voice: "In manus tuas Domine commendo spiritum meum: Domine, recipe spiritum meum!" These words he went on to reiterate many times in English: "Lord, Lord, receive my spirit!"[2] Latimer, aged, frail, and worn, was seen to bathe his hands in the fire; then he died, almost without a pang, crying: "O Father of Heaven, receive my soul!"[3] But the fire was ill made on the other side of the stake, being choked with gorse and piled high with green faggots. Ridley begged them for Christ's sake to let the fire through, and his brother-in-law, as one in such sorrow that he knew not what he did, heaped yet more wood on the fire so that he was nearly covered. The flames blazed up beneath and burned his legs, but the main part of his body was quite untouched. He leapt up and down in the fire, crying: "I can not burn!"[4] And soon they saw that not even his shirt had caught alight. He suffered and struggled as few of the martyrs had to suffer through a long and dreadful ordeal. "Yet," says Foxe, "in all this torment, he forgot not to call unto God still."[5] At last one of the bystanders had the presence of mind to pull off the upper faggots so that the fire could break through, and he bent himself in that direction. The flames soon reached the bag of gunpowder, and his spirit fled as he fell down at last by Latimer's feet. There were signs of sorrow on all sides in Oxford on that fateful mid-October morning; there were hundreds who looked on through a mist of tears while the two friends faced the ordeal by fire. Strype tells us that they were reckoned the two "greatest preachers" in the whole realm at the time when they died in the flames to light that candle of glory in England.[6] They were indeed "lovely and pleasant in their lives, and in their death, they were not divided" (2 Sam. 1:23).

[1] *John Foxe*, Vol. VII, p. 550.   [2] Ibid., p. 550.
[3] Ibid., p. 550.   [4] Ibid., p. 551.
[5] Ibid., p. 551.   [6] Strype, *Eccles. Memorials*, Vol. III, p. 361.

BIBLIOGRAPHY

STEPHEN CATTLEY, *The Acts and Monuments of John Foxe* (8 Vols.), 1841

NICHOLAS RIDLEY, *Works* (Parker Society Edition), 1843

NICHOLAS RIDLEY, *A Brief Declaration of the Lord's Supper* (Edited by H. C. G. Moule), 1895

JOHN STRYPE, *Memorials of Thomas Cranmer* (3 Vols.), 1848

JOHN STRYPE, *Ecclesiastical Memorials* (Oxford), 1824

GILBERT BURNET, *The History of The Reformation of the Church of England* (Edited by Edward Nares) (4 Vols.)

F. W. B. BULLOCK, *The History of Ridley Hall, Cambridge*, 1941

A. F. POLLARD, *Thomas Cranmer and The English Reformation* (New Edition), 1926

ROBERT DEMAUS, *Hugh Latimer: A Biography*, 1881

JOHN CHARLES RYLE, *Nicholas Ridley* (Chapter IX in *Light From Old Times*), 1898

G. W. BROMILEY, *Nicholas Ridley* (No. 19 in "Great Churchmen" Series), 1951

HASTINGS ROBINSON, *Original Letters Relative to the English Reformation.* (Parker Society Edition, 2 Vols.), 1846

THOMAS CRANMER

*Fellow of Jesus College,
Cambridge*

1489–1556

Cranmer "lived in a high region. He preserved the continuity of the Church of England. He gave to the English Reformation largeness and capacity. . . . He was a greater man than any of his contemporaries. His death completed the circle of five men of episcopal degree, who loosed the yoke of Rome from the neck of the Church of England by the sacrifice of their lives: a glorious crown of bishops, the like of which is set upon the brow of no other church in Christendom."

—R. W. DIXON, *The History of The Church of England*, Vol. IV, p. 552.

Thomas Cranmer was born on July 2nd, 1489, in the little village of Aslacton which lies in the Midlands between Grantham and Nottingham, and he was the second son in a home of three boys and four girls who were brought up on their father's small and burdened estate. Cranmer liked to believe that his forbears had first come to England with the Normans, but he knew that they were obscure enough. "I take it," he once said, "that none of us all here, being gentlemen born, but had our beginnings that way from a low and base parentage."[1] It was all that his good father could do to live up to the style of the smaller English gentry, and his younger sons had perforce to turn from the land to the Church. Cranmer was sent to school, but fell under the hand of "a marvellous severe and cruel school master",[2] whose rough treatment and harsh methods left an indelible scar on his mind. The boys came to loathe good literature, and for his part, Cranmer "lost much of that benefit of memory and audacity in his youth that by nature was given to him".[3] But at home his father taught him to hunt and hawk, and he could shoot both with long-bow and with cross-bow. He could always ride the roughest horse that ever came into his stable, and no one could take the saddle with more grace or poise than he as master of the Lambeth household. The death of his father when he was twelve years old did not change his purpose, and his mother sent him up to Cambridge at the early age of fourteen in 1503 or 1504. There was little to spare from his father's estate, and his means must have been narrow; but he lived to declare that he had been better off as a poor scholar at Cambridge than he was as a great prelate at Canterbury.[4] It is assumed that he entered Jesus College, still a recent institution only six or seven years old, founded on the site of a once famous convent which had suffered dissolution. Here Cranmer was "nursled . . . chiefly in the dark riddles of Duns and other subtile questionists: and in these he lost his time till he came to two and

[1] Pollard, pp. 3,
[3] Ibid., p. 9.
[2] Ibid., p. 9.
[4] Cranmer, Vol. II, p. 437.

twenty years of age".[1] He took his Arts degree in 1510 or 1511, and with Thomas Goodrich became one of the twelve Fellows of his College. He was compelled by the statutes to devote himself to theology, and he slowly began to break through the trammels of an outworn system. He turned from Duns and the Schoolmen to the rising star of Erasmus, who had come to take up residence at Queens' in 1511.

But the men from Jesus College used to meet for social relaxation at the Dolphin Inn which stood at the Bridge Street end of All Saints' Lane. It was here that Cranmer fell in love with Joan, a niece of the mistress of the Dolphin, and the match soon ripened into marriage. This meant that he lost his status as a Fellow, but he was appointed as a "common reader" in the recent foundation now known as Magdalen College. But some twelve months later, his wife died in childbirth, and he regained his place as one of the twelve Fellows of Jesus. This was no light tribute "for towardliness in learning".[2] It proves decisively that he was held in high esteem for character and intellect by the men who could best form a judgment. Sorrow and change helped him to yield gladly to the fresh winds which had begun to blow through the long stale air of mediaeval studies. In 1516, Erasmus published his first Edition of the Greek Text of the New Testament, and in 1517, Martin Luther nailed his Ninety-five Theses to the door of the church in Wittenberg. There was no small controversy in Church matters up at Cambridge, and soon Cranmer began to bend his thoughts to the articles of our salvation. "He gave his mind to good writers, both new and old: not rashly running over them; for he was a slow reader, but a diligent marker of whatsoever he read, seldom reading without pen in hand. And whatsoever made either for the one part or the other of things in controversy, he wrote it out if it were short, or at least noted the author and the place that he might find it and write it out at leisure."[3] His high qualities won him promotion in his College and in wider fields of academic life in Cambridge. It was during these years that he took his Master's Degree and was ordained, began to lecture in Divinity at his College, and gave himself up for three years to a patient reading of the Scriptures. In 1523, he became a Doctor of Divinity, and, in 1524, he refused Wolsey's

[1] Strype, Vol. I, p. 3.   [2] *John Foxe*, Vol. VIII, p. 5.   [3] Strype, Vol. I, p. 3.

offer of a Canonry at his newly founded College in Oxford. His mind had now begun to yield to the teaching of the Scriptures, and as early as in 1525, he had begun to pray daily for the abolition of the Papal power in England.[1] About the year 1526, he was asked to examine candidates for Degrees in Divinity, and began to insist that they should furnish proof of a first-hand knowledge of the Scriptures. But new ideas won their way slowly enough in his mind, and there was no sign as yet that he would at length stand out as a friend of Reform.

The years at hand were to see the whole of England from Tweed to Thames stirred by the King's "Great Cause",[2] and the summer months of 1529 produced a series of events which were hardly less momentous for Cranmer than for Henry himself. It was believed that the Papal Legates were to pronounce a verdict in favour of Henry on July 23rd. But when Campeggio appeared in court on that fateful day, it was only to adjourn the case and so shelve the issue. "By the Mass," cried Suffolk, as he smote the table a great blow with his hand, "now I see that the old said saw is true, that never a cardinal or legate did good in England!"[3] But the King gave no sign, and in August he left the court on a progress through the country, accompanied by Edward Fox as his Almoner and by Stephen Gardiner as his Secretary. Meanwhile, there had been an outbreak of plague which had driven Fellows and Scholars away from Cambridge as fast as they could fly. Cranmer had two pupils by the name of Cressy in his care, and he had taken them back to their father's home at Waltham. Thus it happened that when Henry lodged at Waltham, Fox and Gardiner were quartered in the Cressy household at the very time when Cranmer was also there. Fox was Provost of King's College while Gardiner was Master of Trinity Hall in Cambridge; they were both well known to Cranmer, and as fellow-guests in Cressy's home at Waltham, they would have much to share. The three Dons met at the dinner table and soon fell to conversation about the great Divorce problem. Cranmer declared that he had not made a study of the question, but he was in favour of an appeal to the Divines of Oxford and Cambridge. This was not so wide of the mark as we might think, for what other court of

---

[1] Cranmer, Vol. II, p. 327.   [2] Strype, Vol. I, p. 5.
[3] Pollard, p. 38; cp. Pollard, *Wolsey*, p. 234.

appeal apart from Rome in those days could hope to command respect? This he soon went on to explain in words full of common sense and sagacity: "There is but one truth in it, which the Scripture will soon declare, make open and manifest, being by learned men well handled, and that may be as well done in England in the Universities here as at Rome or elsewhere in any foreign nation."[1] A day or two later, when Fox told the King the gist of what had transpired in this conversation, Henry grasped its significance at once. "Marry," he said, "I will surely speak with him, and therefore let him be sent for out of hand. I perceive that that man hath the sow by the right ear."[2] This was the web into which the threads of Cranmer's life were henceforth to be woven.

Cranmer was far from anxious to mind or meddle in this matter, but the choice was not his to make. Henry at once required him to put his views in writing, and sent him to lodge with the Earl of Wiltshire until the task was complete. The Earl was the father of Anne Boleyn, so that Cranmer was brought into contact with the members of her house at a time of great significance. Was it not by his hand that the seed of truth was sown in her heart before ever she could come to the Throne? It was January 1530 before he could submit a full account of his findings, but the King had spoken of him as a "wonderfully virtuous and wise man" whose counsels had brought him great help and comfort.[3] Cranmer's thesis was then circulated among the leading Divines of Cambridge, and he was sent up to explain and enforce the argument. He was able to win over six or seven men of learning who had before opposed the King, but he had left Cambridge before the great vote was taken in the Senate. Henry had made up his mind that Cranmer should be attached to the Earl of Wiltshire, Stokesley, and Lee, who left England early in February as ambassadors to the Pope and to Charles V. When Oxford and Cambridge had given their verdict in his favour, Henry sent it after them to be laid before the Pope. The Royal Ambassadors were in no haste as they journeyed through France, but they did win favourable replies from the Universities of Paris, Orleans, Anjou, Bourges and Toulouse. They found the Pope towards the end of March at Bologna, but he had just crowned Charles V

[1] *John Foxe*, Vol. VIII, p. 7.   [2] Ibid., p. 7.   [3] Pollard, p. 41.

and would now do nothing to cause offence. Wiltshire and Lee retraced their steps through France in the early summer, Stokesley remained at Bologna, Cranmer went on to Venice, and the three Italian Universities of Bologna, Ferrara, and Padua pronounced in favour of Henry. In June, Cranmer offered to debate the issue in Rome itself, but his offer went without a welcome. He soon succumbed to the summer climate of Rome, and was quite ill for two weeks in July. Then he tried to secure a Papal brief for Henry, but he found that he was always choked off through fear of Charles. We would gladly know what Cranmer thought of Church life in Rome; there is just the barest hint in a speech which he made in 1534 and which refers to the various corruptions such as "himself had heard and seen at Rome".[1] But he left Rome in September to return to England with no tangible achievement other than the votes of the three Italian Universities.

Cranmer was thus home in England by the autumn months of 1530 and hoped no doubt to be allowed to take up his life at Cambridge once more. There he might have passed his days in freedom from care, reading, preaching, annotating, examining, leading a stainless life and knowing neither pain nor trouble. But that was not to be. He had no part in the intrigues which lay behind the Sessions of Convocation that year, for he was still quietly employed in a further probe of all the intricacies of the Great Cause. He was appointed the Archdeacon of Taunton and was in close touch with Henry until early in 1532, when he became Ambassador to the Court of Charles V in Germany. His task was to try to conciliate the Emperor, and in secret to sound out the German Princes with a view to a possible alliance with England. Cranmer's diplomatic abilities were of no mean order, and he amassed a huge fund of information. He spent some time with the Imperial Court at Ratisbon, but could make no vital progress with Charles. Then in July, he slipped away to Frederick of Saxony where he met and married a niece of the Lutheran Osiander, a bold step for one who was now in Priest's Orders and on the King's business. On his return to Ratisbon in September, he found that the Turkish menace to Hungary and Germany overshadowed all else, and he followed the march of the Imperial forces, first to Vienna, then to Villach. He learned

[1] Cranmer, Vol. II, p. 77.

much as to the real strength of Charles, and wrote vivid accounts of the desolation wrought by his troops from Spain and Italy. Some eight thousand of them, angry with Charles for his failure to press the war against the Turks, broke away in revolt, "spoiling and robbing all the countries of Austria, Stiria, and Carinthia, more than two hundredth English miles in length, as well churches as other houses, not leaving monstral nor the Sacrament. And the men of arms that come with the Emperor, and other that follow the court, do consume all that the other left in such sort that I, following two days after the Emperor from Vienna, found in no town that was unwalled man, woman, nor child, meat, drink nor bedding; but thanked be God, I found straw, hay, and corn for my horses to eat, and for myself and my servant to lie in; but the people were all fled into the mountains for fear."[1] So he wrote from Villach on October 20th, and part of the letter was in cypher, giving Henry valuable comments on the state of German affairs.

Cranmer crossed the Alps with Charles and got as far as Mantua when he was amazed by a summons to return to England for consecration as Archbishop of Canterbury. This high office had been vacant since the death of Warham in the month of August, and in normal times it might have remained vacant for months to come. There were others, such as Stokesley and Gardiner, who might have felt that the choice ought to have fallen on them rather than on Cranmer, and their relations with Cranmer were embittered for life by the pang of disappointed envy. But the summons brought no joy to Cranmer; he could only regard it as a stern duty to which he must submit. As a husband with strong family affections, he would fear separation from his wife; as a scholar with strong literary habits, he would dread separation from his books. And all for the sake of a most imperious master in the person of King Henry VIII! There is no need to doubt his plain statement that he delayed as long as he could in the hope that the King would change his mind. "There was never man came more unwillingly to a bishopric than I did to that," he said; "in so much that when King Henry did send for me in post that I should come over, I prolonged my journey by seven weeks at the least, thinking that he would be forgetful of

[1] Cranmer, Vol. II, p. 233.

me in the meantime."[1] But the King had found in Cranmer that sweet blend of learning, and virtue, and guileless fidelity, which so suited his plans; he had his own reason for the nomination, and he was quite resolved to have Cranmer consecrated without delay. Cranmer did not land in England until January 1533, but the King had asked the Pope to issue his bulls at once and without fee. Chapuys sent a secret envoy to warn the Pope against Cranmer, but the whip was in the King's hand. Henry let the Pope know that the Act of Annates which had passed the Commons during 1532 would at once be enforced if he delayed. The Pope did not delay: the bull was drawn up and the pall was despatched with remarkable celerity. But Cranmer was troubled by the oath of obedience to the Papal authority which was required of him before consecration: would it not mean conflict with the duty which he owed to the Crown? He sought legal advice and then declared that he would take the oath as a form which had no reality in law; he would not bind himself to do anything contrary to his king or country, or to refrain from the reformation of the Church of England. Most men would have scorned the scruple, and it was to provide his foes with a splendid forensic argument at the end of his life. "He made a protestation one day," they said, "to keep never a whit of that which he would swear the next day."[2] But it was the only safeguard which a man of tender conscience could have taken. Thus the declaration was made, and the oath sworn; and then, on March 30th, 1533, he was duly consecrated as Archbishop of Canterbury.

Cranmer assumed his new duties at a time when the Royal Supremacy filled all men's minds, and he knew that he was required to be no more than "the principal minister of our spiritual jurisdiction".[3] There were stormy years ahead of Cranmer, and the storm burst at once with his verdict on the Divorce question. Cranmer opened his court in May at Dunstable to try the question between the King and Catherine. The Queen denied his right to try the case, would not appear, and made appeal direct to Rome, though no appeal beyond the Realm was now lawful. On May 23rd, Cranmer pronounced the King's marriage to have been void from the outset, on the ground that the Pope did not possess the powers of dispensation which had

[1] Cranmer, Vol. II, p. 216.   [2] *John Foxe*, Vol. VIII, p. 55.   [3] Pollard, p. 74.

been alleged. On June 1st, Cranmer crowned Anne Boleyn in the Abbey, though not even he knew the date of the marriage.[1] Then on July 11th, the Pope prepared bulls of excommunication against Henry, who in reply recalled his Ambassadors, confirmed the Act of Annates, and appealed from the Pope to a General Council. In March 1534, the Right of Succession to the Crown was vested by law in the children born to Henry by Anne Boleyn, and it fell to Cranmer to act at the head of those who were to impose the oath. When Sir Thomas More and Bishop Fisher refused to take the oath in the form in which they heard it proposed, Cranmer tried to persuade Cromwell to let them take it in a form to which they would agree. "If they do obstinately persist in their opinions of the preamble, yet meseemeth it should not be refused if they will be sworn to the very act of succession. . . . And peradventure it should be a good quietation to many other within this realm, if such men should say that the succession, comprised within the said act, is good and according to God's laws: for then I think there is not one within this realm that would once reclaim against it."[2] But the King would not hear of it: he would have no "swearing by halves".[3] Cranmer's plea for leniency failed to save them from confiscation and imprisonment; and he had no part in their subsequent execution on the charge of treason. But the death of More and Fisher aggravated the whole debate as to whether the Pope had any more authority in England than any other foreign bishop, and the whole weight of this quarrel was laid on the shoulders of the Primate. He stood alone against a whole army of monks and other Divines, and met them so firmly from the Scriptures that in November 1534, the Act was passed which laid it down that the King's Majesty "justly and rightfully is and ought to be the Supreme Head of the Church of England".[4]

The Royal Supremacy was the battle-ground throughout the reign of Henry VIII where the two great parties struggled for the direction of English Church policy. Cranmer tried to use it for the reformation of national religion, while Gardiner tried to use it for the extirpation of Lutheran heresy. The King held the balance between the two parties, and he moved from side to side as

[1] Cranmer, Vol II. 246.
[2] Ibid., p. 286.
[3] Strype, Vol. I, p. 59.
[4] Pollard, p. 82.

private or political need might dictate. The Church was to retain its old constitution almost unchanged, except that the King had taken the place of the Pope as supreme; but the form and intent of its formularies were to emerge from the struggle in a profoundly modified spirit through the work of Cranmer. His heart was set on the restoration of a knowledge of the Scriptures among both laymen and clergy; but the goal which he had in view at first was a change in conduct rather than a change of doctrine. He was always on the side of mercy in the case of those who differed from him, and his intervention on behalf of others was a notable element in his career. Thus in 1533, the King was so enraged with the Princess Mary who would neither recognise her mother's divorce nor relinquish her own title that he was on the point of sending her to the Tower to suffer as a subject. But Cranmer felt impelled to plead for her when no other lord or bishop dared to risk the wrath of the King; and he prevailed, although the King told him that it "would be to his utter confusion at the length".[1] In December 1533, he instituted a visitation of the Diocese of Canterbury, and in 1534, he authorised his Commissary to visit the Diocese of Norwich. Then as Metropolitan, he embarked on a visitation of the Southern Province, and was upheld by the King when he met with resistance from Stokesley and Gardiner whose personal jealousies were enflamed. He issued a pastoral to enjoin silence on subjects such as Masses for the dead, prayers to saints, pilgrimages and clerical celibacy, and he induced Convocation to present an appeal for an authorised translation of the Scriptures. But his episcopal jurisdiction was in suspense during the year 1535, while the Visitation of the Monasteries took place under the guidance of Cromwell. Cranmer thus had no part in their Dissolution, but he had no relish for the way in which their estates were farmed out to grasping lords and laymen. He was keenly disappointed in his hope that "from these ruins there would be new foundations in every Cathedral (as) nurseries of learning for the use of the whole Diocese".[2]

The year 1536 was a memorable one for Cranmer and the Reformation, a year in which human tragedy and famous documents both took the stage. It was the year which saw the

---

[1] Strype, Vol. III, p. 363. [2] Ibid., Vol. I, p. 73.

fall of Anne Boleyn, and Cranmer was incredibly shocked by this sad event. "I am in such a perplexity that my mind is clean amazed," he told the King; "for I never had better opinion in woman than I had in her. . . . I think that Your Grace best knoweth that next unto Your Grace I was most bound unto her of all creatures living."[1] He ventured to express the hope that she would yet be found "inculpable and innocent", and he even dared to remind the King that his own life was not without blame before God. Cranmer was the only man who had the courage to speak on her behalf, but she was found guilty and was sent to the block in May. Meanwhile, in the month of February, Cranmer had preached for two hours at Paul's Cross and had strongly attacked the whole idea that the Pope could release souls from durance in a supposed purgatory.[2] Then in March and April, there were daily meetings between Cranmer and the other Prelates, which in due course was to bring about the first definition of the faith under the Royal Supremacy. The whole matter reached a deadlock between the two Houses of Convocation in June, with the result that Henry took the case into his own hands. He penned a new set of Articles, which were then revised by Cranmer and subscribed by Convocation in July. The Ten Articles, five of which dealt with faith and five with ceremonies, were a general compromise between the old and the new. But they disowned the whole system of Indulgence, and the Article on the Eucharist went no further than a statement as to the Real Presence. This was the first historic document in the progress of the English Reformation, and it was a reasonable embodiment of practical rather than doctrinal reform. The sun of truth was still slowly rising, but had as yet only begun to break through the mists of ignorance and idolatry. But the revolt known as the Pilgrimage of Grace in the autumn saw an attack upon Cranmer as the patron of heretics and the author of Catherine's Divorce: this was symptomatic of the forces in the country at large who were opposed to change, and who would have been glad to see Cranmer in prison or exile. But the *Institution of The Christian Man*, commonly known as The Bishops' Book, which was published in the new year as a kind of commentary on the Ten Articles, reaffirmed their statement of doctrine in all respects,

---

[1] Cranmer, Vol. II, p. 324.   [2] Pollard, pp. 101, 102.

except that it allowed for the validity of the Seven Sacraments. Cranmer was glad to leave London as soon as The Bishops' Book was finished, for the plague broke out in July. "They die almost everywhere in London," he told Cromwell, "and in Lambeth, they die at my gate."[1] But the time had now come for which Cranmer had prayed ever since his Consecration, and which was to bring him "as much joy as ever happened to him in all the time of his Prelacy".[2]

Cromwell had issued a series of Injunctions in connection with the Articles, and they were now to bear a rich reward. The Seventh Injunction required every parish priest to get a copy of the Bible in English and Latin before August 1537, "and lay the same in the quire for every man to read . . . as being the Word of God."[3] For this purpose, the King's consent had been secured for the sale of Coverdale's Translation which had just been published. But the Coverdale Translation was by no means perfect, having been made from the Vulgate or from Luther's German Translation. Thus when Matthew's Bible was placed in the hands of Cranmer late in July or early in August 1537, he could hardly tell his delight. This was the work of John Rogers as literary trustee for William Tyndale; it was in fact Tyndale's version of the Scriptures as far as he had been able to carry out the task. The Old Testament in Matthew's Bible represents Tyndale's version as far as the Second Book of Chronicles, and Coverdale's version from that point on to the Book of Malachi; the New Testament was the work of Tyndale, but with the omission of all his marginal comments. On August 4th, Cranmer wrote to Cromwell and sent him a copy of this version, which he declared was more to his liking "than any other translation heretofore made"; and he begged him to get the King's licence to have it sold and read by all, "until such time that we the bishops shall set forth a better translation, which I think will not be till a day after doomsday."[4] The King's consent was soon obtained, and he could not hide his joy when he wrote again nine days later: "My Lord, for this your pain taken in this behalf, I give unto you my most hearty thanks: assuring your Lordship, for the contentation of my mind, you have shewed me more

[1] Cranmer, Vol. II, p. 338.
[2] Strype, Vol. I, p. 125.
[3] Ibid., p. 119, n.
[4] Cranmer, Vol. II, p. 344.

pleasure herein than if you had given me a thousand pound: and I doubt not but that hereby such fruit of good knowledge shall ensue that it shall well appear hereafter what high and acceptable service you have done unto God and the King."[1] In 1539, a new edition of this Bible, revised by Coverdale, supervised by Bonner, was brought out in Paris. It soon became known on account of its size as the The Great Bible, and by Injunction, every church was required to provide itself with a copy of this Bible within twelve months. Thus was Tyndale's prayer at the hour of death honoured by God, and under God, this was by the hand of Cranmer. Cromwell and Henry each had a part to play, but he was the prime mover, and his motive was the simple desire to secure the widest reading of this Book as the Word of God. Cranmer's preface made the editions of 1540 and 1541 known as Cranmer's Bible. "Wherefore," he wrote, "I would advise you all that cometh to the reading or hearing of this Book, which is the Word of God, the most precious jewel and most holy relic that remaineth upon earth, that ye bring with you the fear of God, and that ye do it with all due reverence, and use your knowledge thereof, not to vainglory of frivolous disputation, but to the honour of God, increase of virtue, and edification both of your-selves and other."[2]

Cranmer had forged many close links with the German Divines during his mission in 1532, and he had kept up a frequent corre-spondence with them from his home at Lambeth Palace.[3] They knew that no other English Prelate stood so close to them in theology, and they rightly set high value on his friendship in the cause of Reform. Thus in 1536, Martin Bucer had dedicated his *Commentary on Romans* to Cranmer, and, in 1538, Cranmer was the chief friend of the Protestant delegates who had come to wait on Henry VIII. The trend of his own mind was made clear in 1538 when he proposed that the Blood of St. Thomas in the Cathedral at Canterbury should be examined to see whether it were not "a feigned thing, made of some red ochre or of such like matter".[4] But he still clung to old doctrine in so many details that he was in no sense wholly Lutheran, any more than he was wholly Catholic. Thus he had set his face against Divorce and

[1] Cranmer, Vol. II, pp. 345, 346. [2] Ibid., p. 122.
[3] Strype, Vol. II, p. 396. [4] Cranmer, Vol. II, p. 378.

lax views of marriage just as firmly in the case of Lutheran compromise as in that of Papal Dispensation, and he wrote to Osiander in such strong terms on the Lutheran attitude to such a marriage as that of Philip of Hesse that no one can dispute his own line of independent thought and judgment.[1] Then too, although he was loath to share in acts of persecution, he still believed that as a last resort, extreme measures should be taken in the case of obstinate heretics, and in 1538, however reluctant he may have felt, he was compelled to join in the trial and condemnation of John Lambert. He was as yet only threading his way through the darkness, moving slowly towards the light of a new day. But he was to suffer a rude shock in 1539 when the pall of darkness seemed to thicken more than ever. A Committee of Lords had been appointed at the King's wish to draw up a uniform standard of faith, but the Lords could reach no agreement. After ten days' debate, Norfolk brought the matter before the House of Lords itself, and the King came down to confound them all with his learning. Cranmer would not yield even to the King's learning, holding that the cause was not his, but God's, and he was so intractable in his opposition that the King at last made him leave the House while the Statute of the Six Articles passed into law. Ten years later, Cranmer affirmed that the Act would never have been passed had not the King come down in person: but that was a statement which may only prove how far Cranmer had failed to measure the strength of the forces that were opposed to him.[2] But the King was too wise to ask Cranmer to make any alteration in his private viewpoint, or to crack the whip with its six bloody strings against those who might offend. Thus he remained at his post while men like Latimer and Shaxton retired from their Sees, and it was largely owing to him that the savage penalties were not enforced.[3]

After the marriage of Henry to Anne of Cleves during the first week of 1540, there was growing tension in high places between men of the Old Learning and the friends of the New. But the tension ended when the King struck, and struck against Cromwell with the ruthless ease of a beast of prey. In June, he was accused of treason, stripped of the Garter, and consigned to the

[1] Cranmer, Vol. II, pp. 404:408. [2] Ibid., p. 168.
[3] Pollard, *Henry VIII*, p. 401, n.

Tower. Cranmer at once wrote to Henry, and the only voice that was raised to ask for mercy was the voice of the man who had asked mercy for Anne Boleyn. "He that was such a servant, in my judgment, in wisdom, diligence, faithfulness and experience, as no prince in this realm ever had. . . . I loved him as my friend, for so I took him to be; but I chiefly loved him for the love which I thought I saw him bear ever towards Your Grace singularly above all other."[1] He was condemned unheard, and, in July, he laid his head on the block at Tower Hill. Henry then took measures to secure his divorce from Anne of Cleves; but though Cranmer had to subscribe to the dissolution of the marriage, he had no share in the steps which brought it to pass. It was Gardiner, not Cranmer, who explained the decree of invalidity in a lucid speech to Convocation; it was Gardiner, not Cranmer, who arranged for the King to meet the niece of Norfolk beneath his roof. On July 9th, Convocation declared that the marriage with Anne was null and void; on August 8th, Henry was married in private to Catherine Howard at Oatlands. This meant that the star of Norfolk and Gardiner was now in the ascendant, and the triumph of the men of the Old Learning was even more pronounced by the burning of the preachers Jerome, Garret, and Barnes two days after Cromwell's execution. Cranmer had now to stand alone, the one Prelate whose heart was in favour of the Reformation, and there were as many hands stretched out to seek his ruin as there had been in the case of Cromwell. He had his foes at Court, within the House of Lords, on the Bench of Bishops, among the Squires of Kent, within the precincts of Canterbury, even within the walls of his palace.[2] "And trial was made many ways to bring him to his death, or at least to bring him in disgrace with the King."[3]

It was, in fact, a common saying that Gardiner had "bent his bow to shoot at some of the head deer"[4]: and there is no doubt that his hand was deep in what was called the Plot of the Prebendaries. In April 1542, the Chapter of Canterbury was reconstituted by Royal Charter, so that twelve new Prebends had to be filled. Cranmer's fortune was then in the shadows, and the only friend of Reform among the new Prebendaries was Nicholas

[1] Cranmer, Vol. II, p. 401.   [2] Pollard, p. 144.
[3] Strype, Vol. I, p. 171.   [4] Ibid., p. 244.

Ridley. Gardiner soon found openings to foster an intrigue among the Squires of Kent, and the Prebendaries' Plot was quietly built up against Cranmer. The Plot ripened in March 1543, when two of the Kentish clergy rode to London with a list of charges against Cranmer, and in May, the Privy Council resolved to ask the King to send special commissioners into Kent in order to deal with the accusations. It was thought that Cranmer could be shouldered aside, and that Gardiner could be placed at the head of the Commission. And if such a body of men had been given a free hand in Kent with Henry's authority, it would indoubtedly have fared ill with Cranmer and the cause of Reform. But no master ever had more penetrating insight into the minds of his servants, or less liking for the thought of being made the tool of others.[1] Henry kept his thoughts to himself, until he had to row down the Thames past Lambeth Palace. Cranmer heard the music on the royal barge and came down to the steps as a mark of respect. Henry at once haled him on board so that they could talk in private awhile. "I have news out of Kent for you, my Lord," Henry began; ". . . I now know the greatest heretic in Kent."[2] Then he plucked from his sleeve a series of charges against Cranmer and his preachers signed by certain Kentish Squires and the Prebendaries of his own Cathedral. Cranmer promptly asked for the appointment of a Commission of Inquiry, and the King placed the whole matter in his own hands. Cranmer demurred, as he was the person accused, but the King would take no excuse. "I will have none other but yourself, and such as you will appoint," he said; "for I am sure that you will not halt with me in any thing, although you be driven to accuse yourself."[3] Nothing could shake Henry's trust in Cranmer, and he was determined to sift the whole conspiracy. Cranmer chose as his assessors his Chancellor and Registrar, each of whom had been in the plot, and the result was that six weeks passed by without progress. Henry then summoned Sir Thomas Leigh from York to lay bare the plot, and it was soon exposed. But most of those concerned were allowed to escape with professions of penitence, as when Cranmer faced two of his supposed friends with their own letters: they fell on their knees to crave his pardon, and he forgave them and sent them away "with gentle

[1] Pollard, p. 151.   [2] *John Foxe*, Vol. VIII, p. 28.   [3] Ibid., p. 28.

and comfortable words, in such sort that never after appeared in his countenance or words any remembrance thereof".[1]

Other attempts were made to bring about Cranmer's downfall; the most formidable was the plot which has been woven by Shakespeare into his *Henry VIII*. Certain members of the Privy Council asked the King to commit Cranmer to the Tower on the ground that no one would dare to witness against one in such high office unless he were in durance. Henry agreed that their request should be carried out the next day, but at eleven o'clock that night he sent for Cranmer and told him just what had occurred. Cranmer thanked the King and declared that he would be content to go into durance for the sake of a fair hearing. "O Lord God," cried the King, "what fond simplicity have you, so to permit yourself to be imprisoned that every enemy of yours may take advantage against you! Do not you know that when they have you once in prison, three or four false knaves will soon be procured to witness against you and condemn you; which else, now being at liberty, dare not once open their lips or appear before your face? No, not so my Lord: I have better regard unto you than to permit your enemies so to overthrow you."[2] Henry then told him just how to conduct himself on the morrow. He was to come to the Council but was to ask to be brought face to face with those who had accusations to lay; should the Council refuse, and proceed to commit him to the Tower, he was to appeal direct to the Throne. Henry then gave him a ring: "which ring," he said, "they well know that I use it for no other purpose but to call matters from the Council into mine own hands."[3] By eight o'clock the next morning, Cranmer had his summons to appear before the Council, but he was forced to stand outside the door among the servants and lackeys for half an hour. The King was most incensed when he was told of this. "Have they served my Lord so?" he exclaimed; "it is well enough; I shall talk with them by and bye."[4] Cranmer was at length called inside, and he was told that it was the King's will to commit him to the Tower for trial. He was bluntly rebuffed when he asked to be faced with his accusers, and so perforce made his appeal over their heads. "I am sorry my Lords that you drive

[1] *John Foxe*, Vol. VIII, p. 30.   [2] Strype, Vol. I, pp. 273, 274.
[3] Ibid., p. 274.   [4] Ibid., p. 275.

me unto this exigent, to appeal from you to the King's Majesty; who by this token hath resumed this matter into his own hand, and dischargeth you thereof."[1] When he produced the ring, Russel swore a great oath and said that they might have known that Henry would not permit him to go to prison. The Lords at once repaired to the King who rated them most soundly. "I would you should well understand," he said, "that I account my Lord of Canterbury as faithful a man towards me as ever was prelate in this realm, and one to whom I am many ways beholden by the faith I owe unto God; and therefore who loveth me will upon that account regard him."[2] "This was the last push of the pike that was inferred against (him) in King Henry the Eighth's days," wrote Foxe; "for never after durst any man move matter against him in his time."[3]

Henry's last years imposed many new tasks upon Cranmer's skill and patience, and he was in regular attendance at the Privy Council to the close of the reign. In 1541, while Henry was absent in the north of England, Cranmer's name stood first on the list of those who were responsible for affairs in London; in 1544, while Henry was away in France, Cranmer's name stood first on the list of those who were appointed to the Council of Regency. In November 1541, he was implored by the Council to do what no other man was willing to do, to lay before Henry news and proof of Catherine's misconduct. Meanwhile, Cranmer never ceased to feel the strongest concern for the needs of his own See of Canterbury, and he spared no trouble during these years in the pastoral oversight of clergy and people. He would often preach in the main towns of the See as well as in Canterbury itself, and he refused to rest until he had secured men of learning and of ability to make the truth known in Kent.[4] He had an eye to the future in the cause of Reform, and there were some minor issues in which he won his way. In 1541, he secured the abrogation of certain holy days, and the demolition of certain shrines and relics. In 1542, he was able to defeat Gardiner's plan to revise the English Bible in favour of the Old Learning, and in 1543, he was able to frustrate Gardiner's plan to secure legal recognition for the many forms of worship which were in vogue. But this was all that he

[1] Strype, Vol. I, p. 275.   [2] Ibid., p. 276.
[3] *John Foxe*, Vol. VIII, p. 31.   [4] Strype, Vol. III, p. 379.

could do, for there were still hostile forces at work in high places. This was made clear in the preparation of *The Erudition of The Christian Man*, commonly known as The King's Book, which came out in 1543. The King's Book stood in the same relation to the Six Articles as The Bishops' Book to the Ten Articles, but it did not reach its final form without a struggle. There still exists a most interesting copy of The Bishops' Book with frequent emendations in Henry's hand; Cranmer's comments in reply have also survived. A quiet study of these comments proves that Cranmer seldom agreed with his master and had no qualms in so saying. He said that some of the Royal phrases "obscured the meaning", or were "superfluous"; some were "not grammar", and others were "better out".[1] But The King's Book came out at length despite Cranmer, and it avowed both Transubstantiation and Clerical Celibacy. Thus it is no surprise to learn that when Cranmer in 1545 tried to obtain the King's consent for the demolition of roods, and the abolition of rites such as creeping to the cross or the custom of bell-ringing on All Hallow's Eve, Henry refused.

Meanwhile, his great stores of learning were employed with untiring industry in the preparation of plans which he believed would yet come to maturity. He drew up two schemes for a Church Service which were to prove useful as the basis of the First Book of Common Prayer, and he published certain Occasional Prayers by authority in the language of the people which were to pave the way for an English Service. In 1543, he brought the Book of Homilies before Convocation, and, in 1544, he placed a new draft of Canon Law in the King's hand. These two measures were still before their time; but his work in another direction was about to produce the first great masterpiece of Prayer Book craftsmanship. Henry had more than once ordered the use of a Latin Litany for some special occasion, and had complained that the people had come "very slackly to the procession" because the prayers were in Latin.[2] But in October 1543,[3] Cranmer informed the King that he was now engaged in the translation of some Latin suffrages, and that he was obliged to use a good deal of freedom as the Latin sources were so barren. There were additions; there were omissions; there were many partial alterations;

[1] Cranmer, Vol. II, pp. 83:117.   [2] Ibid., p. 494.   [3] Ibid., p. 412 f.n.

and the whole was cast in a prose that was alive with the music of reverence and devotion. Cranmer wished to have it sung or chanted on some devout or solemn note : " but in mine opinion, the song that shall be made thereunto would not be full of notes, but as near as may be, for every syllable a note ; so that it may be sung distinctly and devoutly".[1] In May 1544, this English Litany appeared in print, and in June it received the King's authority. Wriothesley's Chronicle declared that it was " the godliest hearing that ever was in this realm",[2] and it ran through five editions before the end of 1544. It then formed part of the Primer which was published by the King's Majesty in 1545, and which at once displaced all other Primers in use throughout the realm. It was Cranmer's first great liturgical triumph, and it had taught him to hammer out the rules which were to guide all his later compositions. He made use of older materials, but he wrought them into a new and much finer form of Service. He clothed the old Latin suffrage and its sober rhythm in the purest form of English writing, and the music of his prose lent itself to the deepest strains of awe and pathos that human hearts can ever feel. This is why it has stood the test of time better, perhaps, than any other part of our Prayer Book ; men have always found in it an unsurpassed medium for the expression of their deepest needs and highest aspirations.

Henry VIII, that most surprising Sovereign, imperious, implacable, always at home in the world of music or letters, equal to any trial of strength in the lists or with the hounds, shrewd judge and born master of men and their affairs, was true friend to Cranmer to the close of his reign. Other men might rise and fall with drastic finality ; we can still see shadows across the stage of time at the names of Wolsey, Fisher, Sir Thomas More, Anne Boleyn, Cromwell, the Duke of Norfolk. There was one man, and one alone, towards whom the King's heart never seemed to vary ; and that man was Thomas Cranmer. Henry's clear and penetrating eye saw in him one whose strength and weakness were the opposite of his own, and he knew that he might search his realm in vain for one who combined the same guileless spirit with such stores of learning. There was no trace in him of the self-seeking ambition of prelates and statesmen like Wolsey and

[1] Cranmer, Vol. II, p. 412.   [2] Pollard, p. 173.

Cromwell; there was no man of the time who could have carried out his duties as Primate of England half so well in years of turmoil, not Tunstall, nor Stokesley, nor Gardiner. He took no part in the scramble for wealth or the struggle for power on the Dissolution of the Monasteries, and he paid no regard to the safety even of his own head when he had friend or foe for whom to plead. It may have been "a strange freak of fancy",[1] but a sincere friendship, deep and almost tender in tone, grew up between the King and the gentle scholar. Henry loved him for his simplicity and disregard of self, and "there could neither Councillor, Bishop, nor Papist, win him out of the King's favour".[2] The King's goodwill for him was the envy of friends and the despair of those who sought his fall. "You, my Lord, were born in an happy hour I suppose," said Cromwell, "for do or say what you will, the King will always take it well at your hands. . . . He will never give credit against you, whatsoever is laid to your charge. But let me or any other of the Council be complained of, His Grace will most seriously chide and fall out with us; and therefore you are most happy if you can keep you in this state."[3] When at length the King came to the borders of death, it was Cranmer whom of all his Chaplains he most desired to see. His strength was fast ebbing away on the night of January 27th, 1547, when he sent for Cranmer to come late at night from Croydon. The King could no longer speak when Cranmer arrived, but in response to his words of comfort and his appeal for some token of his trust in the Lord, Henry wrung the hand that held his own in its clasp. "The last support of which he was conscious on earth was the hand of the man whose only support he himself had been in the time of trouble."[4] What would befall Cranmer, the King had once queried, when he was gone? Cranmer had no answer for that question; but he who had been clean-shaven henceforth let his beard grow until his own death as a mark of sorrow at the King's passing.

"Good Lord," wrote Cranmer in later life, "remember not mine ignorances and offences of my youth!"[5] At Cambridge and Lambeth alike, he spared no pains to make himself a ripe scholar

[1] Innes, p. 96.   [2] *John Foxe*, Vol. VIII, p. 24.
[3] Strype, Vol. I, pp. 166, 167.   [4] Pollard, p. 183.
[5] Cranmer, Vol. I, p. 374.

with an exact knowledge of his subject. While at Cambridge, "he read the old writers, so as he despised not the new: and all this while . . . he was a slow reader, but an earnest marker. He never came to any writer's book without pen and ink. . . . He gathered every author's sentence briefly . . . into common places which he had prepared for that purpose; or else if the matter were too long to write out, he noted the place of the author and the number of the leaf, whereby he might have the more help for his memory."[1] Morice tells us that the Archbishop "commonly if he had not business of the prince's or special urgent causes before him, spent three parts of the day in study as effectually as if he had been at Cambridge".[2] Foxe says that he often rose at two or three in the morning and gave almost as much of the night to study as to sleep.[3] But his normal routine was to be at his book by five in the morning and to pass the time in prayer and study until the hour of nine o'clock. He then applied himself to the affairs of Church and State, and would receive friends or suitors until dinner was laid. He would perhaps play chess for an hour after dinner, and would then return to his study. Cranmer always stood at a desk rather than sat at a table, and he thought it no loss to spend "one hour or twain of the day in reading over such works and books as daily came from beyond the seas".[4] At five o'clock, Common Prayer would be read; then he would walk until supper. He was very abstemious, and would often sit at table, not to sup as others, but to regale them with cheerful conversation. He would again walk for an hour at least and then retire to his study until his day came to a close as nine o'clock rang out its chimes. Cranmer's commonplace books, mostly written out by Morice but with marginal additions in his own hand, are now in the British Museum, although six or seven volumes at least which were in the hands of one John Herd in 1563 have now been lost. This system of study undoubtedly helped him to gain a most valuable foothold in royal counsels. "For at all times when the King's Majesty would be resolved in any doubt or question, he would but send word to my Lord overnight, and by the next day the King should have in writing brief notes of the doctors' minds, as well divines as lawyers, both old

[1] *John Foxe*, Vol. VIII, p. 4.   [2] Pollard, p. 317.
[3] *John Foxe*, Vol. VIII, p. 41.   [4] Ibid., p. 13.

and new, with a conclusion of his own mind; which he could never get in such a readiness of none, no, not of all his chaplains and clergy about him, in so short a time. For being thoroughly seen in all kinds of expositors, he could incontinently lay open thirty, forty, sixty, or more somewhiles of authors, and so, reducing the notes of them altogether, would advise the King more in one day than all his learned men could do in a month."[1]

On February 20th, 1547, Cranmer placed the crown on Edward VI in the Abbey, and the door for his long-cherished plans of reform began to swing open. He had welcomed the appointment of Somerset as Protector during the King's minority, for there was no statesman since the death of Cromwell with whom he felt in more accord. His Coronation Sermon had contained a real declaration of war against image worship, and his next step was to publish the *Book of Homilies* for which he had himself composed the Sermons on Salvation, Faith, and Good Works. Then he helped to promote an Act both in Convocation and Parliament in November, which not only repealed the Six Articles of Henry VIII, but all other heresy laws since Richard II. He secured the passage of a bill to authorise Communion in both kinds, so that it only remained for the Bishops to draw up a form of Service for the new rite. This new Order of Communion came out in March 1548 in time for the Easter worship; but it was a very cautious form of Service. It was meant to open the door to the new way of worship, while it did not shut it in the face of the old. Thus the Prayers of Consecration for the Bread and Wine were still in Latin, while some other parts of the Service were framed in English. But the publication of this Office threw light on the growing necessity for an adequate revision of the many Service Books which were still in use throughout England. Cranmer had spent many hours in private on the task of liturgical reform, and it was his intent to mould the old forms of Service into one Book of Common Prayer for all England. He had employed the Breviary of Cardinal Quignon and the Sarum Use in the drafts which he had drawn up in the last years of Henry VIII, and these two drafts were laid before Convocation for the first time in the year of Edward's accession. But it was not until late in 1548 that further measures were taken,

[1] Pollard, pp. 317, 318.

and these marked a huge stride forward from the drafts which Convocation had seen. It is thought that certain Bishops met at Windsor and at Chertsey Abbey in September and October, and that Cranmer laid before them a draft of what was to become the First Book of Common Prayer. This draft was the work of Cranmer, and the Bishops were asked not so much to amend as to approve his work. It was meant to exclude any thought of the Real Presence as well as of Transubstantiation, and there was to be neither Elevation nor Reservation of Bread or Wine. Bonner indeed said that there was "heresy in the book", because the Bread and Wine were still called Bread and Wine after consecration. But Day was the only prelate who refused his consent, and no alteration was made until the book was brought under severe cross-fire in both Commons and Lords.[1]

When this debate took place in the Commons in December 1548, there was conservative opposition to the spirit of change; but in the House of Lords, Cranmer and Ridley argued so ably that the Commoner Traheron said that "Truth never obtained a more brilliant victory".[2] John ab Ulmis said that Cranmer "by the weight of his character and the dignity of his language" had won over many of his hearers.[3] Peter Martyr wrote to Martin Bucer and said: "The palm rests with our friends, but especially with the Archbishop of Canterbury, whom they till now were wont to traduce as a man ignorant of theology, and as being only conversant with matters of government; but now, believe me, he has shewn himself so mighty a theologian against them as they would rather not have proof of, and they are compelled against their inclination to acknowledge his learning and power and dexterity in debate."[4] Cranmer's language in the debate clearly proves that the only Presence in which he now believed was a spiritual presence of Christ in the hearts of His true people by faith. The Real Presence was in fact the great point round which the whole debate revolved; but the result was not entirely decisive. Four more weeks were still to elapse before the Act of Uniformity passed the House of Lords in January 1549, and that allowed enough time to tone down Cranmer's Book so as to secure a majority of episcopal votes in the House. This Act

[1] Pollard, pp. 214, 215. [2] *Original Letters*, Vol. I, p. 323.
[3] Ibid., Vol. II, p. 388. [4] Ibid., pp. 469, 470.

imposed the first Book of Common Prayer on both Church and Realm. But the final form of this book was a disappointment to the leaders of the Reformation, for it had the defects of a tentative compromise between the two parties. It was hardly more than daybreak compared with the full light of the sun which was soon to rise, and it did not secure a real doctrinal settlement of the points at issue; but it marked the coming of dawn after the long night which had gone before, and it was a manual of true devotion. Cranmer had aimed at a Book of Prayer which would be plain and comprehensive, which would be true to the test of simplicity and the teaching of the Scriptures. It was to be Common Prayer, and therefore in the language of the common people, unlike the Latin prayers which had been so meaningless. He would retain all that had been hallowed by the worship of the ages if it bore these hall-marks, while he refused all that was marred by the superstitions or false teaching of the Schoolmen. He would borrow from rites both old and new, Greek and Mozarabic; and what was so borrowed, he would adapt and adorn. Under his hand, the most simple of prayers, rude in form and spirit, were touched with a beauty of thought and style which won men's hearts for ever. "That the English Church survived was due in no small measure to the exquisite charm of her Liturgy"; it gave her a strength and sense of fellowship such as no other Church could boast: "and that was the work of Cranmer."[1]

One great idea which took hold of his mind during these years was to convene a Synod of Divines whose learning and ability would offset the reputation of the Fathers of Trent. He had corresponded for years with the Lutheran Osiander and the Zwinglian Vadianus, and he was well abreast of the trend of Continental thought and theology. Thus in 1548, he was urging John à Lasco and Martin Bucer and Philip Melancthon to visit and reside in England.[2] And in 1552, he wrote to John Calvin and Melancthon and Bullinger to urge that a Council of "the most learned and excellent persons" should be convened "in England or elsewhere . . . in which provision might be made for the purity of ecclesiastical doctrine, and especially for agreement on the Sacramentarian controversy".[3] Calvin's reply was that he would not grudge a journey across the sea for such a purpose,

[1] Pollard, p. 223.　　[2] Cranmer, Vol. II, pp. 420:428.　　[3] Ibid., p. 431.

if there were need; that if it were only to serve the great cause in England, that were reason enough: yet in view of his own weakness, he hoped that he might be allowed to do his part at a distance by his prayers and counsels.[1] That Council was never convened; but the troubles which had broken out on German terrain in 1547 drove many of her leading theologians to seek safety across the sea. Cranmer gladly made them welcome in his spacious home at Lambeth and sought ways in which to use their talents in the service of the English Reformation. In 1547, Peter Martyr, and Tremellius, and Bernardino Ochino, arrived in England; in 1548, John à Lasco, and Martin Bucer, and Paul Fagius, crossed the Channel. There were others like Utenhove of Ghent, and Dryander from Spain; Micronius from Switzerland, and Valerandus from the Netherlands; Alexander of Arles, and Véron from France. And no foreign Divine of note came to England and failed to find lodging beneath his roof until he was otherwise established. In 1549, Peter Martyr became Regius Professor at Oxford, and Martin Bucer at Cambridge; Fagius and Tremellius became Readers in Hebrew at Cambridge. Ochino was given a Prebend at Canterbury, and Alexander of Arles was employed as Cranmer's secretary; John à Lasco took charge of a foreign congregation in London, and Utenhove of the Flemish weavers at Glastonbury. The deaths of Fagius in 1549 and Bucer in 1552 were a great sorrow to Cranmer, who had charged them to work out "a clear, plain, and succinct interpretation of the Scripture according to the propriety of the language".[2] Bucer, Martyr and à Lasco were the three whose contribution to the English Reformation was most direct and whose friendship with the Primate was most fruitful. Reformation thought had also been brought home to England by men like John Knox, who had come from Calvin's school at Geneva, and John Hooper, who had come from Bullinger's school at Zurich; and there were yet others, who had now come home from abroad, such as Rogers and Coverdale, and they were marked out by Cranmer's advice for high office for the sake of Reform.

Cranmer himself was not a man in whose life an absorbing devotion to pure theology played so large a part as was the case with men like Luther, Zwingli, and John Calvin. And yet he was

[1] *Original Letters*, Vol. II, pp. 711:714.　　　　[2] Strype, Vol. II, p. 149.

one of the most able theologians of his age in Europe as well as in England, "a man," declared John ab Ulmis, "of singular worth and learning."[1] His friends at home and the foreign Divines whom he received, his antagonists, his controversies, his commonplace books, and his library all bear witness to his stores of learning. Strype says that his library was a store-house for the theology of the ages, open for the use of scholars from all quarters.[2] His books were soon dispersed after his death, but three hundred and fifty books and a hundred manuscripts have since been traced and are mainly housed now in the British Museum. His library was more extensive and more valuable than that of Cambridge itself in his own day as a student. Roger Ascham said that among his books, there were "many authors which the two Universities could not furnish".[3] He had to beg Poynet, Cranmer's chaplain, to lend him a copy of the Greek text of Gregory Nyssen which could only be obtained elsewhere in Latin.[4] "There were two Hebrew Bibles, and one of them is interleaved with a Latin translation made by Cranmer with his own hand. There was an almost complete set of the Greek and Latin Fathers, and the best of the mediaeval Schoolmen."[5] He was at home in the works of men like Erasmus and the exponents of New Learning. "I have seen almost everything that has been written and published either by Oecolampadius or Zwinglius," he wrote in 1537, "and I have come to the conclusion that the writings of every man must be read with discrimination."[6] He was yet more familiar with the works of Luther and Melancthon, while his commonplace books contain extracts from Calvin, Bucer, Bullinger, Brentius, Eck, and many others; Divines of all schools of thought and of all shades of theology. Latin he wrote and spoke with ease; Hebrew he had mastered in his private studies. Greek he may have acquired after he left Cambridge, and his discovery that $εἴδωλον$ meant the same as IMAGO made an abiding impression upon his mind; and as late as 1550, he made haste to acquire a copy of Robert Estienne's Greek New Testament, and used it with effect in his work on *The Lord's Supper* which was published a year later. He knew German, French, and Italian, and was always glad to con-

---

[1] *Original Letters*, Vol. II, p. 388.   [2] Strype, Vol. III, p. 376.
[3] Pollard, p. 319.   [4] Strype, Vol. III, p. 376.
[5] Pollard, p. 319.   [6] Cranmer, Vol. II, p. 344.

verse with his Continental guests in their own language. Strype speaks of "his favour to places of learning" as well as to men of learning.[1] He was always ready to help scholars such as Erasmus, Alexander Aless, Leland, and Sleidan, but not less ready to help a ploughman's son if he had ability. And his tremendous range of reading, his accurate notes, his scrupulous care, gave him no small advantage when it came to written controversy.

Cranmer was a conservative in thought and in nature, and the movement of his mind was very cautious. "It was of that academic cast which weighs and deliberates, and seeks for new lights and fresh data, and for ever finds an infinite deal to be said on both sides."[2] Thus new ideas only won their way by slow and painful steps to the control of his mind and were only avowed after years of mature study in the ever-growing light of Scripture. This renders it impossible to date with certainty each stage in the development of his Reformation Theology. Thus in 1533, he was against John Frith who "thought it not necessary" to hold that "there is the very corporal presence of Christ within the host and sacrament of the altar", but was inclined to the views of Oecolampadius: "And surely I myself sent for him (Frith) three or four times to persuade him to leave that his imagination."[3] And, in 1537, he was very displeased when the Zwinglian writer, Vadianus, sent him a book against the doctrine of the Real Presence: "For unless I see stronger evidence brought forward than I have yet been able to see, I desire neither to be the patron nor the approver of the opinion maintained by you."[4] Nevertheless, it was during these years that he came to disown the doctrine of Transubstantiation, and he avowed this in 1538 in his statement on the case of Adam Damplip: "He confuted the opinion of the Transubstantiation, and therein I think he taught but the truth."[5] Did he then pass at once from the mediaeval dogma to the Zwinglian doctrine of the Eucharist? In his trial at Oxford in September 1555, he was accused of having taught "three contrary doctrines" at different times, and he replied: "Nay, I taught but two contrary doctrines." It was then claimed that when he gave up the Roman doctrine, he had held the Lutheran concept of the Real Presence, and had for this reason

[1] Strype, Vol. III, p. 279.   [2] Innes, p. 162.   [3] Cranmer, Vol. II, p. 246.
[4] Ibid., p. 343.   [5] Ibid., p. 375.

agreed to the burning of Lambert in 1538 as a Zwinglian. "Then," it was said, "from a Lutheran, ye became a Zwinglian, which is the vilest heresy of all." Cranmer replied: "I grant that then I believed otherwise than I do now; and so I did, until my Lord of London, Doctor Ridley, did confer with me, and by sundry persuasions and authorities of doctors, drew me quite from my opinion."[1] We do not know what he meant in saying that he had taught but two Sacramental doctrines, but it is not improbable that he had then come to regard the Real Presence like Transubstantiation as Roman doctrine.[2] He had plainly declared in his Answer to Smith in 1553 : "This I confess of myself that . . . I was in that error of the Real Presence, as I was many years past in divers other errors: as of transubstantiation, of the sacrifice propitiatory of the priests in the mass, of pilgrimages, purgatory, pardons, and many other superstitions and errors that came from Rome."[3] He was, in fact, believed by the Zwinglian party to be no more than a misguided Lutheran for some ten years, and it was not until 1546 that his conversations with Ridley led to a decisive change of view. This was made clear to all for the first time in the debate in the House of Lords in 1548; and his final doctrine was to receive its most elaborate treatment in his written controversies with Bishop Gardiner.

The great weakness in the Book of 1549 lay in the fact that the Order of Communion was capable of a different construction by the two parties who were so strongly opposed to each other in their Eucharistic doctrine. Cranmer therefore set out to prove that the Reformed doctrine alone could claim true Scriptural and Patristic support, and, in 1550, he published *A Defence of The True and Catholic Doctrine of The Sacrament*. Peter Martyr wrote of this work with great admiration, and went on to say that "Cranmer had so great skill in this controversy as one could hardly find in any one besides; that there was none of the Fathers which he had not diligently noted; no ancient or modern book extant that he (Martyr) had not with his own eyes seen noted by the Archbishop's hand". Cranmer had not only reduced all that pertained to the controversy into his chapters on Councils, Canons, Papal Decrees, and such like, but had done it "with so great labour that unless he (Martyr) had been an eye-witness of

[1] *John Foxe*, Vol. VIII, pp. 56, 57.   [2] Cranmer, Vol. I, pp. 3, 4.   [3] Ibid., p. 374.

it and seen it, he could not easily have believed others, if they had told him, in regard of the infinite toil, diligence, and exactness wherewith the Archbishop had done it".[1] However, Gardiner, who had now been confined to the Tower, at once took up the challenge and prepared *A Confutation* which was published in the same year. He was no match for the Primate in logic or learning, and he needed all his skill in debate for this clash with Cranmer. But he had a great deal of rough common sense, as well as leisure in his imprisonment to think how best to state his case. He thought good to pretend that though Cranmer's *Defence* bore his name, it could not really have been his work since it expressed views so hostile to those which he was known once to have held; and from that point, he went on to put the Roman doctrine with no little ability and much moderation. Cranmer's reply was *An Answer* which appeared in 1551; a stout volume which printed in sections first his Defence, then Gardiner's Confutation, and then his own Answer. Gardiner was still under restraint, but he had been furnished with books and scribes, and, in 1552, he brought out in Latin a fresh reply under the pen-name of Marcus Antonius Constantius. Not one copy of this work is extant, but we know that Cranmer was referred to only as "the Sectary". Cranmer himself was most anxious to compose a reply, but the gale was by then in his own face. Sir John Cheke turned his first Answer into Latin, and, in 1553, this was published as a temporary measure. Cranmer reviewed this book while in prison, making annotations in the margin, adding authorities from the Fathers. This fell into the hands of the Exiles at Embden, and, in 1557, it was printed, with the device of a hand to point out Cranmer's annotations. Cranmer could not carry out his desire to draw up a reply at length; he was hindered by want of books, ink, and paper, and the unfinished manuscript was to perish before it could see light of day.

Cranmer's *Answer* may, therefore, be taken as his maturest utterance on the points at issue, and his own great Testimony to Truth. "I am glad, even from the bottom of my heart," he declared, "that it hath pleased Almighty God in this latter end of my years to give me knowledge of my former error and a will to embrace the truth, setting apart all manner of worldly respects

[1] Strype, Vol. II, p. 322.

which be special hinderances."[1] The first pages state his intent with admirable clarity. "This therefore shall be mine issue: that as no Scripture, so no ancient author known and approved hath in plain terms your transubstantiation: nor that the Body and Blood of Christ be really, corporally, naturally, and carnally under the forms of bread and wine: nor that evil men do eat the very Body and drink the very Blood of Christ: nor that Christ is offered every day by the priest a sacrifice propitiatory for sin. Wherefore by your own description and rule of a Catholic Faith, your doctrine and teaching in these four articles can not be good and catholic, except you can find it in plain terms in the Scripture and old Catholic Doctors; which when you do, I will hold up my hand at the bar and say 'Guilty'; and if you can not, then it is reason that you do the like, per legem talionis."[2] Thus his work was marked by exhaustive reference to the Fathers and was perhaps the most important document in the literature of those years on the Mass. It was conceived on a much more elaborate scale than Ridley's work on *The Lord's Supper* and was far more direct and pointed in controversy. How well he had learned what Ridley had to teach him is clear from the way in which he spoke of Bertram[3]; and how little he had to fear from his antagonists is clear from the ease with which he could turn to his authorities.[4] "Here you confess," he wrote, "that you cited Hilary untruly, but you impute the fault to your copy. What copy you had I know not, but as well the citation of Melancthon as all the printed books that ever I saw have otherwise than you have written; and therefore it seemeth that you never read any printed book of Hilarius."[5] Cranmer's learning could not be brushed aside, and he was sure of the ground on which he had made his stand. "Although in such weighty matters of Scripture and ancient authors, you must needs trust your men, without whom I know you can do very little, being brought up from your tender age in other kinds of study, yet I, having exercised myself in the study of Scripture and Divinity from my youth, whereof I give most hearty lauds and thanks to God, have learned now to go alone, and do examine, judge, and write all such weighty matters myself."[6] Cranmer was to revert to this statement in most

[1] Cranmer, Vol. I, p. 64. [2] Ibid., p. 13. [3] Ibid., p. 14.
[4] Ibid., p. 163. [5] Ibid., p. 163. [6] Ibid., pp. 223, 224.

significant terms in a letter to the Queen in 1555. "Forasmuch as I have alleged in my book many old authors, both Greeks and Latins, which above a thousand years after Christ continually taught as I do; if they could bring forth but one old author that saith in these two points as they say, I offered six or seven years ago, and do offer yet still, that I will give place unto them."[1]

Cranmer asserts time and again that the Presence of Christ consists not in material substance like bread and wine, but in spiritual reality known by faith in the heart. The bread and wine were "nude and bare tokens" to them that "to the outward eating of the bread join not thereto an inward eating of Christ by faith".[2] But they were not empty tokens for those who would receive the truth. "Figuratively," he said, "He is in the bread and wine, and spiritually He is in them that worthily eat and drink the bread and wine; but really, carnally, and corporally, He is only in heaven, from whence He shall come to judge the quick and dead."[3] As a result of this positive argument, Cranmer would not spare false ways of worship. "Thus our Saviour Christ . . . hath given us warning beforehand of the perils and dangers that were to come, and to be wise and ware that we should not give credit unto such teachers as would persuade us to worship a piece of bread, to kneel to it, to knock to it, to creep to it, to follow it in procession, to lift up our hands to it, to offer to it, to light candles to it, to shut it up in a chest or box, to do all other honour unto it, more than we do unto God; having alway this pretence or excuse for our idolatry, 'Behold, here is Christ'!"[4] And he pressed home the whole attack with remarkable vigour. "And now that I have brought you to the ground, although it be but a small piece of manhood to strike a man when he is down, yet for the truth's sake unto whom you have ever been so great an adversary, I shall beat you with your transubstantiation, as they say, both back and bone. How say you, Sir? is whiteness, or other colours, the nature of bread and wine, (for the colours be only visible by your doctrine;) or be they elements? or be accidents the bodily matter? Lie still, ye shall be better beaten yet for your wilfulness. Be the accidents of bread substances, as you said not long before? And if they be substances,

[1] Cranmer, Vol. II, p. 453.   [2] Ibid., Vol. I, p. 17.
[3] Ibid., p. 139.   [4] Ibid., p. 238.

what manner of substances be they, corporal or spiritual? If they be spiritual, then be they souls, devils, or angels? And if they be corporal substance, either they have life or no life. I trust you will say at the least that bread hath life, because you said but even now almost that 'the substance of bread is the soul of it'. Such absurdities they fall into that maintain errors!"[1] And so he closed: "I will not here answer for myself, but leave the judgment to God Who seeth the bottom of all men's hearts, and at Whose only judgment I shall stand or fall; saving that this I will say before God Who is everywhere present and knoweth all things that be done, that as for seeking to please men in this matter, I think my conscience clear, that I never sought herein but only the pleasure and glory of God."[2]

The Book of Common Prayer was as far as the Reformation could be carried in 1549, and the Act of Uniformity was as mild as any such act could be in its design to bring in the change of worship with as little offence as possible. But the Roman party used the Prayer Book to whip up the popular discontent which had broken out in many rural districts the year before as a result of the enclosure of common lands. There was a mass rising by the men of Cornwall in which the two issues were most sadly confused. A series of fifteen complaints had been drawn up to represent their grievances, but the hand of the priests had shaped many of them against the new Prayer Book. It fell upon Cranmer to draw up the reply, no hard task in itself. He took the true and most charitable point of view when he said that the rebels as a body did not know the meaning of that for which they were constrained to ask; but he wrote with rather more of asperity on the whole than was his custom. Perhaps he sensed the fact that these troubles in the country at large would pave the way for a change of authority which to him could only seem disastrous. In September 1549, Somerset, Cranmer, Cecil, and Paget were with Edward VI at Hampton Court, little aware of the storm that was now brewing elsewhere; but in October, the storm burst. Somerset carried on a war of words with Northumberland, but his cause was hopeless. Cranmer and Paget tried to mediate between the two parties and obtained a promise that Somerset would not suffer in lands, in goods, or in honour. Somerset's

---

[1] Crammer, Vol. I, p. 284.   [2] Ibid., p. 374.

submission was thus secured; but the Council then sent him to the Tower, drove his friends from office, and gave Northumberland, a brilliant but unscrupulous adventurer, supreme control. Cranmer had little in common with the Duke of Northumberland and began to absent himself from the Council. The brief freedom which the Church had enjoyed under Somerset's government had gone. It was not long before Northumberland seized the Chantry lands as the best means of supply available. Ridley's statements make it clear that Cranmer incurred grave risk by his protests with regard to Somerset's confinement and the "spoil of church goods".[1] And where there was spoliation, persecution did not lag far behind. Cranmer and Ridley had agreed that the Princess Mary should be allowed to have the Mass in her private household; but the licence was now withdrawn. Cranmer was named as head of a commission for the trial of Gardiner; but he took no part in the trial, did not sign the sentence, and was not present at the Council when it was confirmed. Cranmer alone spoke out boldly against the bill which came before the Lords to charge Tunstall with high treason, and it only failed when sent down to the Commons.[2] The dark days had set in.

Nevertheless, the last years of Edward's reign were to see certain developments of the greatest value for the English Reformation. "The labour of the Most Reverend the Archbishop of Canterbury," wrote Peter Martyr to Bullinger in January 1550, "is not to be expressed. For whatever has hitherto been wrested from them (the Bishops), we have acquired solely by the industry and activity and importunity of this Prelate."[3] It was true that in the Commons, Acts were passed for the destruction of all the old Service Books except the Primer of Henry VIII, and for the appointment of two new Commissions which were to draw up a new code of Canon Law and an Ordinal for the Church in England. In March 1550, the new Ordinal made its appearance and swept away all the highly ornate features of the Roman Pontifical. The Ordination of Deacons allowed for the use of "a plain albe", and of a tunicle for the reading of the Gospel; but this direction fell out of the Service in 1552. The Ordination of Priests required the Bishop to convey to the newly

---

[1] Ridley, *Works*, p. 59.   [2] Strype, Vol. II, p. 405.
[3] *Original Letters*, Vol. II, pp. 479, 480.

ordained "the Bible in the one hand, and the Chalice or Cup
with the Bread in the other"; whereas in 1552 the Bible only
was thus prescribed. The Consecration of Bishops retained
certain ceremonial acts in connection with the Bible and the
Pastoral Staff which were omitted in 1552. But Cranmer had
preserved all that was judged necessary for a true and valid
ordination, while the forms of Service marked a great step
towards the goal of true simplicity. Yet it provoked opposition
from the extreme members of both parties. Heath was sent to
prison in the Fleet because he would not subscribe to a Service
which he deemed too Protestant; and Hooper followed him
because he would not submit to a Service which he deemed too
Catholic. But the appointment of a Commission to work out a
new code of law for the Church in England did not come to so
favourable an issue. It touched one of Cranmer's oldest and most
deeply cherished designs, for he could not escape from the fact
that, under the King, he was the first authority in the realm on
Church Law. But no man knew better that the Canon Law had
been in ruins ever since the downfall of the Papal jurisdiction,
and he had toiled long and arduously to effect its reform. But
there was much delay even after 1549, and not until February
1552 did he receive authority to go on with the task. His main
colleagues were Sir John Cheke, and Peter Martyr, and Walter
Haddon; but they could not complete their work before the
three-year term imposed by the 1549 Act had expired. The chief
document of the Commission was known as the *Reformatio
Legum Ecclesiasticarum*, but its failure to gain the King's consent
deprived the Church of the note of internal discipline for which
Cranmer had toiled so earnestly.

But the need for further liturgical reform had been made clear
by the controversies which had followed the Prayer Book of
1549. That book had brought English people the great gift of
Common Prayer in contrast with the many mediaeval service
books which had been in use; and it was framed in the language
of the common people instead of in Latin like the old prayers,
which had had so little meaning for the mediaeval congregations.
It had meant that for the first time men and women in city and
hamlet from Thames to Tweed could join in the worship of the
parish church with understanding and a sense of family unity

throughout the realm. This was great gain; it was undeniable in the blessing that it brought to England. Yet there were still ambiguities of doctrine, infelicities of language, in which un-reformed opinion could find harbour. A book which each party felt that it could construe in its own way was still lacking in qualities of permanence; the task that still remained was to shut the door so firmly in the face of the Old Learning that the formularies of Church worship would speak with no equivocal testimony. Cranmer, therefore, sought the advice of Martin Bucer and Peter Martyr as well as of the tried friends of Reform on the Bench of Bishops. But his own hand remained supreme in the preparation of the Second Book of Common Prayer with all its noble wording. This book passed through Commons and Lords, and a second Act of Uniformity was approved in 1552, and the new book was used for the first time on All Saints' Day in St. Paul's Cathedral. Thus it became by law the one Book for England, and no one could doubt its emphatic intention. All that the first book had done to assert Reformation Theology was now retained, but not only retained; it was sealed and confirmed by the deliberate way in which the ground for controversy had been removed. There were no large alterations in the body of this Prayer Book, but the Communion Service was so remodelled that no room for mistake was left. The Mass now gave place to The Lord's Supper wherein we may feed on Christ in our hearts by faith with thanksgiving. The whole book, so saturated with the language and the spirit of Holy Writ, throws light on the liturgical craft of Cranmer at its finest stage of development. The book excels in dignity and devotion, in rhythm and movement, in music and beauty of thought and phrase. The most careful study of all subsequent revisions proves that the Prayer Book of 1552 is in substance the Prayer Book of to-day, for it possessed a sense of poise in the midst of troubles which has withstood the storms and strains of four hundred years.

But there was yet another document which was drawn up during those years. It had been found necessary by each of the Reformed Churches in turn to draw up a set of Articles as a Confession of Faith. The fact that the Council of Trent was in session had been much in Cranmer's thinking, for he knew that the Church of Rome had set out to define its own dogma with most explicit clarity. It was just as necessary for the Church in England to state on the one hand where she differed from Rome and the Council of Trent, and to declare on the other hand that she held firmly to the great Creeds of the whole Church. Thus in 1549, Cranmer had prepared a draft of the kind of articles to which subscription might be required for the issue of a preacher's licence, and in 1551, this list or a similar list of articles was placed before the Bishops for advice. In May 1552, he was required to bring this list before the King in Council and to show whether it had been "set forth by any public authority or no".[1] As a result, he was asked to revise it in detail, and in September he sent his new draft to Sir John Cheke and Cecil. Then in October, on the order of the Council, it was passed on for the judgment of six of the Royal Chaplains, and in November, it was returned with various amendments to Cranmer. Four days later, he sent it back to the Council with the request that the Articles might now be authorised by the King for subscription by all the clergy. "And then," he wrote, "I trust that such a concord and quietness in religion shall shortly follow thereof as else is not to be looked for many years."[2] But they did not receive the King's signature until June 1553, and less than a month was to pass before the King lay dead. The Forty-two Articles found themselves in abeyance, and it was not until 1571 that they reappeared with full authority, in Latin and English, with addition and omission, as the Thirty-nine Articles of The Church of England. But "the broad soft touch of Cranmer"[3] was not wholly retained in this ultimate rescension; his draft was more comprehensive and more charitable in tone than the subsequent revisions. However, the Thirty-nine Articles were still in substance the work of Cranmer, and they remain as "a noble witness to the strong deep foundation truths of the Gospel, and to the principles of Church Order and Ordinance" which were recovered for us at the Reformation.[4]

Cranmer had been called from his books and his pupils to an office in which he had to thread his way through a singularly complex age of change and crisis. His great concern was to do his duty in that place to which God had called him and to preserve

[1] Pollard, p. 284.   [2] Cranmer, Vol. II, p. 441.
[3] R. W. Dixon, *History of the Church of England*, Vol. III, p. 520 (1878).
[4] H. C. G. Moule, *Our Prayer Book*, p. 170.

a conscience void of offence under the three Tudors in whose reigns he was at Canterbury. He had to take up his rôle as Primate under the King who had broken Wolsey without care or regret, and who had forced Warham to yield up the keys of spiritual independence. He had to pursue the path of Reform in the reign of Edward VI, with an interval of peace and freedom under Somerset, and then through a period of strife and anxiety under Northumberland. He found himself at last under a Queen whose rule reduced him to hopeless conflict in his own soul: he was in bonds to a doctrine which held that to resist the Crown would be against the Law of God, and yet in bonds to a conscience which held that to submit would be an act of spiritual disloyalty to Christ. Cranmer had neither the ruggedness of a Luther nor the loftiness of a Calvin to fit him for his task. He was much more akin to men such as Martin Bucer or Philip Melancthon, mild and gentle in spirit, ripe and expert in letters, less a man of affairs than a scholar at home with his Greek and Latin Divines, less a Prince or Prelate than a host whose purse and palace were so un-failingly open to men of true faith and learning. He had been won over to the Reformation Theology through the reading of the Scriptures to which he had given himself from his student days at Cambridge, and it was this patient study of Scripture rather than some profound struggle of spirit which had brought him slowly to the cross-roads where he had to turn his back on Roman dogma. But the inner sincerity which had led him to pray for years for the abolition of the Papal Supremacy would not suffer him to decline his share in toil and sacrifice for the common weal of the Church. "He chose the better part, but it was one of labours and sorrows."[1] He gave men the English Bible and the English Prayer Book; his hand shaped and prepared the Litany and Homilies, the Ordinal and Articles. And the fact that his work has stood the test of time almost unchanged is a remarkable witness to the accuracy with which it lights up the feelings of the common people. It was because the Prayer Book of 1552 touched real chords in English hearts that it lives to-day.[2] This affords an insight into his own inner spirit which we cannot neglect. Cranmer was like Nathanael, a man in whom there was no guile, simple-hearted and single-minded in the purest

[1] Pollard, p. iv.   [2] Ibid., p. 309.

sense of each term. Simplicity was the fundamental key of his soul.

Cranmer was slight in build, with fresh features and a long beard which had grown white and thick by the time of his death; "and yet, being a man sore broken in studies, in all his time never used any spectacles."[1] He was a most affectionate husband and friend, and no scandal ever spun its web round his name. After the death of his girl-bride from the Dolphin, he had risked his future in a second marriage with the German niece of Osiander. This wife he had to hide during the dark days of the Six Articles, but she took her place at Lambeth in the reign of Edward VI. But when Mary came to the throne, he saw to her safety and sent her across the sea to Osiander. There were one son and two daughters from this marriage, but they had no issue and the line of descent died out with them. He was always tender, trustful, and kind in heart, and he leant hard on the friendship of others. He loved and grieved for Anne Boleyn, Cromwell, and Somerset, scarcely knowing how to accept their fall. He was often in debt to the friendship of Sir William Butts and Sir John Cheke and William Cecil at the Court of Henry VIII or Edward VI. Old Father Latimer seems to have lived with him during the first years of Edward,[2] and with Ridley and John Poynet was the closest of his friends and colleagues in Church life and activity. No one could doubt his true paternal affection for his Chaplains such as Rowland Taylor and Thomas Becon, or the foreign Divines such as Martin Bucer and Peter Martyr. He was in turn deeply loved by his friends, and his personal attractions won a favourable testimony even from his antagonists. "He had in his favour," one of them wrote, "a dignified presence, adorned with a semblance of goodness, considerable reputation for learning, and manners so courteous, kindly, and pleasant that he seemed like an old friend to those whom he encountered for the first time."[3] After the defeat of the Scottish Army in 1542, the Earl of Cassilis was quartered at Lambeth, and through Cranmer's kindness, was won over to the Reformation, in whose cause he was to stand in Scotland.[4] Osiander had once remarked that he had "an incredible sweetness of manners, . . . and . . . a singular love

[1] *John Foxe*, Vol. VIII, p. 43.   [2] Latimer, *Sermons*, pp. 127, 205, 209.
[3] Pollard, p. 20.   [4] Strype, Vol. I, pp. 224, 225.

towards his country".[1] And Ralph Morice, who was for so many years his private secretary, wrote of him with engaging affection: "I think there was never such a master among men, both feared and entirely beloved."[2]

And "as he was a man of most gentle nature,"[3] he was singularly free from any trace of rancour, and his forgiving attitude was a proverb even within his own lifetime. "Do my Lord of Canterbury a shrewd (bad) turn," as Shakespeare made Henry say, "and he is your friend for ever."[4] "My Lord," said Heath one day, "I now know how to win all things at your hand well enough." "How so?" asked Cranmer. "Marry," he said, "I perceive that I must first attempt to do unto you some notable displeasure; and then, by a little relenting, obtain of you what I can desire." Cranmer was a little nettled, and bit his lip as his manner was, and said in reply: "You say well; but yet you may be deceived. Howbeit . . . I may not alter my mind and accustomed condition, as some would have me do."[5] It was the same innate simplicity which gave tone and colour in those matters which were within his own control. Thus he alone in the court of Henry VIII refrained from the selfish grab for lands and titles, and it was well that men should see such a Prelate after the pride and the greed of Wolsey. He told Cromwell in 1535: "I pray God never be merciful unto me at the general judgment, if I perceive in my heart that I set more by any title, name, or style that I write than I do by the paring of an apple, farther than it shall be to the setting forth of God's Word and will".[6] He told Cecil in 1552: "I took not half so much care for my living when I was a scholar of Cambridge as I do at this present. For although I have now much more revenue, yet I have much more to do withal; and have more care to live now as an Archbishop than I had at that time to live like a scholar."[7] It was not love of ease that ruled his mind and soul: it was the quest for Light, for Truth, and for the Will of God; and in that quest he was faithful until it led him beyond human sight. But the weak point in his moral armour showed up when his sense of right and wrong was mastered by a stronger will than his own, and his story is that

---

[1] Strype, Vol. III, p. 414.   [2] Ibid., p. 371.   [3] Ibid., p. 371.
[4] *Henry VIII*, Act V, Scene III.   [5] Strype, Vol. III, pp. 358, 359.
[6] Cranmer, Vol. II, 305.   [7] Ibid., p. 437.

of a man whose conscience was caught in the whirl of momentous happenings which he could not control. His acquiescence in the fall of Anne Boleyn and of Thomas Cromwell marked the extremes to which Cranmer might go, though not without tears and travail of soul. But it was the weakness of one who could not trust his own judgment if it were opposed by that of another in whom he had learned to confide without reserve.[1] There were at times conflict and mistake; he seemed to be pliant and irresolute. "But unless I misread his mind," as Pollard so finely says, "he surveyed his life's work in the hour of death and was satisfied."[2]

After the fall of Somerset, Cranmer "came not so often to court, or transacted business there unless sent for".[3] In March 1552, Cranmer and Lord Stourton were the only peers to oppose the bill against Tunstall in the House of Lords, and so to incur the wrath of Northumberland. In 1553, he was in fresh conflict with the Duke when he sought legislative sanction for his new code of Canon Law, and he was threatened with rough usage if he did not look to his own business. Then Somerset's execution "exceedingly grieved (him), . . . and begat in him fears and jealousies of the King's life".[4] But there was grave enough cause to fear for Edward on the ground of his health, and March 1553 found him too ill to attend the opening of Parliament. This forced the Duke towards extremes; his plan was to unite all claims to the Throne in his own daughter-in-law, Lady Jane Grey, against those of Mary and Elizabeth. He won Edward's consent by an appeal to the dying King to protect his realm from a Catholic reaction, and the luminaries of the law were told to devise a form that would settle the crown on the Lady Jane Grey. This form was at length drawn up and signed by the Lords of the Council and more than a hundred others. Cranmer in the meanwhile still knew nothing of it. The Duke's heart, he wrote, "was not such toward me (seeking long time my destruction) that he would either trust me in such matter or think that I would be persuaded by him."[5] But the Council summoned him as the first subject of the Crown to subscribe the deed after all the other names had been signed. Cranmer refused, since he had already sworn in favour of Mary's succession. He asked for a private

[1] Innes, p. 164. [2] Pollard, p. v. [3] Strype, Vol. II, p. 273.
[4] Ibid., p. 340. [5] Cranmer, Vol. II, p. 444.

audience with the King in the hope that Edward would change his mind. But the Council sent two Peers in with him: "and so I failed of my purpose."[1] That scene must have been as painful for the dying King as for the Primate, but his Tudor obstinacy made him insist that he had the right to dispose of the Crown as he would. "This seemed very strange unto me," wrote Cranmer, "but . . . methought it became not me, being unlearned in the law, to stand against my prince therein."[2] But still he could not bring himself to yield until the King begged him not to oppose his will so much more than any one else in the Council. "And so at length I was required by the King's Majesty himself to set to my hand to his will; saying that he trusted that I alone would not be more repugnant to his will than the rest of the Council."[3] His plan to turn the King from his purpose had brought down the wrath of Northumberland, and for that he cared not at all; but the King's faint reflection on his loyalty grieved him deeply, and at last he subscribed. Edward died on July 6th, and on July 10th heralds announced the accession of the Lady Jane Grey. But nine days later, her reign was over, for on July 19th, the City of London hailed the proclamation of the Princess Mary with wild delight.

Mary came to the Throne on a wave of popular reaction against Northumberland, who went to the scaffold. On July 20th, Cranmer signed the Council's letter which owned Mary as Queen, and on August 8th, he buried Edward VI according to the rites of the Second Book of Common Prayer. His friends, he urged to seek safety in flight across the sea, and the group of Divines who went into voluntary exile began to grow apace. "I exhort you," he wrote, ". . . to withdraw yourself from the malice of your and God's enemies into some place where God is most truly served. . . . And that you will do, do it with speed, lest by your own folly you fall into the persecutors' hands. And the Lord send his Holy Spirit to lead and guide you, wheresoever you go."[4] There were rumours abroad that he would be sent to the Tower, and his friends urged him to make for safety. But he declared that it would not become a man in his office to fly; neither was he afraid to own his work in the cause of Reform.[5]

[1] Cranmer, Vol. II, p. 443. [2] Ibid., p. 443. [3] Ibid., p. 443.
[4] Ibid., p. 445. [5] Strype, Vol. III, p. 37.

"Therefore," wrote Ridley, "if thou, O man of God, do purpose to abide in this realm, prepare and arm thyself to die: for . . . there is no appearance or likelihood of any other thing, except thou will deny thy Master Christ."[1] The test was not deferred. Stories were soon afloat that he had restored the Mass in his own Cathedral, and that he had offered to say Mass before Mary in St. Paul's. This was too much even for the mild and gentle Cranmer, who drew up one of the bravest statements ever composed in such circumstances. "Although I have been well exercised these twenty years in suffering and bearing evil bruits, reports, and lies, and have not been much grieved thereat, but have borne all things quietly: yet when untrue reports and lies turn to the hindrance of God's Truth, then are they in no wise tolerate or to be suffered. Wherefore this is to signify to the world that it was not I that did set up the Mass in Canterbury. . . . And as for offering myself to say Mass before the Queen's Highness at Paul's, or in any other place, I never did it, as Her Grace well knoweth. But if Her Grace will give me leave, I will . . . prove against all that would say the contrary, that all that is said in the Holy Communion set forth by the most innocent and godly prince, King Edward the Sixth, in his court of Parliament, is conformable to that order that our Saviour Christ did both observe and command to be observed."[2] He went on to offer to prove in a public debate that "all the doctrine and religion set forth by our Sovereign Lord King Edward the Sixth is more pure and according to God's Word than any other that hath been used in England these thousand years".[3] Cranmer gave a copy of this statement to John Scory, and it was soon being passed round from hand to hand. On September 5th, it was read aloud in Cheapside, and the next day, "every scrivener's shop was occupied in writing and copying out the same."[4]

On September 14th, he was summoned before the Star Chamber, where he boldly confessed: "I am sorry that it so passed my hands: for I had . . . minded to have set it on Paul's Church door, and on the doors of all the churches in London, with mine own seal joined thereto."[5] Although Cranmer did not

[1] Ridley, *Works*, p. 62.
[2] Cranmer, Vol. I, p. 429.
[3] Ibid., p. 429.
[4] *John Foxe*, Vol. VIII, p. 38.
[5] Ibid., p. 38.

carry out this design himself, Peter Martyr said that placards to this effect were nailed up in London.[1] Meanwhile, Cranmer was sent from Star Chamber to Tower, and the gates which clanged shut behind him spelt the end of his freedom. Treason was the charge laid before the Council, treason of a kind in which not a few who sat on the Council were more deeply implicated than he. They had received the royal pardon and were high in the Queen's favour. But there was no pardon for him; nothing short of his death could meet the Queen's implacable desire to avenge her mother's divorce. Thus on November 13th, Lady Jane Grey, Cranmer, and two or three others, faced their trial for treason, and were condemned to die in four days' time. But then it was found that by the laws of the Church, Cranmer could not be put to death until he had suffered degradation from his Orders. This brought him a temporary reprieve, and he prepared a most touching appeal to the Queen for whom he had once interceded. He implored her pardon for his consent to her brother's last will, settling the crown on the Lady Jane Grey: "Which will, God, He knoweth, I never liked; nor never anything grieved me so much that Your Grace's brother did: and if by any means it had been in me to have letted the making of that will, I would have done it." He went on to describe how he had at last signed his name only at the King's most earnest request, and then, with the purest and most transparent honesty, he wrote: "Which, when I had set my hand unto, I did it unfeignedly and without dis-simulation."[2] But this appeal was quite hopeless, and he remained in the Tower in a most anomalous situation. Mary now wished to have Cranmer deprived by the authority of Rome and burnt as a heretic; but the papal jurisdiction had not yet been restored, nor the laws de haeretico comburendo revived. Therefore he was merely sequestered for the time being from his See and was even allowed to walk in the Tower garden. In Lent 1554, he was lodged in the same room with Latimer, Ridley, and Brad-ford, and the four friends sought to strengthen their faith by long study and the reverent discussion of the New Testament. Then early in April, Cranmer, Ridley, and Latimer were sent up to Oxford to take part in the now famous Disputation with the Divines from Oxford and Cambridge. Cranmer was there im-

[1] *Original Letters*, Vol. II, p. 505. [2] Cranmer, Vol. II, p. 443.

prisoned in the Bocardo, part of the northern gate of the city, and the charge of treason was shelved for the charge of heresy: "which liked the Archbishop right well, and came to pass as he wished, because the cause was not now his own, but Christ's."[1]

The plans for this debate on the Eucharistic doctrine were quite elaborate, and it was thought that since each man was to dispute alone and was not to hear the case put forward by the others, they would be trapped into unintended contradictions. On Saturday, April 14th, the Oxford and Cambridge Divines were all seated within the choir of St. Mary's Church when Cranmer was brought in "with a great number of rusty billmen".[2] He stood with his staff in his hand while the Prolocutor Weston asked if he would subscribe the Articles of Inquiry. Cranmer read them over three or four times, and then declared that they were all contrary to God's Word. He was told that he must commit his reasons to paper and then defend them in debate on the Monday. He was dismissed with a promise that he would be furnished with such books as he might require. Cranmer's written statement was sent to the Doctors on the Sunday evening, and he left the Bocardo on the Monday morning to join in the Disputation at Exeter College. He sat with the Mayor and Aldermen opposite the Vice-Chancellor and Prolocutor, who with certain Divines and scribes were grouped round a table. Weston began with a statement to the effect that their object was not to call Roman dogma into question, but "to confound the detestable heresy" of the Reformers on the Sacrament. Cranmer declared that the Disputation in that case was useless. "It is indeed no reason that we should dispute of that which is determined upon before the truth be tried," he said; "but if these questions be not called into controversy, surely mine answer then is looked for in vain."[3] Nevertheless, Chedsey who was his chief antagonist began with a scholastic argument to which Cranmer made a reply clear as crystal: "His true body is truly present to them that truly receive Him: but spiritually."[4] He then handed a copy of his written statement to Weston and asked him to read it aloud. It was scholarly in style, moderate in tone, constructive in thought. Men should attend, he had written,

[1] *John Foxe*, Vol. VIII, p. 38.   [2] Ibid., Vol. VI, p. 441.
[3] Ibid., p. 444.   [4] Ibid., p. 445.

"not to the visible nature of the Sacraments, neither have respect only to the outward bread and cup, thinking to see there with our eyes no other things but only bread and wine: but that lifting up our minds, we should look up to the blood of Christ with our faith, should touch Him with our mind, and receive Him with our inward man."[1] But the Prolocutor waved it aside, and the debate went on. Chedsey, Weston, Tresham, Young, and others all tried their skill against Cranmer, and all appealed to the Fathers to bear them out. But they found that Cranmer was too well read for them to score very often, and he told them plainly that their way of understanding many things was childish. "This is new learning," he said; "you shall never read this among the Fathers!"[2] Nevertheless, Weston closed the Disputation at two o'clock with the boastful words "Vicit Veritas", and the Doctors adjourned to a College repast while the Mayor led Cranmer away.[3]

Thus for almost six hours, from eight o'clock till two, Cranmer faced his antagonists in this disorderly contest, sometimes carried on in Latin, and sometimes in English. At one stage while Cranmer was still speaking, there was so much noise and interruption that his mild voice could not be heard at all. Weston himself gave the signal for the people to hiss, and clap their hands, and shout him down, while he stood and waited with quiet patience.[4] Cranmer wrote an account of the Disputation for the Council, and expressed his surprise: "I never knew nor heard of a more confused disputation in all my life. For albeit there was one appointed to dispute against me, yet every man spake his mind and brought forth what him liked without order. And such haste was made that no answer could be suffered to be given fully to any argument before another brought a new argument. And in such weighty and large matters, there was no remedy but the Disputations must needs be ended in one day . . . whereas I myself have more to say than can be well discussed in twenty days. . . . But why they would not answer us, what other cause can there be, but that either they feared the matter, . . . or else . . . they came not to speak the truth, but to condemn us in post haste before the truth might be thoroughly tried and heard?"[5]

[1] *John Foxe*, Vol. VI, p. 447.   [2] Ibid., p. 466.
[3] Ibid., p. 444.   [4] Ibid., p. 454.   [5] Cranmer, Vol. II, p. 446.

On Tuesday, Ridley faced the ordeal, and on Wednesday, Latimer made his appearance. Then on Thursday, Cranmer was asked to be present when John Harpsfield was to dispute for his Doctor's Degree. Cranmer's questions soon turned into general argument in which all the Divines took up arms to defend Harpsfield. But in spite of so much unmannerly treatment, Cranmer came through with an unruffled courtesy, and in the end Weston paid high tribute to his bearing: "Your wonderful gentle behaviour and modesty, good Master Doctor Cranmer, is worthy much commendation: and that I may not deprive you of your right and just deserving, I give you most hearty thanks in my own name and in the name of all my brethren." And so saying, Weston and the Doctors "gently put off their caps".[1] But on Friday, April 20th, Cranmer, Ridley, and Latimer were once again arraigned in St. Mary's and were asked by Weston whether or no they would subscribe. Cranmer was told that he had been routed in the Disputation; but this he was bold to deny. He said that he could not oppose as he would, nor reply as was required, "unless he would have brawled with them, so thick their reasons came one after another: ever four or five did interrupt him that he could not speak."[2] Then the sentence was read: the three Prelates were no true members of the Church. They were asked if they would recant, but they simply told them to read on in the Name of God. They were condemned as heretics; but Cranmer said: "From this your judgment and sentence, I appeal to the just judgment of God Almighty; trusting to be present with Him in heaven, for Whose presence in the altar I am thus condemned."[3]

But this Disputation was an academic affair and could not seal their fate. The Oxford and Cambridge Dons might condemn them as obstinate heretics, but there was no law de haeretico comburendo as yet in force. Months were to drag by in prison, while their fate was postponed until they could be put to death with the forms of law and order. On April 23rd, 1554, Cranmer wrote to the Lords of the Council to beg them to secure the Queen's pardon on the charge of treason, and to voice his protest on the conduct of the Disputation. Weston agreed to carry the letter up to London, but read it on the way and liked it so little

[1] *John Foxe*, Vol. VI, p. 518.   [2] Ibid., p. 533.   [3] Ibid., p. 534.

that he refused to deliver it.[1] Cranmer busied himself in the
months that followed with his Answer to the Latin work put out
by Gardiner under the name of Marcus Antonius Constantius.
There was occasional correspondence between the three friends
by means of letters carried by their servants, but one letter from
Ridley to Cranmer shows how strict was Cranmer's durance.
"My man is trusty," so Ridley could say; "but it grieveth both
him and me that when I send him with anything to you, your
man will not let him come up to see you, as he may to Master
Latimer, and yours to me."[2] But in January 1555, the tides began
to turn against them all, for the authority of Rome and the laws
of persecution were once again restored to the statute book of
England. Rogers, Hooper, Rowland Taylor, and perhaps fifty
more within the next six months followed in each other's steps
to the stake. But since Cranmer had once received his pall from
Rome, it was held that his trial could not take place without
direct Papal authority. Thus Philip and Mary had him "denounced" before the Pope, who then placed the case in the hands
of the Prefect of the Holy Inquisition, and he in turn delegated
the whole conduct of the trial to Brooks of Gloucester. Brooks
reached Oxford early in September, and on the 7th, Cranmer
was cited to appear at Rome within eighty days in person or by
proxy. But this was mere pretence. On Thursday, September
12th, Brooks set up his court in the Church of St. Mary, where he
sat just beneath the high altar on a chair decked "with cloth of
state, very richly and sumptuously adorned."[3] Cranmer was
brought in "with bills and glaves for fear he should start away,
being clothed in a fair black gown, with his hood on both
shoulders, . . . and in his hand a white staff."[4] He raised his cap
and bowed to the two Royal Proctors, Martin and Story, who
sat on either side of Brooks; but he replaced his cap, and he refused to bow to Brooks as the sub-delegate of a jurisdiction
which he had once forsworn. Brooks then declared that he had
not come to dispute but to inquire, and he went on to urge him
to return into the fold of Rome. "It is ten to one," he argued,
"that whereas you were Archbishop of Canterbury and Metropolitan of England, it is ten to one, I say, that ye shall be as well

[1] Strype, Vol. III, p. 123. [2] Ridley, *Works*, p. 363.
[3] *John Foxe*, Vol. VIII, p. 44 [4] Ibid., p. 45.

still, yea, and rather better!"[1] Was he trying to bribe Cranmer with the supposititious offer of a Cardinal's hat?

Cranmer's first words were to protest that he would not answer Brooks at all as the Pope's sub-delegate, but that for conscience' sake he would address himself to the two Royal Proctors. He then made a formal statement as to his faith, in which no words were minced. As to Papal claims, he bluntly declared: "I will never consent that the Bishop of Rome shall have any jurisdiction within this realm."[2] And as to the Sacrament, he said: "I have taught no false doctrine of the sacrament of the altar: for if it can be proved by any doctor above a thousand years after Christ that Christ's body is there really, I will give over. My book was made seven years ago, and no man hath brought any authors against it. I believe that whoso eateth and drinketh that Sacrament, Christ is within them, whole Christ, His nativity, passion, resurrection, and ascension, but not that corporally that sitteth in heaven."[3] Then he asked for leave to reply to Brooks, and so went on to say: "My Lord, you have very learnedly and eloquently in your oration put me in remembrance of many things touching myself, wherein I do not mean to spend the time in answering of them. I acknowledge God's goodness to me in all His gifts, and thank Him as heartily for this state wherein I find myself now as ever I did for the time of my prosperity; and it is not the loss of my promotions that grieveth me. The greatest grief I have at this time is, and one of the greatest that ever I had in all my life, to see the King and Queen's Majesties, by their Proctors, here to become my accusers, and that, in their own realm and country, before a foreign power. If I have transgressed the laws of the land, their Majesties have sufficient authority and power, both from God and by the ordinance of this realm, to punish me; whereunto I both have, and at all times shall be content to submit myself. Alas! what hath the Pope to do in England? whose jurisdiction is so far different from the jurisdiction of this realm that it is impossible to be true to the one and true to the other."[4] Martin and Story both cross-examined him, interrupted him, and asked Brooks to silence him in the course of the day's trial; but Brooks let him alone until the trial came to

---

[1] *John Foxe*, Vol. VIII., p. 48. [2] Cranmer, Vol. II, p. 212.
[3] Ibid., p. 213. [4] Ibid., p. 221.

an end at two o'clock. Brooks had not been authorised to pronounce a sentence; his task was to submit a full report to Rome, where it would in due course receive the Pope's verdict. Cranmer wrote to the two Proctors as soon as the trial was over in a way that lights up the whole story: "You promised I should see mine answers to the sixteen articles, that I might correct, amend, and change them where I thought good: which your promise you kept not. And mine answer was not made upon my oath, nor repeated; nor made 'in iudicio', but 'extra iudicium', as I protested: nor to the Bishop of Gloucester as judge, but to you, the King's and Queen's Proctors. I trust you deal sincerely with me, without fraud or craft, and use me as you would wish to be used in like case yourselves."[1]

Cranmer's next step was to pen a remarkable letter to the Queen in which he vindicated his own faith and conduct, and in which he also expressed his deep sorrow that the Queen should cite him before a foreign court. "I think that death shall not grieve me much more than to have my most dread and most gracious Sovereign Lord and Lady, to whom under God I do owe all obedience, to be mine accusers in judgment within their own realm, before any stranger and outward power."[2] And as if one letter were not enough, Cranmer addressed the Queen again, pointing out that her oath to the Pope was inconsistent with that other oath to her own realm of England. He told her that he had been cut off from friends and books and counsel, but that he was ready to answer his summons at Rome: "And I trust that God shall put in my mouth to defend His truth there as well as here."[3] But that was not to be. Cranmer's trial was followed by the trial of Ridley and Latimer at the request of Pole as the Papal Legate, and it issued in a sentence of death. On October 16th, they passed beneath Cranmer's window on their way to the stake while he was in debate with a Spanish Friar. But he ran to look after them with a look of exceeding tenderness, and then fell on his knees to pray for them in their time of trouble and at the hour of death.[4] It was not until November 20th that the Cardinal-delegate at Rome brought a report of Cranmer's trial before the Papal Consistory. Five days later, he was

[1] Cranmer, Vol. II, p. 447.　　[2] Ibid., p. 447.
[3] Ibid., p. 454.　　[4] Strype, Vol. III, p. 200.

pronounced contumacious, and sentenced to degradation and death. Meanwhile, Cranmer had drawn up an appeal from the Pope to a General Council, and it was a notable document in which he spoke his mind freely: "Whereas I was kept in prison with most strait ward so that I could in no wise be suffered to go to Rome, . . . and though I would never so fain send my proctor, yet by reason of poverty I am not able, for all that ever I had . . . is quite taken from me."[1] But he also wrote a letter in Latin to Peter Martyr in which his heart is most clearly disclosed. His one regret at the time was the fact that no answer had yet appeared to the work of Marcus Antonius Constantius; such a reply would not still be wanting did he himself not want both for books and freedom. "Yet," he also wrote, "I have not deemed it right to pass over this one thing which I have learned by experience, namely, that God never shines forth more brightly, and pours out the beams of His mercy and consolation, or of strength and firmness of spirit, more clearly or impressively upon the minds of His people, than when they are under the most extreme pain and distress . . . that He may then more specially show Himself to be the God of His people when He seems to have altogether forsaken them; then raising them up when they think He is bringing them down and laying them low." And he concludes: "I pray God to grant that I may endure to the end!"[2]

It was only in the hearts of the few that the light of Truth and Freedom had shone with real lustre before, but it had been kindled into a new and brighter flame all through England by the moral shock and indignation which the burning of the martyrs had now evoked. This was greatly increased by the thrill of admiration which was aroused by the noble bearing of the martyrs themselves, for those who had suffered had to a man borne the pains of death in splendid triumph. They may have had faults and failings which had shown up in the stress of controversy; but the one thing which all men now saw or heard of was the faith, the patience, the courage, the unfailing dignity, with which they met jibe, and insult, and death by fire. This called forth a wave of "horrified sympathy which a more commonplace harshness and a more commonplace (ordeal)

[1] Cranmer, Vol. II, p. 225.   [2] Ibid., pp. 457, 458.

would never have evoked".[1] All men knew that those who suffered
were martyrs and heroes, and "the appeal of manifest heroism
is well-nigh irresistible".[2] And would it not be so in the case of
Cranmer? For of all men in the country, recantation would be
for him the most unthinkable. He was chief and captain of the
English Reformation and had sought to guide it step by step
with all the authority of his great place. It was he who, when
his enemies recovered power, had outfaced them all with a
strength and resolution which no one had surpassed.[3] Was it
likely that he would fail where so many friends and colleagues
had stood without flinching? It was well known that his sense
of moral duty had at times armed him with courage of the
highest order on behalf of others, and there had been many
moments of high drama and great historic interest in his career
when he had stood, and stood alone. It was Cranmer who had
once tried to win better terms for More and Fisher, who had
dared to plead for Princess Mary and Anne Boleyn, and who
spoke when no man else would speak for Thomas Cromwell and
for Cuthbert Tunstall. And the courage which made him bold
for the sake of others also made him bold in the cause of conscience. It was Cranmer who strove against the Act of Six
Articles when "he alone against them all stood in the defence of
the truth".[4] It was Cranmer who stood out longer than all
others against Northumberland's conspiracy, when he only
yielded at the urgent request of the dying Edward. He who
advised his friends to fly the land without hint of reproach chose
for his own part to remain, and he braved the fear of prison and
death by his resolute confession of faith and his declaration
against the Mass. Nor did he show the least sign of yielding until
he had suffered imprisonment for well over two years, and the
fires of persecution had for twelve months burnt round many of
his closest colleagues. And yet he did falter when the end was at
hand, falter in an hour of supreme trial and weakness: but this
one great failure was at the last redeemed by a heroism which
has seldom found its equal in the tale of human courage.

Cranmer was caught in the torment of a conflict between
doctrine and doctrine, between duty and duty. It is said that for

---

[1] Innes, p. 156. [2] Ibid., p. 157.
[3] Ibid., p. 158. [4] *John Foxe*, Vol. VIII, p. 23.

some weeks he had been assailed by two Spanish Friars, and that they had induced him to sign two statements in the early part of 1556. These two statements head the Submissions and Recantations which were published by Bonner soon after his death; but they bear no date, and we do not know just when they were composed. They are not real recantations at all: they are no more than a general submission to the authority of the Queen and her laws. But they throw light on the troubled state of conscience which long debates with the friars and more than two years of imprisonment had now induced. He would submit to the authority of Rome in so far as this was enjoined by the laws of England: so the logic of his political doctrine seemed to require. But then, he had sworn to renounce the Pope, and his conscience was soon at war with his logic. This was his state of mind when on February 13th, Bonner and Thirlby arrived in Oxford to carry out the ceremonies of degradation in the choir of Christ Church. Bonner approached the task with a coarse and open relish for which it is hard to offer excuse; but for Thirlby, who had owed so much to Cranmer's friendship, the whole scene must have been painful indeed. Cranmer could not contain his wrath when they affirmed that he had lacked nothing for his defence at Rome, and that his cause had been heard with justice. "O Lord, what lies be these!" he cried; ". . . God must needs punish this open and shameless lying."[1] Cranmer was then arrayed in the vestments of the seven Orders as well as the apparel of an Archbishop, except that the vestments, and the mitre, and the pall, were all made of clouts and rotten canvas. It was with him as once it was with his Divine Master, when they put on Him a scarlet robe and a crown of thorns, and thrust a reed into His hand, to mock Him as a King. Bonner began to mock and crow with an air of brutal triumph; but this was too much for Thirlby, who tugged vainly at his sleeve to stop him. They went on to wrest the staff from his hand, while he drew from his left sleeve his Appeal to a General Council. As they removed his pall, he said: "Which of you hath a pall, to take off my pall?"[2] But he was stripped of all his robes, his head was shaved, and his very fingers and nails were scraped as if to do away with the unction bestowed at his Consecration twenty-three years before. "All this needed not,"

[1] *John Foxe*, Vol. VIII, p. 72.   [2] Ibid., p. 79.

he declared; "I had myself done with this gear long ago."[1] Thus he stood at last in "a poor yeoman-beadle's gown, full bare and nearly worn, . . . and a townsman's cap on his head".[2] Bonner could not refrain from one last jibe: "Now are you no lord any more."[3] He was handed over to the secular authorities and was taken back to the Bocardo. But his own mind was at peace as he said: "Now that it is past, my heart is well quieted."[4]

Thus when Bonner went to visit him in prison the next morning, he could only extract from him a third statement which offered to submit his books to the judgment of a General Council. But on February 16th, he signed the first dated Recantation in which he made his first direct statement as to faith and doctrine: "As concerning the Sacraments of the Church, I believe unfeignedly in all points as the said Catholic church doth and hath believed from the beginning of Christian religion."[5] Bonner then returned to London with these statements, and it only remained for the Queen to decide his fate. The Queen had made up her mind that Cranmer must die; but she would have him so recant that his death would put out the flame of Latimer's candle. Therefore it was resolved to play alternately on the chords of fear and hope so as to obtain a more detailed recantation from the author of the Reformation formularies. Therefore on the 24th, the Queen signed a warrant which would commit Cranmer to death by fire; but no date was fixed, and he was simply informed that the writ had been signed. Cranmer had now been in prison for two and a half years, cut off from friends, from books, even for the most part from the means of writing. He was perplexed by the conflict within; he was appalled by the prospect without. He had looked out after Ridley and Latimer on the morning of their execution, and may even have seen them die, and his impressionable imagination in the loneliness of the Bocardo would feel the terrors of death in advance. But as soon as there had been time for such fears to work their havoc in his mind, the treatment was changed. The doors of his prison were flung open, and he left the comfortless Bocardo for the delightful residence of the Dean of Christ Church. There he played bowls

[1] *John Foxe*, Vol. VIII, p. 79.   [2] Ibid., p. 79.   [3] Ibid., p. 79.
[4] Ibid., p. 80.   [5] Cranmer, Vol. II, p. 563.

on the green, and walked in the gardens, conversed with men of wit and learning, and "lacked no delicate fare".[1] And false men laid siege to his heart, flattering, threatening, promising, cajoling in turn. Brooks had wagered at his trial that he would yet be restored to his honours if he would but recant. Now he was put in hope that he should have his life, and be restored to his office: all these things would be his, if he would but subscribe to a few words with his own hand! On the other hand, were he to refuse, "there was no hope of health and pardon: for the Queen was so purposed that she would have Cranmer a Catholic, or else no Cranmer at all".[2] It would seem that he broke down at this point through want of the moral support of warm personal affection; he had leant so much on his friends that his long and aggravated isolation now told on his emotional nature.[3] He was overcome by human loneliness and human frailty, and he subscribed his name at last to a statement which had been drawn up in advance. His name, written on that scrap of paper, does not reflect his intrinsic character so much as the collapse of his nerve and his self-control.[4]

This was the fifth statement, but the first real recantation which he had thus subscribed. It was printed by Bonner in Latin, but Foxe gave an English version. "I, Thomas Cranmer," so it ran, "do renounce, abhor, and detest all manner of heresies and errors of Luther and Zwinglius, and all other teachings which be contrary to sound and true doctrine. And I believe most sincerely in my heart, and with my mouth I confess, one holy and catholic church visible, without the which there is no salvation; and therefore I acknowledge the Bishop of Rome to be supreme head in earth, . . . the highest bishop and pope, and Christ's vicar, unto whom all Christian people ought to be subject. And as concerning the Sacraments, I believe and worship in the Sacrament of the Altar the very body and blood of Christ, being contained most truly under the forms of bread and wine; the bread through the mighty power of God being turned into the body of our Saviour Jesus Christ, and the wine into His blood. . . . And God is my witness that I have not done this for favour or fear of any person, but willingly, and of mine own mind, as well to the

---

[1] *John Foxe*, Vol. VIII, p. 80. [2] Ibid., p. 81.
[3] Innes, p. 169. [4] Ibid., p. 171.

discharge of mine own conscience as to the instruction of others."[1] But he was at once sent back to the dark loneliness of the Bocardo, and his dreams of freedom were at an end. The Doctors and Prelates gave his recantation to the printers, and it was soon in all men's hands. But since it had been drawn up in Latin and was witnessed by a Spanish Friar, there were many who quite bluntly refused to think of it as an authentic document. There was in fact so much popular misgiving that the printers were summoned before the Privy Council, and a writ was issued for the burning of all copies. It was on March 13th that this step was taken, and plans were then prepared to make Cranmer sign yet another confession. This may have been partly to remove for ever all suspicion of forgery, but the major object was to blacken the whole Reformation with indelible shame. Cranmer was required to accuse himself as the sinister architect of all the wrongs which had overtaken both Church and Realm, and the language of this recantation was drawn up so as to shame and humiliate him in the last depths of disgrace. He was forced to yield at every point the things for which he had fought, and to yield in terms which were to grind his soul in the dust. On March 18th, this Sixth Recantation was laid before him in prison. Cranmer, humbled, broken, sore at heart, in shame of conscience, succumbed for the last time. He had for so many years held himself in stern control, but now for a brief space his sense of poise was swept away. He signed his name to a statement which placed in the hands of the Queen all that she could desire: for when the chief Prophet of the Reformation had cursed it in terms like these, who would rise up to bless or defend?[2]

It was on March 19th that this recantation was lodged in the hands of the Queen: "But of her purpose to put him to death, she would nothing relent."[3] On March 20th, orders were despatched to Oxford that he should die by fire on the morrow. Dr. Cole, Provost of Eton, was sent up to preach the sermon at his execution, and Lord Williams of Thame was warned to guard against uproar. But did Cranmer in his prison know that he was to die on the morrow? Foxe has it that he was left to guess at his fate from the conduct of Cole on the morning itself. But in

[1] *John Foxe*, Vol. VIII, p. 82.   [2] Pollard, p. 374.   [3] *John Foxe*, Vol. VIII, p. 83.

Bonner's published account of the Recantations, there was a seventh document, and the language makes it plain that this was meant for reading aloud at his execution. But it remained unsigned and bore neither date nor witness. The Sixth Recantation had bent the bow to the utmost; it would neither give nor bend a fraction beyond. But that recantation must have been in his hands, and he must have known the truth the night before; else how could he have found time to amend that last recantation with such care and detail so that it took the form of the written statement from which he read at last? And if he knew that the stake was to be set up in the morning, how did he spend that last night of trial and sorrow? We do not know. But we almost feel the throb of pain in that last lonely vigil, with its tears and shame, the shadow of failure, the trouble of conscience, and the longing for peace. Perhaps he would pour out his heart in the plaintive strains of his own beautiful Litany. Do we see that slender figure kneeling in the soft light of the candles, and can we hear his voice as it rehearsed those matchless words: "That it may please Thee to bring into the way of truth all such as have erred, and are deceived: That it may please Thee to strengthen such as do stand; and to comfort and help the weak-hearted; and to raise up them that fall; and finally to beat down Satan under our feet: That it may please Thee to succour, help, and comfort all that are in danger, necessity, and tribulation: That it may please Thee to forgive our enemies, persecutors, and slanderers, and to turn their hearts: That it may please Thee to give us true repentance; to forgive us all our sins, negligences, and ignorances; and to endue us with the grace of Thy Holy Spirit to amend our lives according to Thy Holy Word." He was still deep in the valley of doubts and fears, but there was a glimmer of light at last; and so into his very soul there came the Grace of God, and out of weakness he was made strong.[1]

For his enemies had so overreached themselves that the whole course of things was changed. Morning broke with angry skies and driving rain in Oxford, but the crowds were early at St. Mary's with hope and fear alternating in their uncertainty of mind. Cranmer gave no sign at all as to his thoughts that morning. A high sense of drama, of history and destiny, seems to have made

[1] Pollard, p. 375.

him hold his peace. But the procession from the Bocardo to St. Mary's was led by the Mayor and Aldermen, while he walked just behind with a Spanish Friar on each side to keep up a dirge of Psalms. As they approached the doors of St. Mary's, the significant strains of the Nunc Dimittis were raised. The two Friars led him into the church to a stage which faced the pulpit, and there he stood while Cole preached his sermon. Cranmer was clothed in a ragged and thread-bare gown, with an old square cap on his head, "an image of sorrow",[1] lifting up his hands once or twice while his lips moved in prayer, and the tears rolled down his face as down the face of a child. That last sermon was "not unmerciful",[2] but its purport was clear. "It seemed meet, according to the law of equality," said Cole, "that as the death of the Duke of Northumberland of late, made even with Thomas More, Chancellor, that died for the Church, so there should be one that should make even with Fisher of Rochester: and because that Ridley, Hooper, Ferrar, were not able to make even with that man, it seemed meet that Cranmer should be joined to them to fill up their part of equality."[3] Meanwhile, Cranmer stood and listened, "with what grief of mind" his looks and bearing declared better than words could do[4]: one while lifting his eyes up to heaven in hope, and then again for shame letting them drop towards the ground, his great sorrow welling up and pouring down in a rain of tears, his fatherly face "retaining ever a quiet and grave behaviour".[5] But the sermon came to an end with Cole's summons to the people, and to Cranmer. "Brethren," he said, "lest any man should doubt of this man's earnest conversion and repentance, you shall hear him speak before you; and therefore I pray you, Master Cranmer, that you will now perform that you promised not long ago, namely, that you would openly express the true and undoubted profession of your faith that . . . all men may understand that you are a catholic indeed."[6] Cranmer was thus marked out as the pivot of the English Reformation: it was to stand or fall with his conduct, and not a doubt but that they thought it must fall.

Cranmer first knelt with the congregation in prayer. Then he

[1] Strype, Vol. III, p. 247.   [2] Pollard, p. 378.
[3] *John Foxe*, Vol. VIII, p. 85.   [4] Ibid., p. 86.
[5] Strype, Vol. III, p. 247.   [6] *John Foxe*, Vol. VIII, p. 86.

rose, put off his cap, drew out a piece of paper, and so began to read. He thanked the people for their prayers, and then went on to say: "And now will I pray for myself, as I could best devise for mine own comfort."[1] He knelt again and prayed in the sublime words of the last prayer he was to compose: "Thou didst not give Thy Son unto death for small sins only, but for all the greatest sins of the world: so that the sinner return to Thee with his whole heart, as I do here at this present. Wherefore have mercy on me O God, Whose property is always to have mercy: have mercy upon me, O Lord, for Thy great mercy."[2] Then he addressed four short exhortations to the people, that they might have somewhat whereon to think after his death. He would have them care less for this world, and more for the world to come; obey the King and Queen, not for fear of them, but for fear of God; love each other, and do good to all men; and think on the needs of the poor, for news of their penury had reached his ears in the Bocardo. This was all in the style common to the age and the man, but he gave it his own special turn in this last summons to think kindly of those in need. But this was all so far no more than an introduction to the real end which was in view, although with great skill he kept his purpose hidden until the very last moment. "And now," he said, "forasmuch as I am come to the last end of my life, whereupon hangeth all my life past and all my life to come, . . . I shall therefore declare unto you my very faith how I believe, without any colour or dissimulation: for now is no time to dissemble, whatsoever I have said or written in times past."[3] Cranmer had now come to the great work which was to make that day for ever memorable. When he had poured out his heart in prayer, the voice of repentance had been so manifest to all; but it was repentance, not for Reformation truth and teaching, but for his denial of them. But the meaning did not reach the congregation as they heard his first words, for they had been led to expect quite a different confession. He held them in deliberate suspense while he went on with a recitation of the Creed in English: and then at last followed the words which his antagonists would all construe in their own way until their real meaning staggered them with utter dismay.

---

[1] Strype, Vol. III, pp. 247, 248.   [3] *John Foxe*, Vol. VIII, p. 88.
[2] *John Foxe*, Vol. VIII, p. 87; Strype, Vol. III, p. 249.

Cranmer had now completely recovered the poise which he had lost when he signed the Recantations, and he meant to restate his full accord with the Reformation and its theology. But he managed his speech with such skill that he was allowed to run on at some length before its real drift was perceived. Yet the tension must have become almost unbearable as he neared the climax. "And now," he said, "I come to the great thing that troubleth my conscience more than any other thing that ever I said or did in my life, and that is the setting abroad of writings contrary to the truth: which here now I renounce and refuse, as things written with my hand contrary to the truth which I thought in my heart, and written for fear of death and to save my life if it might be; and that is, all such bills which I have written or signed with mine own hand since my degradation: wherein I have written many things untrue. And forasmuch as my hand offended in writing contrary to my heart, therefore my hand shall first be punished; for if I may come to the fire, it shall be first burned. And as for the Pope, I refuse him as Christ's enemy and anti-Christ, with all his false doctrine. And as for the Sacrament—"[1] He could get no further; all the pent-up fury of a thunderstruck audience broke out. The Lord Williams of Thame ordered him to reflect on his Recantations, and to refrain from dissembling. "Alas my Lord," Cranmer replied, "I have been a man that all my life loved plainness, and never dissembled till now against the truth: which I am most sorry for."[2] And he seized the chance to bear his witness to the Sacramental doctrine which he really believed. "And as for the Sacrament," he cried, "I believe as I have taught in my book against the Bishop of Winchester: the which my book teacheth so true a doctrine of the Sacrament that it shall stand at the last day before the judgment of God!"[3] Then Cole thundered out to stop the heretic utterance and to have him away. Cranmer was dragged from the stage and hurried off to the stake. He had nothing to say, nor did he lag as they hastened along, and so light and fleet were his steps that the Friars were hard put to keep pace. He had emerged from the toils of conscience and its war with logic, and he was now possessed of an inner freedom which made him soar in hope and long for the hour of release.

[1] Strype, Vol. III, p. 252.   [2] Ibid., p. 252.   [3] *John Foxe*, Vol. VIII, p 88 .

The route lay down Brasenose Lane and out through the gate near St. Michael's to the site in front of Balliol where not six months before Ridley and Latimer had been called out to play the man. On the same site, the stake was set up for Cranmer. It was in vain that the Spanish Friars warned and threatened now; he was beyond their reach. He knelt on the bare ground beside the stake and gave himself briefly to prayer. Then with cheerful spirit, he put off his upper garments until he stood with bare feet in a long shirt which reached to the ground. When his caps were removed, not a hair was to be seen on his head; but his long white beard flowed down on his chest and gave him an air of wonderful dignity. He gave his hand in a final clasp of goodwill to the friends who stood by, and so bade them farewell. Then he was bound to the stake with a steel band round his waist, and the fire was kindled at his feet, where a hundred and fifty faggots of furze and a hundred faggots of wood were piled. The fire leapt up, and he stretched out his arm and held his right hand in the flame: there he held it, without flinching, except that once it was withdrawn to wipe his face, until it had burnt to a stump, while he cried out the while: "This hand hath offended."[1] It was by this famous gesture that he proclaimed his faith and came at last to his triumph. This was recantation of a kind which none could undo; a Sign of Faith which no one could misread.[2] His patience in torment, his courage in dying, won admiration even from hostile members of the crowd which looked on. He stood firmly in the same place, ringed with flame, lapped with fire; and stirred no more than the stake to which he was bound, only lifting up his eyes and crying so long as his voice would allow, "Lord Jesus, receive my spirit!"[3] But while the flames might scorch his limbs, there was nothing but peace within. Would he not hear the Voice of God speak to his soul through the Scriptures which he had so loved and laboured to put in the homes of England: "Fear not: for I have redeemed thee, I have called thee by thy name; thou art mine. When thou passest through the waters, I will be with thee; and through the rivers, they shall not overflow thee: when thou walkest through the fire, thou shalt not be burned; neither shall the flame kindle upon thee" (Isaiah 43:

---

[1] Strype, Vol. III, p. 254.   [2] Pollard, p. 383.
[3] *John Foxe*, Vol. VIII, p. 90.

1, 2). On that cold, wet morning of March 21st, 1556, in the sixty-seventh year of his life, Thomas Cranmer was caught away in a chariot of fire to soar aloft at the call of God in glory; while to those who stood by, the doom of the Primate of All England, his sorrow and triumph, struck home with a moral grandeur such as no mere words could ever inspire.

BIBLIOGRAPHY

STEPHEN CATTLEY, *The Acts and Monuments of John Foxe* (8 Vols.), 1841

JOHN STRYPE, *Memorials of Thomas Cranmer* (3 Vols.), 1848

THOMAS CRANMER, *Writings and Disputations Relative to The Lord's Supper* (Parker Society Edition; cited as Vol. I), 1844

THOMAS CRANMER, *Miscellaneous Writings and Letters* (Parker Society Edition; cited as Vol. II), 1846

A. F. POLLARD, *Thomas Cranmer and The English Reformation* (New Edition), 1926

A. F. POLLARD, *Henry VIII* (New Edition), 1934

ARTHUR D. INNES, *Cranmer and The Reformation in England*, 1900

ROBERT DEMAUS, *Hugh Latimer: A Biography*, 1881

NICHOLAS RIDLEY, *Works* (Parker Society Edition), 1843

HASTINGS ROBINSON, *Original Letters Relative to The English Reformation* (Parker Society Edition—2 Vols.), 1846

INDEX

INDEX

Ulmis, John ab, 203, 206
Utenhove, John, 205

Vadianus, 204, 207
Valence, Peter de, 4
Valerandus, 205
Vaughan, Stephen, 71, 72, 78, 82
Vergil, Polydore, 138
Véron, Jean, 205

Walsh, Lady, 75
Walsh, Sir John, 50, 51, 52, 54, 78
Warham, William, Archbishop of
  Canterbury, 19, 54, 60, 61, 103,
  186, 217
Warner, Dr., 40, 41
West, Nicholas, Bishop of Ely, 95, 96
Westcott, Bishop, 76

Weston, Dr. Hugh, 93, 125, 127, 128,
  163, 164, 224, 225, 226
White, John, Bishop of Lincoln, 129,
  130, 131, 168, 169, 170, 171, 172
Williams, John, Lord of Thame, 131,
  161, 235, 239
Wilson, 106
Wiltshire, Earl of, 184, 185
Wolsey, Thomas, Cardinal, 10, 14, 15,
  16, 19, 20, 22, 23, 24, 25, 26, 32, 33,
  50, 54, 60, 61, 62, 64, 68, 69, 96, 97,
  182, 199, 217, 219
Wyatt, Sir Thomas, 158
Wycliffe, John, 26, 45, 53, 90, 160

Young, 225

Zwinglius, 4, 205, 206, 234